WINNER TAKE ALL

A Brutally Honest and Irreverent Look at the Motivations and Methods of Top Traders

D1246154

WILLIAM R. GALLACHER

McGraw-Hill

New York   San Francisco   Washington, D.C.   Auckland   Bogotá
Caracas   Lisbon   London   Madrid   Mexico City   Milan
Montreal   New Delhi   San Juan   Singapore
Sydney   Tokyo   Toronto

McGraw-Hill

A Division of The **McGraw·Hill** Companies

2 3 4 5 6 7 8 9 0 BB 9 0 2 1 0 9 8 7

ISBN 0-7863-1191-6

Printed and bound by Braun Brumfield

This publication is designed to provide accurate and authoritative information in regard to the subject matter covered. It is sold with the understanding that neither the author nor the publisher is engaged in rendering legal, accounting, or other professional service. If legal advice or other expert assistance is required, the services of a competent professional person should be sought.

> *—From a Declaration of Principles jointly adopted by a Committee of the American Bar Association and a Committee of Publishers.*

McGraw-Hill books are available at special quantity discounts to use as premiums and sales promotions, or for use in corporate training programs. For more information, please write to the Director of Special Sales, McGraw-Hill, 11 West 19th Street, New York, NY 10011. Or contact your local bookstore.

To Frank, who got me out of the brokerage business—forever.

CONTENTS

PREFACE

Winner Take All was first published in Canada in 1983, in a small edition. The book received mostly excellent reviews and did well enough in Canada—a limited market for books of any kind but especially for a book on commodities. *Winner Take All* was never officially distributed in the United States, but it sold steadily, if unspectacularly, through a few specialty outlets, mostly, I presume, by word of mouth.

Then, in 1992, almost nine years after publication, a rather curious thing happened. *Winner Take All* was belatedly reviewed in the American press, and demand for the book suddenly mushroomed. The last few hundred copies gathering dust in a Toronto warehouse were snapped up in weeks. Shortly thereafter, Probus Publishing of Chicago asked me if I would update the book and prepare it for publication in a second edition. After so many years in the twilight zone, how could I refuse?

Of course, this meant I had to read *Winner Take All* yet again, and reflect upon statements made ten years earlier. Thankfully, almost all of it has withstood the test of time. I felt, however, there were a few things to be revised and a number of things to be added. As a consequence, the second edition is a good deal thicker than the first.

On the surface, some of the biggest changes in the commodity scene are the result of advances in electronic gadgetry. Today's trader has massive amounts of computing power at his disposal, and he has access to any number of sophisticated software programs to aid him in decision-making. Yet, despite the availability of these new trading tools, traders are finding the markets as difficult as ever—perhaps even more difficult.

Short-term price volatility seems to be increasing as more and more money gets committed to the market on purely technical grounds. Long term, the character of the markets has probably not changed very much at all. Fundamental shifts in supply and demand still dictate price, notwithstanding the gigabytes of computer RAM searching for hidden order in the historical price series.

Some of yesterday's star players are still around, but mostly the faces are new; commodity traders march as a parade rather than loiter as a crowd. But if faces have changed, success patterns emphatically have not; the same human behaviors ensure that money flows out of the pockets of those who don't deserve to keep it and into the pockets of those who position themselves to take it.

One thing for sure has changed, the speed and ease with which traders can display and manipulate data. Ten years ago, only wealthy fanatics could afford to have real-time price information piped into their homes. Now, such devices as miniature personal quotation monitors are commonplace, as are personal computers programmed to summon up real-time data and massage it, instantaneously, in a thousand ways. At the press of a key, today's trader can display oscillators, moving averages, and any "stochastic" his heart may desire—in time intervals from as short as a minute to as long as a month.

Media coverage of the markets has greatly expanded. We have a television channel, CNBC, devoted entirely to business, with instant expert analysis on every piece of breaking news—both the significant *and* the inconsequential.

In short, advances in information transfer technology have radically altered the environment in which trading decisions are made and the speed with which ideas get translated into market orders. As a result, while markets may have become more efficient, they have also become more unstable. I have a number of things to say about short-term price instability and what it means for traders' expectations.

On the research front, the electronic information explosion—with its massive data processing capabilities—has compelled a number of trendy hacks to seek the hidden order in the market using "artificial intelligence" and neural network theory. I have a few things to say about where *that* might lead.

There are more people than ever wanting to manage your money. Commodity funds proliferate, despite their consistent failure to deliver. Promoters and advisors still stalk the seminar circuit, and the gullible still pay to listen. In the first edition of *Winner Take All*, I discussed some of the more flamboyant operators of the day and assessed their claims to fame. That was a decade ago. Amazingly, most of them are still around, as persistent, predictable, and irritating as black flies in May on the French River. The circus never leaves town, and I have fresh tales of excess for connoisseurs of the paranormal in marketing.

Stock market futures, bonds, and currencies continue to attract business away from the traditional commodities. The reason for this is simple: financial instruments, including gold, are the hardest markets to forecast fundamentally, and therefore the easiest markets on which to hold strong, *uninformed,* and indisputable opinions. Meanwhile, pork bellies—the market most amenable to economic forecasting—has fallen from favor, reflecting the well-entrenched trend away from fundamental and towards technical trading.

Sections of the first edition I have retained in their entirety. But there are substantial additions. Options on futures are much more popular now than they were ten years ago, and I have devoted an entire chapter to the trading of options. I have also added a new chapter on money management, and I have gone into greater detail on the fundamentals affecting individual commodities and commodity groups.

It's my belief that expertise in trading comes in large part from understanding how others fail. So, it is with no apology that I devote many pages to looking at ways unsuccessful traders try to beat the market. I also take issue with many ideas espoused by market analysts whose thinking, though widely accepted, does not stand up to critical scrutiny. I strongly suggest the traders develop a healthy skepticism towards all so-called expert opinion. I am not kind to experts, it's true, but I attack only unsound ideas, outlandish claims, and the deliberate concealment of the truth.

As the reader will quickly discover, I am a staunch believer in the fundamental approach to commodity trading, and in the do-it-yourself school of decision-making. This puts me very much in the minority camp—a camp that is shrinking, as technical analysis continues to win converts.

Of the writers named in this book, I am personally acquainted only with Dr. Alexander Elder, President of Financial Trading Seminars of New York. Although Alex Elder is a technical trader and holds to a very different trading philosophy than I do, he has been an avid promoter of my previous book and in no small way has been instrumental in getting my second edition into print. My special thanks to him, and also to Kevin Commins at Probus for his helpful suggestions.

For the sake of convenience, I consistently refer to the trader as he, commodity trading being a predominantly male preserve. I trust my female readers will accept this convention.

As a trader with twenty years of trading experience, I feel well qualified to warn the reader of the many foolish things traders do under pressure, since I have done all of these things myself. I still do foolish things in the market. On the other hand, I can claim to have made a few smart moves along the way, and I have only written one check to a commodity broker.

Many people have heard of commodity trading, but relatively few have tried it for themselves. A commodity author, therefore, must think seriously about who he is writing for. I structured this book to appeal to the broadest of audiences. It presupposes no knowledge of the commodity business, and I believe it can be read and understood by anyone with natural curiosity, intelligence, and a keen interest to learn. I have striven for clarity throughout, kept jargon to a minimum, and avoided fancy mathematical formulae as much as possible.

That is not to say the contents have been simplified to the point where an experienced trader would find them obvious or old hat. On the contrary, I have looked for material that is fresh, and tried to present this material from a novel and provocative viewpoint.

Though I realize a number of analysts are going to be infuriated at having their pet theories ripped apart, my duty is to inform the reader as best I can. Experts *are* what they write, and I would rather influence people than win friends.

Bill Gallacher
French River, Ontario

Don't put your hope in ungodly men, or

Be a slave to what somebody else believes.

If you need somebody you can trust,

Trust yourself.

—Bob Dylan

1

INITIATION

Attractions

In the fullness of time, commodity prices fluctuate in response to changing conditions of supply or demand. It follows, therefore, that the forecasting of futures prices is a problem in *economics*. Surprisingly, not a lot is written on this subject—at least in book form. Perhaps it is because economic statistics date so quickly. Perhaps it is because the universe unfolds in a highly unpredictable way and often makes a mockery of the most carefully researched forecasts.

Predicting futures prices from a study of economic fundamentals involves flexible and *dynamic* thinking. Many commodity trading books—the majority in recent years—recommend a *systematic* approach to trading, based on the belief that futures prices may be predicted solely from previous price patterns and without reference to economics at all. Such books are heavily into statistics (not always rigorous), chart interpretation, and mechanical rule following. These books appeal to so-called *technical traders* and are pretty dry stuff for the general reader.

I have taken a much broader approach, examining both the dynamic and the systematic philosophies of trading. I also take a look at the commodity stage—the players, the brokers, the money managers, the advisors, and the fringe circus of self-proclaimed market gurus. The commodity market provides many fascinating insights into human psychology and for that reason alone merits description at some length.

"I travel for travel's sake," wrote Robert Louis Stevenson, "to come down off this featherbed of civilization and feel the globe granite underfoot, strewn with cutting flints." Make no mistake about it. For the most jaded spirit, the commodity market offers cutting flints aplenty.

Good trading, like good travelling, is an art requiring both imagination and real effort. The trader who masters it will find himself trading for trading's sake—perhaps not quite—and thoroughly enjoying what he is doing. The trader who fails to master it may find himself, or herself, trading for revenge, and sinking into a quagmire from which it is very difficult to escape.

Commodity trading ought to be an exhilarating experience, an opportunity to test one's skill in applied economics using real money. The prospect is financial independence, with sporting diversion along the way. Although gamblers love it, trading, at least smart trading, has little to do with nerve. It does have something to do with brains, but mostly it has to so with imagination; trading without imagination is like painting by numbers—and is about as rewarding.

Temptations

People trade commodities to make money, or, more precisely, to take money from other traders who are trying equally hard to take theirs. Commodity speculators don't force prices up in periods of shortage, nor force prices down in periods of surplus. Economic realities dictate prices, except perhaps, in the very short term. Speculators, then, are price *takers*, not price *makers*, as any number of condo owners in Toronto or Miami will happily verify.

"How's the market treating you today?" I am often asked by well-meaning non-commodity friends, as if the market woke up in the morning feeling benign or grumpy.

"How am I treating the market is the real question," I reply, "The market is as it always is, diabolical, inscrutable, and seductive."

In commodities—unlike condos, or stocks for that matter, there is no such thing as a *bad* market, only a market that is making some people happy and others unhappy. This is just as true in a falling market as in a rising market. Tap the shoulder of short-seller watching a market collapse, and you will find him grinning from ear to ear.

While it is customary to talk about trading on the exchange or trading the market, traders are actually engaged in private wars with each other. The rules by which these wars are fought are straightforward enough, but few can fight and win consistently, because the right moves are never obvious. A winning trader must learn to deal with such obstacles as his own fickle temperament, with a stream of incomplete and sometimes misleading information, and with a great deal of fatuous advice from people who don't know a silk purse from a sow's ear.

Anyone reading this book is either trading already or, presumably, at least thinking about trading. Perhaps the reader has just received an unsolicited call from a salesman who knows someone who knows someone else who has a sure-fire trading system that will double his money every year from now until eternity. Perhaps someone the reader knows has suddenly acquired a large sailboat called *September Wheat*.

If you have never traded before and are tempted—for whatever reason, how should you proceed? Is there really opportunity to make a killing, or will you be the one more likely to be killed? Remember, those closest to the action—brokers, advisors, and money managers—want you in there, and want you badly. Why? Because recruiting new players to replace the burned-out cases is the name of the game and is the one constant of this peculiar and volatile business. Those furthest from the action, on the other hand, will warn you to stay away from commodities, citing the usual litany of shop-worn horror stories about lost shirts and unwanted piles of pork bellies arriving on your front lawn.

Let's say you cast caution to the wind and take a position in a commodity. What are your chances? It is a widely held belief that the great majority of traders lose in the long run—perhaps the only widely held belief in this business that is absolutely correct. Is commodity trading an impossible game? Or are there big winners really out there, and if so, how do you become one of them? I don't *guarantee* to answer these questions, but I certainly intend to address them before I reach the back cover of this book.

Even thoughtful and generally able people don't always ask the right questions about commodities. Some people don't ask any questions at all, and blunder right off the bat into a first trade initiated on the strength of an unknown salesman's recommendation. The pitch may sound convincing. If he is towing the company line, his research report may look authoritative and read like the word of God. But consider what you are getting; it is likely *one analyst's opinion*, an analyst who may or may not have any insight whatsoever.

Imagine, under this scenario, that your trade turns out to be profitable, which is, after all, the object of the game. Is this a good result? I would argue that it is not. First, the exhilaration of quickly nailing down a first profit will blind you to the dangers lurking just ahead. Second, you will have made a profit by taking someone else's advice, creating a dependency that may be hard to break. And third, while you may be a few dollars ahead, you will have learned absolutely nothing.

Unless you, yourself, know enough about a commodity to make an independent assessment of how fairly it is priced, you really ought not to be trading that commodity. Acquiring the understanding to make such an assessment is not as difficult as you might imagine, but it does take a little work.

Odds are, however, that your first trades will be made mostly on someone else's suggestion, along the lines of the example I gave above. After a string of misses, you may begin to wonder at the wisdom of trading this way. Bad trading habits can be corrected, but what a pity to develop them in the first place.

Your own imagination is your greatest strength. Give free rein to it. This is the direction I am going to steer you in. *Learn to make your own decisions.*

Learn to trust yourself.

Possibilities

Statistically, the average trader is up against formidable odds. That's understandable, though, because the average trader expects to beat the market without doing very much thinking. You cannot beat the market thinking like an average trader. Unless you are able to develop a considerable trading edge over the crowd, you're going to wind up just another accident statistic.

If your expectation in commodities is to make it fast, with little or no work, you've picked up the wrong book. Sorry. I can't tell you whether gold is going to $1,000 or $100, and I can't direct you to a seasonal pattern that has worked nineteen out of the past twenty years; that's the stuff of $3,000 commodity seminars and $399 textbooks, and there are plenty of these on the market.

Any book dealing with investment advice, mine included, should be regarded with a certain degree of skepticism. Some are thinly disguised promotions, calculated to appeal to that most basic of human instincts, greed. A textbook, for example, may contain a hidden agenda, an indirect pitch to the reader to subscribe to a system or some other product that the author—or someone in cahoots with the author—may be marketing. You may have to read the whole book to discover this. So, let me state at the outset that I have no formula or system to sell, nothing to promote beyond the book itself, and no personal knowledge of, or ties to, any of the individuals you will see mentioned in later chapters.

A great deal of nonsense continues to be written about commodity trading. I can recognize nonsense very quickly now, but I have been trading for a long time. People with less experience may not recognize nonsense right away. The most useful service that I can perform with this book may well be that of the debunker, for there is a great deal needing to be debunked.

But you, the reader, want and deserve more than that. You want direction. I have written a trading guide whose appeal should be to the trader with a genuine interest in developing a winning trading style. Not a winning formula, but a winning philosophy.

Why should you care about my philosophy of trading? Only if I can convince you that it makes sense—and works. And I do not intend to do this by regaling you with tales of great trades past. People who trumpet their prowess at trading usually have little useful to say; empty vessels really do make the most sound. Do I always follow the disciplines I recommend? No, although I should. But my doctor, whose diagnoses I would never question, should also quit smoking. The most important credential I can offer the reader is simply this: In the twenty odd years I have traded the market, I have endured my share of bad runs, but I have only been behind once—on the very first trade I ever made. That may not seem like much of an excuse to write a book, but there are few who can truthfully claim as much.

In *Science and Humanism*, Erwin Schrödinger, a famous quantum physicist, wrote: "If you cannot—in the long run—tell everyone what you have been doing, your doing has been worthless." It's just possible I may have something useful to say about the commodities market.

Players

When I first traded commodities, there was a lot more social interaction among traders, perhaps because of the quaint technology of the times (1971). Richardson Securities of Toronto, for example, had an enormous mechanical price board, a behemoth of clacking gear wheels with lights that flashed green or red whenever a contract made a daily high or low.

Traders would congregate in front of this monster for their daily adrenalin fix. Some would hang around all day; others would sneak in during their lunch break. A lot of hot air must have passed in front of the "Great Board," but it was fun to gossip about the latest news, listen to the other players' reasons for holding this or that position. It was certainly a social environment with something of the feel of the racetrack—except the thoroughbreds were hogs and the race never stopped.

Alas, technology has changed all that. With instantaneous access to price information through any number of electronic toys, plus all-day network business reporting, there is little reason for traders to come into contact with each other. The underlying trading habits of the players, however, are probably little changed. The big difference is that now you can stick your foot through your home computer screen instead of through your broker's quote machine. It happens.

What will never alter much is the composition of the orders that stream to the trading floors of the commodity exchanges, and the reasons why these orders are placed. By and large, trading orders are the product of spur-of-the-moment decisions taken by whimsical people *looking for action*. And nothing is more fascinating for a trader than to monitor the electronic chaos, he, himself, is helping to create. What opportunities to make an impression on the world, if only for an instant. With one phone call *you* may change the course of history (or at least the financial page of the *New York Times*). As a bonus, you get to see the result on TV, flashed back at you at the speed of light!

It is 2:25 pm in New York. On the floor of the silver exchange, where there are just ten seconds left for trading, silver is hovering just under

$4.00 per ounce, a level it has not seen in months. In Geneva, Switzerland, a giant *trend-following* commodity pool is watching closely. Tomorrow they will buy, but only if their charts look positive—that is, if today silver can close in New York above $4.00 per ounce. Knowing nothing of this, *you* put in a buy order for ten contracts right on today's close, and that little piece of buying pressure causes silver to close at $4.001—instead of $3.999, where it would have closed without your order.

The following morning the giant commodity pool strikes, ramming silver 25 cents higher just after the opening. Suddenly, the total psychology of the market changes. Silver looks strong on the charts. With few fundamental constraints in the short run (demand is whatever the market wants it to be) silver shoots even higher. Buyers appear from nowhere, suddenly afraid of being shut out of the action. The rumor mill clicks into gear. Reasons are found "explaining" why silver just *had* to go higher. This adds more fuel to the fire; now short sellers begin to panic and rush to cover their short positions.

In Rochester, New York, Eastman Kodak (a big silver consumer) worries that today's action will lead to sharply higher silver prices down the road. Plans for a major plant expansion are put on hold. This news hits the media. Stock analysts get skittish and recommend selling Kodak stock. The weakness in Kodak stock begins to contaminate the whole market. Now the computers jump in to try and catch the trend. We have a wash out on Wall Street that leads eventually to a global depression. And all this because of your single small order in silver.

Impossible? Who knows? We live in a chaotic world, and a world that looks increasingly inward for answers, where no answers are to be found. I introduce the hypothetical silver scenario only half facetiously, as a caveat against trying to read too much into a price chart. A lot of market action is *endogenous* and defies rational understanding.

But enough of imaginary silver trading. Today, July 20, 1993, soybeans are the talk of the market. For the last week, CNN has been showing pictures of the flood-ravaged Mississippi basin. From these pictures, one might easily believe that the entire Midwest is under water. We see hogs sunning themselves on rooftops and having their rations delivered by power boat. The few soybean plants that appear to have survived the flood resemble seaweeds waving in the Sargasso Sea.

In the past two weeks the price of soybeans has rallied over $1.00, and soybeans are now quoted at $7.00 per bushel. For some players, sublime truths are unfolding: chart points hold, trendlines remain intact, and the "one o'clock Tuesday reversal" phenomenon is evident again. All systems are go; beans, it seems, are headed for the teens.

Or are they? Exactly half the players do not seem to think so; they have sold short. Why are they not afraid to sell a crop that appears to have been destroyed? And particularly, why do they think beans will go down? Are they blind? Deaf? Are they trading from Somalia? They are certainly getting shafted today, because beans are rallying back to contract highs. In offices around the world, brokers who have bet the long side congratulate their clients on their foresight, while those caught short on the bull's horns commiserate with their clients, or counsel bravery as the client's mood demands.

Soybeans may be dominating the talk in brokerage offices today, but other markets are moving and other players are watching and listening, too. At a country club, a golf ball hooks viciously into deep rough as a "market alert" goes off at the top of someone's backswing. Elsewhere, a wrong tooth is being pulled because pork bellies have gone down the limit. In Zurich, gnomes gnash their teeth with every down tick of the Swiss Franc. And this game is not just for suits. Heartland USA is in there playing; we have no-necked oilmen from Texas, and good ole' boys from Tennessee.

Across the globe, insomniac eyes are focussed on the latest news from the trading pits of Chicago and New York. Citizens of every country, convinced that only *they* have never had it so bad, are trying to protect themselves by short-selling their own currencies. And, closer to home, we have players who couldn't give a damn about the height of the Mississippi, or whether it rains from now until kingdom come. These are the chart watchers, the computer freaks, and a host of technical analysts searching for meaning in the price action itself. From out of this chaotic battlefield of fears, hopes, greed, whimsy, and perhaps a little objective thought, there emerges a curious and very temporary standoff—the instantaneous price of a commodity.

Players who believe—or act as though they believe—that commodity fundamentals are unimportant are surprisingly numerous. Though vaguely and uneasily aware of fundamental traders who make decisions for economic reasons, chart watchers, particularly *day traders*, feel that they must be in constant touch with the very latest price. People who sit around brokerage offices, eyes glued to quote machines, are usually day traders. Typically, they have strong bladders and blurred vision.

Chronic failure does little to diminish the day trader's confidence. As long as the market is open, he will try to outsmart it. Regular contributors to the kitty, and especially to his broker's monthly income, he is always a welcome participant in the game. For the day trader, no news is good news. In fact, news is an intrusion. News demands interpretation, and interpretation demands thought. Who the hell needs data on grain exports, on crop planting intentions, on pork belly storage stocks, on cotton consumption or copper production? "Fundamentals are bullshit," says the day trader. "News is already factored into the market by the time the public hears about it."

By and large, day traders are small fish—one or two contracts at a time seem about their speed. Whether, on balance, they are right or wrong has little bearing on their fate; commission costs will chew them up, regardless. Traders who take a longer view of the market—*position traders*—stand a much better chance. But even position traders can get severely burned if they're not careful. Substantial sums, fortunes to many, are squandered regularly by otherwise level-headed entrepreneurial individuals who believe that their capacity for wheeling and dealing in the business world should extend to the commodity market—an understandable but devastating misconception. Having succeeded elsewhere by being persistent and resolute, they are prone to stick with positions until they are proven right. No one, however, can be right in the market every time.

When such traders are wrong, they can become impotent and defiant. Probably the biggest casualty I have come across in the market was a large scrap-metal dealer who could not get himself out of a long copper position, holding on as it sank from $1.30 to 65 cents, and angrily buying more and more as the price declined. If lotteries are a tax on the poor, commodity trading is most definitely a tax on the rich. The inclination to defy the market afflicts so-called "experts," too. In the seventies, the professional traders at Rowntree's chocolate company shorted into a bull market in cocoa, became paralyzed, and finally lost tens of millions of dollars for their firm. A few years ago, when the Canadian dollar staged a remarkable recovery from 68 cents to 90 cents, financial commentators in Canada were screaming: "Sell, sell, the Canuck buck is going to hell." A sizeable chunk of Canada's annual deficit must flow through the currency pit of the Chicago Mercantile Exchange.

Inexperienced traders do not always understand that a commodity futures contract is a bet on a *future* event. I once knew a very able and innovative boat builder who made one of the finest sailboats in the world. He was smart but impatient. Always in control of events in his own area of expertise, he had become used to getting his own way. One day I found him in a rage over soybeans. I did not know he had any interest in futures—if I had, I would have warned him. A broker had persuaded him to buy soybean futures, and the trade wasn't working.

"Why are you upset?" I asked him. "They could have gone up, you know. They just didn't. There's no one to blame."

"You bet there is," he said. "You know that sonovabitch who calls himself a broker. When I asked him where the soybeans are, he said they haven't even been planted."

"Well, so what?" I said, intrigued.

"So what?" he yelled. "If I had known *that*, I would never have bought the damn things."

If these are the losers, who are the winners? You don't hear a lot from them—the real winners, I mean, not the blowhards. What do winners do that losers don't? Anyone who wins with consistency, I imagine, plays a unique game, but a game employing logical disciplines. A winner, I imagine, has little use for the very latest price, but rather spends his time keeping himself informed about the important things that affect prices in the long run. A winner, I imagine, has learned not to clutter his thoughts with irrelevant information. A winner, I imagine, puts on a trade for very good reasons, with an expectation that it will be successful, but with a fallback position in the event the trade is unsuccessful. I imagine all these things because I have to. Real winners don't talk a lot.

Speculators and Gamblers

Commodity futures exchanges came into being in the last century for purely economic reasons: to permit producers and consumers to contract to deliver and receive specified quantities of a commodity at some date in the future, but at a price determined in the present. Such forward buying and selling, or *hedging* as it is known, allowed for more stable economic activity, by removing to some extent price volatility as one of the unknowns in the business planning equation. In general, the needs of consumers to buy did not coincide with the needs of producers to sell. In stepped the speculator.

Although commercial interests still do a lot of hedging, particularly in the crop markets, speculators have come to dominate the action. Indeed, it could be argued that futures markets exist now mainly to satisfy the needs of speculators.

Does speculation for its own sake, and on this scale, serve any useful function? Should this question even be asked? After all, Las Vegas exists purely to satisfy the desires of the gambling public. Gambling is considered a legitimate business when viewed as entertainment. But speculation is not normally thought of as entertainment. However much it may be denigrated in some philosophies, speculation is still considered an economic activity, possibly, just possibly, conferring some benefit on society at large.

> A basic freedom that we have in virtue of living in a capitalistic country is that we are free to speculate on the movement of prices. This freedom does not require any additional justification, such as promoting the interests of commercials. All that is required is that the general public not be harmed and that the market place be organized according to fair rules and procedures.

> *—The Rosenthal Report* circa 1976

Commercial interests—those supposedly in the market to hedge their bets—are in practice speculating much of the time. Be that as it may, let us concede that the exchanges, true to their original charter, do continue to provide hedging facilities to legitimate commercial interests, at least in the *real* commodities such as grains, metals, meats, and so on, and therefore do serve a true economic function.

The legitimacy of some recently organized futures markets has been seriously questioned—stock index futures, for example. (A stock index future is an instrument that allows a trader to bet on the movement of the stock market as a whole.) There are indeed solid grounds for opposing index futures trading in principle. First, since index traders as a group are much more active market participants than stock-holders, it may well be that stock futures indexes *lead* the stock market rather than reflect it, and thereby add a volatility to stock prices that otherwise might not be there. In the last decade or so, there has been an increase in the volatility of the stock market, an increase paralleling the rise in popularity of index futures trading, and one has to wonder whether the phenomenal decline in the Dow Jones Industrial Average in October of 1987 would have occurred to the same extent in the *absence* of index trading. Is increased volatility necessarily a bad thing? I think it is. Remember that futures exchanges were initially organized to promote price stability and to create a less uncertain environment for business.

Trading stock index futures is radically different from buying and selling stocks on a stock exchange, where buyers bid up the price of successful companies, and offer down the price of less successful companies. Insofar as a company can raise investment capital on the strength of its stock price, the free trading of stocks can be viewed as an efficient mechanism for allocating society's resources where they may be most successfully employed.

But the trader of stock indexes couldn't care less about the relative performances of individual companies. The index is, by definition, an average, a measure of the overall state of the economy as reflected in investors' willingness to hold stocks. An index futures position is a bet on the health of the economy as a whole and would not appear to serve any useful economic function. So it can be argued that, whereas the trading of stocks is a speculative activity and in the public interest, the trading of stock futures is close to pure gambling and is *not necessarily* in the public interest.

In some circles, speculation per se is viewed with suspicion. Should the public care about speculators in its midst? I don't think so. With the possible exception of stock index traders, speculators are price takers, not price makers. If you are long a contract, and I am short the same contract, one of us will win what the other one will lose. Whatever the outcome, it is a private matter between us, and it's hard to see where the community would either derive benefit or incur harm from our wager. On the other hand, I would be hard pressed to defend our contract as adding a dime of value to anything. For, although it is true that traders are simply trying to take each other's money, in the process they are also wasting a great deal of each other's time. They are also directly and indirectly sustaining a horde of commodity brokers, research analysts, advisors, money managers, and the manufacturers of a lot of electronic gadgetry of questionable utility. If asked whether society would be more productive were commodity traders to channel their manic energies elsewhere, a rational person would have to say yes. A cynic might even question whether futures trading is truly commerce or little more than "a tale told by an idiot, full of sound and fury, signifying nothing."

While I am certainly a skeptic, I am not a cynic, and it would be hypocritical of me to deride futures trading. Although speculating in commodities may indeed signify nothing, the world would surely be a much duller—and perhaps unsafer—place without it.

I had occasion to visit the Soviet Union before Gorbachev came to power. Just for the hell of it, I took along a copy of the first edition of *Winner Take All*. Although it seems laughable now, less than a decade ago the Soviet authorities were quite paranoid about subversive materials entering the country, and had they divined its contents, my book would certainly have been confiscated and its author probably booted unceremoniously out of the country.

"Pushkin, da," said the grim-faced customs apparatchik, lifting the first book off my carefully arranged stack of Russian classics.

"Tolstoy, da," he went on, working his way down, into the hard-core propaganda.

"Lenin, da, hurashaw," he said, without enthusiasm. Just his luck to get a sycophantic sympathizer. He looked up from Lenin's grim stare.

"No Playboy?" he said.

"No Playboy," I repeated.

His face fell.

"Kommunizm, hurashaw," I said, just to be sure.

He grunted, stamped the papers, and sent me on my way.

Winner Take All was through. It went on to become an object of intense curiosity in the information-hungry dissident circuits of Moscow. Five years later, communism collapsed, and the first primitive commodity exchanges were established in the former Soviet Union. Now, you might call that a coincidence, but I have another theory. . . .

Overload

On October 19, 1987, the Dow Jones Industrial Average plunged over 500 points, twenty percent of its value, in a single day. The S & P stock futures index plunged by a similar amount. The event made world headlines. Futures traders had never seen anything like it. Buyers of contracts stared in catatonic disbelief, as their account equities morphed into whopping deficits before their very eyes. Short sellers were equally dumbfounded at the embarrassment of riches suddenly thrust upon them. No one could fathom it.

True, the market had been falling hard in the days leading up to the day of the debacle, but there really was no clue that the decline would turn into a massacre. What followed the massacre was, in some ways, even more extraordinary. The market began a long, steady recovery and within two years was back at an all-time high. In retrospect, the bear market turned out to be a one-week wonder. Mysteriously it came, and just as mysteriously it went.

When the signal from an amplifier is fed back through a microphone to that same amplifier, the sound very quickly builds to an unbearable shriek. This is called positive feedback. When a preponderance of passengers on a very heavily laden ferry moves to one side of the ferry, they may cause it to tilt slightly to that side, and, gravity being what it is, the tilt may cause other passengers, subconsciously, also to favor the low side, thereby adding to the tilt. If the tilt becomes acute enough, more passengers, against their will, may be forced to join the crowd, and if the ship is poorly designed or grossly overloaded, it may flip over.

Trading on European stock markets begins several hours before North American markets open. On the morning of the great stock market debacle, traders in Europe were not happy about Wall Street's performance the previous day. They had driven down the European stock indexes hard, even before trading began in New York. Traders in New York did not like what they saw in Europe, nor were they feeling very happy about the losses from the previous week. Wall Street opened to a barrage of selling that increased in intensity throughout the day. By the close, when the averages had been averaged, the average stockholder found that his holdings were worth twenty percent less than they had been worth just twenty-four hours earlier. The leapfrogging phenomenon—where bad news from one time zone induces similar sentiment in another—is common enough. Usually, such an imbalance corrects itself, quickly and sharply, as the illogicality of the leapfrog effect becomes apparent. On this occasion it did not. And one of the reasons it did not may well have to do with the *growing instability of the markets due to positive feedback.*

Tune your television to one of the many financial news networks, on a morning when some closely watched statistic like the unemployment figure is released by the government. Bond traders are particularly interested in this number, which comes out just after bond futures have opened for trading. Typically, the news anchor will have a representative from a brokerage office standing by in the studio to give an instant analysis.

There is something faintly comic about high-priced analysts trying to divine the future by counting the unemployed. But swallow the irony if you can and listen in. Commodity brokers will be watching the program on one screen, as they study real-time quotes coming from the floor on another. Chartists will be gazing at their charts to see if any "key chart levels" are about to be penetrated. The unemployed, the source of all this attention, will presumably be asleep, watching old movies, or filing next week's jobless claims. Meanwhile at the studio:

> ANCHOR: (to viewers) Well, there you have it, folks. Last month's jobless rate in at 7.3 percent. That's a tad higher than most analysts had been expecting. Reaction in the bond market to this number will be appearing momentarily on the corner of the screen.

There it is ... and as you can see the bellwether 30-year bond, which had been trading down 16/32's before the release of the number, has suddenly reversed and gone positive ... in fact it is now up 12/32's. We'll keep that number on the screen for the next ten minutes or so.

ANCHOR: (to the suit) What do you make of the market's reaction to the jobs number?

SUIT: Bond traders obviously like the number. The long bond is moving higher, as it usually does on gloomy economic news. However, I would question the economic significance of the numbers we are seeing.

ANCHOR: How do you mean?

SUIT: The numbers are derived from a survey done in the third trading week of the month. Don't you remember the big blizzard last month? Put a lot of people out of work, temporarily. I think the unemployment numbers are telling us this.

ANCHOR: You think they're overstated, is that it?

SUIT: I just think we have to be a little cautious in our interpretation.

Meanwhile, the bond market rallies further, penetrating a previous "resistance" price and causing chartists to jump in on the long side and touch off stop-loss orders from the short sellers.

ANCHOR: Bond traders sure seem to believe the number.

SUIT: For the moment.

ANCHOR: You don't think this rally can continue? Surely this morning's news puts a damper on inflation fears?

SUIT: Yes and no.

ANCHOR: How do you mean?

SUIT: Even if we accept the government's figures, I don't see the increase in unemployment numbers as being necessarily positive for long-term interest rates.

ANCHOR: Care to explain?

SUIT: It will increase the likelihood of the Clinton administration's stimulus package getting through Congress.

ANCHOR: Which means inflation may be just down the road?

Bond futures, which had been rallying sharply, have meanwhile fallen back to almost unchanged.

SUIT: Possibly.

ANCHOR: Well, apparently the bond market seems to be agreeing with you. I see now it's back almost at the unchanged level ... So, let me see if I have this straight. You're saying that increasing unemployment, which is normally thought to be positive for bonds, may in fact be negative?

SUIT: That's possible.

ANCHOR: On the other hand you don't believe the unemployment number is necessarily correct.

SUIT: That's possible, too.

ANCHOR: So the effect of the number could be either positive or negative, depending on ...

SUIT: Depending on how the politicians see it.

ANCHOR: And what's your guess on that?

SUIT: I wouldn't like to make a call on that. I'm an economist, you see, not a politician.

ANCHOR: (to viewers) Well, there you have it folks, I'd like to thank this morning's guest for his insight into the latest jobless numbers. As you can see on the screen, the bond market, which initially opened lower, then rallied on the disappointing employment news, has now settled back to unchanged. Time now for a look at currency futures and how the European stock markets are faring.

Some statistics, like producer and consumer price indexes, are significant fundamental numbers that traders should most certainly be aware of. Employment trends, too, are important. But snap analysis of a single number can be misleading, and some numbers are subject to a great deal more analysis than they deserve. Now we have to watch the bond market's reaction to such obscure polls as the purchasing manager's sentiment index, a highly unreliable number subject to wide revisions and swings. And after we have watched the reaction, more experts will be along to analyze the reaction to the reaction.

There is no question that the amount of information available to the trader is much greater than it was ten years ago. There is gadgetry now to keep the trader instantaneously apprised of all the latest price quotes from all the exchanges. There are personal computers working with real-time data, computers than can draw and display charts on any time scale and with any amount of history. The latest toys can display spreads, moving averages, oscillators, and indexes on high resolution monitors and in any number of color combinations. The trader can listen to the financial news continuously throughout the trading day—and trade twenty-four hours a day, if he has the stamina.

Has the media revolution led to any improvement in the average trader's chances? Not a hope. Quite the contrary in fact. Short-term price behavior is becoming increasingly erratic—which should be a surprise to no one. An increase in short-term volatility in the markets is entirely consistent with the notion that traders are suffering from information overload.

Does that mean the markets are becoming more unpredictable? Yes, for the trader who allows himself to be swayed by every neurotic reaction in the media. No, for the trader who adjusts to the new reality. If you are so close to the market that you are watching every price tick, and making decisions based on what you are observing, you are going to be influenced by the random actions of mostly unthinking people. Your own thinking will become very short term. You will forget what is important and what is not. You will be prone to jump on every bandwagon and to abandon ship at the slightest yaw.

All of the hi-tech gadgetry that is supposed to keep you in close contact with the action is working directly against your best interests. It is expensive, time wasting, and bad for your trading health. If you don't have it, don't get it. If you have it, get rid of it, for you will save yourself a bundle on charges, and an even bigger bundle on *foolish trades avoided*.

The gadgetry you need to trade adds up to no more than pencil and paper—and a telephone to make the occasional call to your broker. You also need an uncluttered mind to give free rein to your imagination. The key to success in trading lies in learning to trust yourself.

2

THE CIRCUS

Commodity Clients

A number of years ago I was trading the markets in sufficient volume to justify the costs of operating a small commodity brokerage firm. I hired an intelligent and capable young woman, who had just obtained her trading license, to manage the office when I was not around. She brought occasional small accounts into the firm and appeared to service these efficiently. In the fall of 1978, I was out of town for a couple of weeks. Not wishing to be updated on every minor up and down in the market, I left Liz with instructions to call me only in the event of an emergency.

When I returned to the office two weeks later, Liz was oddly quiet. The markets had certainly not been quiet; gold had fallen from $250 to $200 in just a few trading sessions. We were not involved in gold, so this decline was of academic interest—I thought. Then I looked at the positions in the trading accounts; one of these showed a deficit of $25,000 and was still holding five open gold contracts—purchased several days earlier. I didn't recognize the name of the trader.

"Who's Frank?" I asked.

"A friend of mine," said Liz, swallowing hard.

"Why is he holding 500 ounces of gold with minus twenty-five thousand in his account?"

"We couldn't get out," she said, rather limply.

I checked the charts; the drop had been steep, but there were no gaps. They could have got out at any time. Liz read my thoughts.

"What I mean is ... we couldn't bring ourselves to do it. It all happened so quickly. I couldn't put the sell order in. I was *sure* the market would bounce back."

I stared at her in disbelief.

"But it's all right," she insisted. "Frank is coming round to see you this morning. He'll straighten things out."

Later that afternoon, Frank slunk into the office. He had egg on his tie and liquor on his breath.

"Seems we ran into a little problem last week," he said.

"We? Who's we?" I asked, with a sinking feeling.

"We," said Frank. "You and me. It's Bill, isn't it?"

I nodded, staring at the egg spot.

"But it's all right," said Frank. "I have the solution."

"I'm glad to hear it," I said. "You had me worried for a moment."

I waited for Frank to produce the check to cover the deficit. But instead of producing the check, he got up off the chair and dropped to his knees.

"I'm really sorry, Bill," he went on.

"Frank," I said, "this isn't necessary, a check will do just fine."

Frank wasn't thinking about checks.

"I want you to come down here beside me," he said.

I looked up from the kneeling figure on the floor. Liz was standing in the doorway, covering her face with her handkerchief.

"Don't you understand, Bill?" said Frank, smiling beatifically. "There is only one solution. We have to pray to the Good Lord Jesus Christ."

I picked up the telephone and called the exchange.

"Sell five December gold ... "

"No," wailed Frank, still on his knees.

" ... at the market."

I saw Frank again about a year later. He was sitting on a tattered settee on his front lawn, surrounded by his furniture and all his worldly goods. I had just come from the trust company that held the mortgages on his property. To secure title, I had been forced to pay off two years of defaulted mortgage payments plus all his tax arrears. Frank was now into me for over $35,000 (the final bill would be much higher).

It was a bitterly cold day, and Frank was huddled under a blanket, sipping tea from a battered mug. I suspected his piece of theater was a set-up for a photo shoot and could see the headline in the next day's tabloid: "Ruthless Broker Evicts Derelict Man of God."

"I suppose you're satisfied," said Frank, looking up.

"Yes, Frank," I replied. "Nothing I enjoy more than paying off another man's tax arrears."

"It's all your fault, you realize."

"How do you figure that, Frank?"

"You liquidated my position without my approval."

It was true; I had.

"I also wrote a check to the Commodity Exchange for twenty-five big ones on your behalf," I said.

Frank waved the morning's newspapers at me and began shouting. Some of his words were not Sunday school words.

"I would have been worth a quarter of a million, you beep, beep, Scottish mother-beep."

And you know what? It was true. Gold had just reached a new all-time high of over $700 per ounce. I quit the brokerage business shortly thereafter, and I never saw Frank again.

Commodity Brokers

Heard on the street:

"What do you call a hundred commodity brokers lying at the bottom of the ocean?"

"An excellent start."

In the eyes of many of their clients, commodity brokers rank just slightly ahead of grave robbers and malpractice lawyers. This is a little unfair, but only a little. Talk to a commodity broker and it will likely cost you money. People sometimes ask me to recommend a good commodity broker. What they are looking for, of course, is someone who will show them how to beat the market. Fact is, people who truly know how to beat the market are not likely to be hawking their expertise. It is those who *cannot* beat the market who are going to be making a pitch for your buck.

Could it be that the non-speculating public has a perception of stock and commodity brokers as a professional elite privy to trade secrets? If so, that perception is hopelessly wrong, for the reality is that brokers are just as much in the dark as the public—possibly, more so. Many brokers are conscientious enough, but few have any imagination, and there is a veritable army of completely uninformed brokers. It is from this latter category you are likely to get an unsolicited phone call. He, or sometimes she, may spin a good line as to why silver prices just have to go up. This is a favorite opener, though after a ten-year bear market in silver, the yarn is beginning to wear pretty thin.

Do not imagine you can succeed in the market by following the recommendations of commodity brokers. Consider what a broker does. Every day, from 8:30 a.m. until 4:15 p.m., a broker sits staring at a television monitor that flashes an endless stream of price quotations direct from the trading floors of the exchanges. For those with a financial stake in the outcome, these numbers make for obsessive and compelling viewing; they are hypnotic enough to suppress the rational thinking processes of anyone who dares to watch them.

While watching the flashing numbers, a commodity broker will also be receiving a constant barrage of telephone calls from clients demanding to know the latest prices from up to fifty actively traded markets. Furthermore, these same clients will usually be holding positions—mostly losing positions (a statistical fact), and they will invariably be vastly uncertain as to what they ought to do next. As you might imagine, conversations between brokers and clients tend to be rambling, convoluted, inconclusive, and sometimes recriminating affairs.

"You know, we're probably the first real commodity brokers these cows have ever seen."

When not soliciting clients, a commodity broker functions alternately as a punch-bag and a talking quote machine. Occasionally, he will be required to transmit a customer's order to the floor of the correct commodity exchange. And he must do this accurately, for his clients will be ready to jump down his throat and demand compensation if he makes any mistake. Some brokers are natural salesmen who might just as easily be selling appliances or used cars. Some are simply failed traders who have found an excuse to stay in contact with the "action." Trading commodities *can* become highly-addictive, and even proven basket cases have to be dragged kicking and screaming from the arena. A few brokers are quite successful financially, but rarely, if ever, through trading. A surprising number of brokers are barely scratching a living.

One of the attractions of becoming a broker is that so little skill, training, or experience is necessary. There are a few formal examinations to be written, but no one pretends these would tax the most basic of intellects. Many salesman make no pretence of having market expertise themselves; they rely on others, and open accounts by touting the firm's research capabilities or the expertise of a "hot" trader they know. But mainly, the commodity broker will be offering himself. He may make phony claims about his track record, boasting of buying lows and selling highs—while you may have been struggling or doing the opposite. Exaggeration is central to his presentation, for the broker needs a steady stream of wide-eyed hopefuls to keep his business afloat.

Ask your broker if he trades for himself and makes money, and he is sure to answer, yes. He will likely stare off at the screen as he answers, avoiding your eyes, but he will answer, yes. He can hardly answer no. So, be gentle on your broker. Don't make him squirm, needlessly. Why ask questions when you know the answers already? The qualities you want in a commodity broker are accuracy, honesty, and a willingness to get you information when you request it. Remember the broker's lot in life. He spends every day crowded over a machine, like a moth fixated on a light bulb, listening to egomaniacs boasting, whining, or threatening legal action.

Think about it. If a broker *really* had anything valuable to tell you, he would hardly be where he is, doing what he does. Never take the advice of brokers. Trust yourself.

Elliott's Wave and the Ghost of Fibonacci

Naturally, brokerage firms advertise themselves as experts. But it is a mistake to think that picking the right commodity brokerage firm will materially improve your prospects. A trader doesn't talk with a brokerage firm; he talks with salesmen, or brokers, who may or may not be following specific recommendations put out by the company they work for. Opinions within a firm are just as diverse as opinions between firms.

Brokerage-firm loyalty amongst salesmen is rare. Brokers are a highly mobile breed, and are constantly shopping rival firms in search of the highest commission payout. Usually, they take their clients with them when they change firms. Surprisingly enough, despite the frequent recriminations that pass between broker and client, broker-client alliances are much stronger than firm-client alliances, which suggests that brokers may well be adept at telling their clients what they want to hear, or at least are able to give their clients the necessary psychological support they need to function as traders.

For insight into how some commodity brokers do come up with sales pitches, consider the training a licensed broker is likely to receive. All licensed brokers must pass an examination. The study material for that examination is the *Futures Trading Course and Handbook*, published by the Futures Industry Association Incorporated. Allow me to quote verbatim from Lesson Ten of that study guide: "Advanced Technical Analysis—The Elliott Wave Theory."

Elliott observed that all natural phenomena are cyclical and set out to determine whether this same cyclicality can be found in market price behavior. After several years of study he arrived at the conclusion that prices do move in waves and that these waves have certain identifiable characteristics which can be utilized in price forecasting ...

... Elliott also discussed the so-called Fibonacci numbers, named after a thirteenth-century Italian mathematician. The Fibonacci series is infinite, with each number being the sum of the preceding two numbers:

0, 1, 1, 2, 3, 5, 8, 13, 21 ...

... Although reputedly designed by Fibonacci merely as an exercise for his students, the Fibonacci Relationships have received close attention from statisticians—including commodity market technical analysts. Elliott's totals for the numbers of major, intermediate, and minor moves in a bull and a bear market are all Fibonacci numbers. Some technicians have devised entire trading methods based on the Fibonacci numbers.

This is a direct quote from the study guide, and a revealing one in that Elliott's philosophy is presented, uncritically, as a rational approach to trading the market. The Elliott Wave Theory and the Fibonacci Numbers have as much credence with professional statisticians as astrologers have with the National Weather Bureau. But they do have a devoted following. (A magazine called *The Elliott Wave Theorist* is available for devotees of the philosophy.)

Elliott's "wave" and Fibonacci's "numbers" have long been favorites of the far-out trading fringe. The arcane interpretations and mystical overtones appeal to a certain type of commodity mind. Reading the examination material, I kept waiting for the punch line, the disclaimer, but it never came. Elliott and Fibonacci *have* to be taken seriously. Otherwise, you could be denied your broker's license!

There is little point in exploring the Elliott Wave Theory because it is not a theory at all, but rather the banal observation that a price chart comprises a series of peaks and troughs. Depending on the time scale you use, there can be as many peaks and troughs as you care to imagine. Elliott thought that a bull market consisted of five peaks interrupted by five troughs. Trouble is, no two people can agree on what constitutes a peak or a trough, so there are as many interpretations as there are chartists.

Much is made of Elliott's observation that all natural phenomena are cyclical. But this is no more than a statement of the obvious, and the market is not going to reward anyone for observing the obvious. We all know that another earthquake is coming in California, but no one knows *when*. If natural phenomena—and by extension, commodity prices—were *periodic* then they would be forecastable with some precision. They would not be tradable for a profit, however, since everyone would know the answer in advance.

In truth, Elliott's greatest strength is that he is no longer around to be asked a few elementary questions. Elliott was a stockbroker, and a rather unsuccessful one. To reverse his sinking fortunes, he hit upon the idea of incorporating the Fibonacci numbers into his pitch. His fame is entirely posthumous, for he is reputed to have passed away in 1946, penniless, in a lunatic asylum in New Jersey. To be fair, this story may have been put out by one of his disgruntled subscribers who was promised periodicity but found only cycles. Elliott's most prominent present day incarnation is Robert Prechter, publisher of *The Elliott Wave Theorist*. Prechter gained fame about a decade ago with a couple of major correct calls in the stock market. His star has waned in recent years—after he got his signals crossed during the stock market crash of 1987.

And Fibonacci? Surely the medieval mathematician would be astounded at his impact on twentieth-century commodity man. His mathematical series was constructed from observations on the incestuous copulation patterns of rabbits. Let's see, you start with a male and a female, then you take the first female offspring and you ... well, better not get into it.

The Legacy of W. D. Gann

When we have knowledge of the Divine Law of supply and demand and know how to draw upon the universal laws which supply all our desires, then we are free from fear and worry. Therefore ... seek the truth, the Divine Law ... find it and be free.

—W. D. Gann

Enjoying a place in the Commodity Hall of Fame along with Fibonacci and Elliott is the legendary W. D. Gann, who left us his theory of Gann Angles, Gann Cycles, Gann Fans, Gann Numbers, and Gann Lines—a set of contradictory geometric theorems allegedly applicable to all price charts. Gann is also remembered for his market catechism—twenty vague, self-evident warnings mostly about money management.

Advisory services such as *Gann Angles Incorporated* publish material of abiding interest to Gannophiles—as his groupies are called. Perhaps W. D. Gann's enduring appeal lies in his attempt to forecast prices using geometry. Gann had so many lines on his charts, so many rules open to multiple interpretations, that no one then or now could hope to refute or confirm any of his claims. However, some gems of his muddled thought are illustrated by one of his present-day admirers, Frank A. Taucher, in *The 1990 Supertrader's Almanac*. Taucher uses the weekly price chart of the S & P index to demonstrate one of Gann's favorite themes. I have seen this chart used elsewhere by Gannophiles, and the reason it is so popular is its curious geometric form—a huge break, resembling a cliff, followed by a steady climb up from the base of this cliff. As with all demonstrations of the power of Gann, it's a big help to start off with an oddball chart supportive of the claim. Here's Taucher, interpreting Gann:

> Gann's geometric angles are trendlines drawn from tops or bottoms at certain specific angles which represent the relationship between price and time. One of Gann's most important theories was that when price meets time, change is imminent. The angle representing time and price is the 45 degree angle.
>
> In an uptrend, that line is drawn upward to the right from a market low. In a downtrend, it is drawn down to the right from a market high. On this line, *one unit of price equals one unit of time*. Price penetration of this line usually indicates a major trend reversal.

How, you may well ask, can one unit of price equal one unit of time? Price is expressed in dollars or cents; time is expressed in what? Days, weeks, months? Gann saw no logical absurdity in this equation. Time could be any unit he wanted, and if price per pound wouldn't make his angle fit, why not change it to price per kilo? Taucher (presumably with Gann's silent approval) wants to draw a line on the S & P chart—defined by the equalization of price and time—downward to the right from the high point of the chart (Figure 2-1). Once the price penetrates this line on the upside, something important is supposed to happen. Let's see how he constructs this line:

Since the drop in the S & P futures market covered 342.35–181.00 = 161.35 points, the point in the future where this line should intersect with the horizontal line drawn off the market low should be 161 weeks. [The above is edited slightly to make Taucher's point more clearly.]

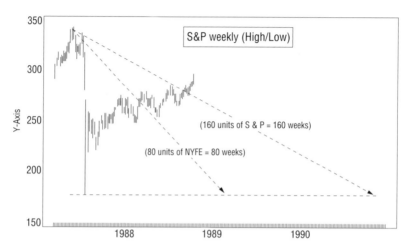

Figure 2-1 Gann's Paradox

By altering the scale on the Y-axis, any unit of price can be made to equal any unit of time. This leads to multiple contradictory interpretations of the same data. Few technical analysts seem to notice.

Now we have it. The Divine Law of supply and demand is revealed at last: *one point* of the S & P index equals one week of time. But, what is divine about *one point* of the S & P index? Far from being divine, this quantity is an arbitrary interval entirely dependent on scaling.

If, for example, Gann's divine law were applied to the NYFE index—a stock index approximately *half* the size of the S & P index, Gann's angle would have to intersect the horizontal at 80 weeks. (A decline of 160 points in the S & P would correspond with a drop of about 80 points in the NYFE index.) This is quite a different line, but one, presumably, that should be interpreted in the same way. Gannophiles working the S & P chart would get a buy signal at a completely different time from Gannophiles working the NYFE chart, *even though they could be looking at identical charts!*

The absurdity of getting a signal on one chart and no signal on an identical chart, *purely as a result of scaling,* has escaped the notice of many technical analysts, among them John J. Murphy, whose *Technical Analysis of the Futures Markets* is considered by many to be the bible of technical analysis. According to Murphy:

> Combining *price* and *time* forms the basis of much of [Gann's] theory. Gann saw a definite proportional relationship between the two. One of his methods for finding tops or bottoms is based on *the squaring of price and time*—that is, when a unit of price equals a unit of time. For example, Gann would take a prominent high in a market, convert that dollar figure into a calendar unit (days, weeks, months, or years), and project that time period forward. When that time period is reached, time and price are squared and a market turn is due. As an illustration, if a market hit a prominent high at $100, Gann counted 100 days, weeks, months, or years forward. Those future dates identified possible turning points.

Well, let's see. Gold peaked at $900 per ounce in 1980. It was lower 900 days later, but there was no major turn—that much we know. The next milestone is in 1998, when the 900 weeks should be up. Anyone care to stick around for 900 months, or 900 years? Of course, if we express the price in grams, we can look for a turn perhaps as early as next year.

I'm sure many readers will be astonished, as I was, that an analyst of Murphy's stature is prepared to parrot such drivel without critical comment. Perhaps we should not be so astonished. Chartists, as we shall see, will believe in almost *anything*. This is good news. A great many of the people who will be trying to take your money in the commodity market will be technical analysts of one stripe or another. And the more of them who believe in the "squaring of price and time" the better.

There are as many stories surrounding Gann's career as there are permutations of Fibonacci numbers. Here's Dr. Alex Elder, writing in *Trading for a Living*:

> Various opportunists sell "Gann courses" and "Gann software." They claim that Gann was one of the best traders who ever lived, that he left a $50 million estate and so on. I interviewed W. D. Gann's son, an analyst for a Boston bank. He told me that his famous father could not support his family by trading but earned his living by writing and selling instructional courses. When W. D. Gann died in the 1950's, his estate, including his house, was valued at slightly over $100,000. The legend of W. D. Gann, the giant of trading, is perpetuated by those who sell courses and other paraphernalia to gullible customers.

Yet, according to Taucher, Gann made $54 million trading the markets. I fancy Alex Elder's figure is closer to the mark. All the same, $100,000 in 1950 was not a sum to be sneezed at. Some might have considered it a small fortune. I know of *two* surefire ways to end up with a small fortune from the commodity markets. The first is to convince the public that you amassed a large fortune trading, and then have the public pay through the nose for your secret. The second and more common way to wind up with a small fortune is to start out with a large fortune.

Readers who wish to pursue Gann's wisdom further may contact the Kansas City Board of Trade, which offers a helpful protractor called the "Opportunity Angles" tool. It costs $3.95, and is designed specifically to help you draw Gann angle lines. Sounds like one hell of a bargain.

Seers and Profiteers

The mechanics of trading are simple enough. All you need is some evidence of your net worth—and some cash. Any brokerage firm will be happy to open your account and execute your orders. While you may be content to trade for yourself, you will find no shortage of self-styled experts offering to manage your money for you.

A fellow trader whose judgment I respect has cautioned me not to discuss the subject of promoters, on the grounds that I may come across as "small-minded and vindictive." His reasoning is that fools cannot be protected from themselves, and that anyone who does not see through a promotion deserves to be taken. I'm not so convinced. It's true that experienced and savvy investors are unlikely to be hoodwinked, but I am writing for the general reader, too. So, I see no harm in raising a few red flags, for a promotion may entrap the merely curious, as well as cater to the persistently credulous.

Promoters' advice comes in many guises, but it is always expensive. It could come in the form of a ridiculously priced textbook with a restricted circulation list; it could be a *trading system*, which the buyer is instructed to operate mechanically according to a set of rules; it could be software for a personal computer pre-programmed with a "magic" formula. To convince you that they have a product you cannot live without, promoters may ask you to swear an oath of secrecy, with a threat of legal action if you reveal details of the product to third parties.

Promoters do have one thing in common. For some reason, they find it more profitable to market their advice than to apply it for their own benefit. Such is the gullibility of the public at large that the obvious question: "If *you're* so smart, how come you need *my* money?" does not get asked until it is too late. No doubt there will be a market for commodity advice as long as there are markets for astrologers and fortune tellers.

To catch your attention, promoters invariably make outrageous claims for whatever they are selling. An outrageous claim—if it is not willfully and fraudulently made—is based on a selective interpretation of history. Normally one would attack an unsound idea by debunking it, exposing its inherent fallacy. Commodity trading, however, is not a normal field of study. To foster the illusion of exclusivity, so-called "theories" may be kept secret, and subscribers may be asked to accept a stated performance record on faith alone. Almost all commodity promoters, especially the heavy advertisers, imply that by following their advice a trader can extract huge profits from the market with little or no risk. And I mean *huge* profits, never less than 100 percent per annum. Later, I will demonstrate how such returns, on a consistent basis, are impossible to achieve.

It hardly matters whether promoters are unscrupulous or simply honest dupes with an exaggerated sense of their own importance and a desire for recognition. Anyone who sets himself up as a public soothsayer deserves a little scrutiny. So let's take a look at what is being sold out there and by whom. Who knows? Even in folly we may uncover some unexpected pearls of wisdom.

The basis of many commodity promotions is the discovery of a "trading system," usually after "years of painstaking research." People who invent trading systems are likely to be computer-oriented individuals with speculative leanings. They get hold of data banks containing daily price histories of actively traded futures and tweak the numbers until they come up with trading rules that yield enormous profits. Trouble is, all a historical price sequence reveals is the consensus at different instants of time past, and how the consensus shifted as the future became the present. It is very, very simple, after the fact, to come up with a decision rule that looks highly profitable when applied to a price series, and to make an erroneous conclusion about that rule's predictive value. I have done a lot of fiddling with historical price data myself, searching for predictive patterns, and I can remember many occasions when I was convinced I had discovered something akin to Gann's Divine Law, only to be brought resoundingly crashing to earth when the future turned out to be remarkably *unlike* the past. Thankfully, none of these amazing "discoveries" made it into print.

The same cannot be said of J. Welles Wilder and Larry Williams, two highly visible and enduring presences on the promotion-advisory circuit. In the first edition of *Winner Take All*, published in 1983, I reviewed, in less than glowing terms, the ideas these individuals were propounding and the claims they were making. Not that many people paid any attention to what I said. Since then, Wilder and Williams have thrived and prospered, discovering "ultimate secrets" every other year, and continuing to bamboozle an ever-gullible trading public. Most of what follows here I wrote in 1983. It has aged remarkably well, and I believe it is every bit as true now as it was ten years ago.

When such "amazing truths" dawn in the uncritical mind, prophets are born, and sometimes born again. For example, in his book, *New Concepts in Technical Trading*, J. Welles Wilder, an inveterate chart interpreter, perceives himself as a man with a messianic message to deliver. His discovery, it appears, has a celebrated historic parallel: "Sir Isaac Newton was not the first to formulate general concepts regarding space and time, but he was the first to define these concepts into an exact mathematical discipline."

C'mon Wilder, get down to earth. Isaac Newton you most assuredly are not. What you have discovered about space and time is how to forecast last year's soybean prices. Unfortunately, we cannot trade last year's soybeans. Wilder has marketed two very expensive trading instruction manuals based on the most banal of observations: the *apparent* nonrandomness of price sequences. The trouble with people like Wilder is that they never stop to consider the essential *unpredictability of natural processes* that lie behind *all* commodity price changes. If they did, they would realize that price movement cannot be explained from *itself*, and that there is no necessary link between today's prices and those of yesterday, or last week. Given sufficient latitude to play with the numbers (and Wilder demands a lot) the past can always, superficially, be made to *appear* deterministic. Some discovery; some nerve.

You can't be around the markets very long before you run into a Welles Wilder scheme, or a Welles Wilder advertisement. The latter are masterpieces of design, combining the pictorial immediacy of the FBI's most wanted list with the typesetting flair of the National Enquirer. I'm not saying you will lose your shirt if you buy into his system (because he *is* selling a system), but I doubt you will make anything either. And you will be bored stiff. Furthermore, you will be subjected to a non-stop flow of revisions, rehashes of his old systems, seminar invitations, demonstrations, computer offers, plus whatever else he may have in the pipeline. Like all system gurus, Wilder is in a permanent "discovery" mode, which means he has to reinvent himself whenever the future turns out not to be like the past at all—which is all the time.

Welles Wilder was not the first to see wine in water, but he is among the most conspicuous. His penultimate book, which he unluckily named *The Ultimate Trading System*, went for $1,000 per copy. His latest, *New Concepts in Technical Trading Systems* is yours for a mere $65. Deflationary times ahead, perhaps?

Another highly conspicuous promoter operating on the comic fringe of commodities is Larry (The Professor) Williams, who first surfaced in 1974 with *How I Made a Million Dollars Trading Commodities Last Year*. It is not clear what happened to his commodity trading thereafter, but in the late seventies, Williams was popping up at trading seminars and advertising heavily in the commodity press. His interests now seemed to lie in promoting rather than in trading.

Unlike Wilder, who makes a few concessions to probability principles, Williams goes for dead certainties: events which repeat themselves, year after year, with clear patterns he can exploit. In his textbook, Williams is quite blunt: "I believe that one can, with amazing accuracy, forecast the markets ... using the moon! I have repeatedly watched several commodities respond with precise accuracy to new moon sell signals and full moon buy signals."

Williams is a victim—or rather his readers are victims—of the talented coin syndrome. You set out to find a talented coin, one that likes to come up heads rather than tails. You start with fifty coins, say, toss them all, and discard those that come up tails. You then toss the remainder and once again discard the tails. Finally you are left with one or two coins that have always come up heads. All the evidence suggests that these particular coins prefer to come up heads. They have never failed in the past; why should they fail in the future? They are sure things.

And so, for the modest sum of $50 (real value $300 to $500) we are offered a talented coin in the shape of *Sure Thing Commodity Trading* by Larry Williams. We are told that $100,000 was invested researching these sure things. One thing for sure is that sales will be brisk. With a claimed profit of $687,492 (time period and number of trades unspecified), it will be hard for many to resist.

Sure things notwithstanding, Larry Williams is not above hedging his bets. He also markets a system under the name of *Striker*, a system "so complicated that it cannot be taught but must be placed in a computer." According to Williams this is a system you simply must have because it makes all other systems obsolete (including, presumably, *Sure Thing Commodity Trading*). The "professor" tells us he is running for the US Senate in Montana and must bow out of the commodity scene for six years. I doubt very much he will be elected, in which case I don't think we've seen the last of him in commodities. (I was right about that—in spades.)

Doubtless, any of these operators will be able to produce testimonials from happy clients. But that will prove nothing. In a chaotic environment where a multiplicity of systems are signaling contradictory trade recommendations, volume and chance alone will throw up some success stories. But what about the trades that bomb? Will we hear about them? Not likely. An astute promoter will build into the client contract the threat of litigation to forestall inevitable and potentially damaging complaints from irate subscribers.

I made these observations on Williams and Wilder back in 1983, and ten years later very little has changed. It is a tribute to the power of marketing and the eternal triumph of greed over common sense that so many of the same people are still around, selling the same dreams in different packaging. Over the last decade, Welles Wilder has retired, made a comeback, flirted with altruism, and most-recently become embroiled in a rather amusing public vendetta with another high-profile promoter, Bruce Babcock Jr.

Promotion-wise, Wilder's latest gizmo is a variation on one of his old favorites, *The Delta System*. Wilder sold the Delta secrets to seventy-two investors in 1984, at a price of $35,000 each, with the usual promises of exclusivity and the usual warnings to possible tattletales. Now, one of the original hapless seventy-two has threatened to reveal the system, so Wilder is going public with the *Delta Phenomenon*, which he has made available in book form for $175. What's in the Delta Phenomenon? Frankly, I wouldn't pay $1.75 to find out. For the curious, however, there are clues. It seems that Wilder, who originally proffered himself as a mathematician, has gone lunar this time out. As usual, Wilder confuses the comic with the cosmic:

> I think I have opened a door to a science of predicting markets that will make what is now known about technical analysis pale by comparison. One thing I'm sure of: The total interaction of the sun, moon, and earth is the basis of all market movement. Nothing else has the potential for predicting markets.

And what about Larry Williams, who himself confesses to being moonstruck on occasions? Williams forms so many ephemeral alliances with other promoters that you never know where he will surface next. Recently, he has been promoting the secrets of the *Turtles*, an exclusivity of self-proclaimed supertraders. Whatever one may think about Williams' analytical ability, there's no denying his resilience. He is back with a service called *Commodity Timing* (plus his turtle secrets, of course), seemingly unfazed by the humiliating losses he endured trying to trade pooled money under public scrutiny.

How do people like Williams and Wilder manage to sell themselves so effectively? Well, for one thing, commodity trading is not a science, in the sense that mathematics and physics are sciences; nor is it like the study of archaeology, say, where the community recognizes a body of common knowledge, and where innovation, while welcome, is subject to scrutiny. Lacking any controls to rein them in, promoters can say pretty well what they like, and get away with it. They may express totally absurd ideas with little fear of ridicule or exposure. I already showed how the myth of W. D. Gann is perpetuated through uncritical repetition by people who ought to know better. The commodity community is not much interested in the methods of science. Traders are greedy, and they crave action. What turns them on are promises of large gains with no work involved. Few will question the basis of a theory if it's nicely packaged and has a big name attached. Publishers don't care what their advertisers say as long as they pay their bills.

But what do commodity advisors really believe? A good proportion will simply be deluding themselves; they may honestly believe their systems will work, despite actual trading results to the contrary. Even if an advisor has done well at one time, he may still have nothing of value to tell you. Did he make a million one year and lose it the next? The dice will always throw up the occasional big winner, so why admire, seek to emulate, or ascribe wisdom to a big chance winner?

Would you expect, for example, to learn anything from a lottery winner? It's remarkable how many people take up writing after winning the lottery. Chances are the one-time charlie who makes it big will want to write about his experience, especially when he finds that he cannot repeat his success. A theory may evolve in his mind explaining the successful trade. If he writes artfully, he may attract a following, even publish a newsletter. In short, he may come to believe in his own bull. Put yourself in the position of the chance winner who cannot repeat. Wouldn't you rather think yourself smart than lucky?

For a few, trading becomes a form of preaching. Gurus emerge with congregations of true believers. (A true believer does not have to adapt to reality because he or she solves problems either by denying their existence or by placing them in the hands of a savior.) A commodity discussion with a true believer—be it a Gannophile, an Elliott Wave Theorist, or a Japanese Candlestick Maker would be no more illuminating than a conversation with the Pope about evolution, or with Saddam Hussein about disarmament.

Like all quasi-religious figures, commodity gurus exploit man's need for faith, or, perhaps more accurately, man's need to blame someone else for his own failure. A guru is secretive by nature; he will be happy to sell you a black box—as long as you don't ask to look inside. He will tell you the box contains diamonds, because he knows that the promise of diamonds is a powerful antidote to that which he must suppress at all costs—*your* common sense.

Winner Take All believes in common sense. What it offers the reader is an unorthodox look at the commodity business from an unusually critical vantage point. We will start with no preconceived notion of what will work in the market and what will not. If commodity prices turn out to be random walks, too bad; at least we will know to avoid trading techniques that assume otherwise. If an approach looks promising, we'll explore it further. If it still looks good, we may incorporate it into a trading philosophy. There is no turf to defend here, no sacred cows that cannot be touched.

The market can only be challenged if its workings are understood. That is the goal of the next several chapters. Paying someone to tell you what to do, or to make your decisions for you, is a dismal prospect for the soul. Besides, it won't work. And it could prove costly. Ask subscribers to *Larry Williams' Financial Strategy Fund*.

Hail to the Champion

In 1987, Robbins Trading Company—a commodity futures brokerage firm—sponsored a trading contest titled, rather immodestly, *The World Cup of Futures Trading*. To enter this competition, a contestant had to open a $10,000 account with Robbins. The prize was to go to whoever made the most money during the course of a year's trading. In other words, *real money* would be traded.

The prize was incidental. The real attraction for any trader entering a trading contest is the exposure he or she will get from winning the contest, and the investment dollars such a victory will attract. The principal attraction for a brokerage firm sponsoring a trading contest is the expectation that the investment money pulled in by the publicity will be traded through that firm. One of the entrants to the contest was Larry Williams.

During the course of 1987, while the contest was still running, Robbins Trading Company began taking out full-page advertisements in *Futures*, a monthly magazine devoted to commodity trading. Understandably, Robbins wanted to capitalize on the publicity the contest was generating. "Managed Accounts by the World Cup Trading Team" proclaimed their ad copy, which showed a quartet of well-known commodity advisors, presumably the team in question. There were a number of problems with this solicitation that would eventually land Robbins Trading Company in hot water with the National Futures Association (NFA)—an industry watchdog organization, one of whose mandates is to scrutinize promotional material put out by its members.

The first problem with the advertisements was that the World Cup of Futures Trading was billed as a contest for individuals, not teams, so that the concept of a World Cup Trading Team didn't make sense. Second, while the contest was still under way, Larry Williams, a contestant, was already being identified as a member of this World Cup Trading Team. What could it mean? Was Williams' victory being taken for granted before the contest was half over? He certainly had got off to a flying start. In its May 1987 issue, *Futures* magazine, the principal conduit for the advertising of the trading contest, informed its readers:

> First quarter results for the World Cup of Futures Trading, for example, are the most spectacular in the event's five-year history, says Joel Robbins, President of Robbins Trading Co., sponsor for the competition. Current leader Larry Williams began trading the initial $10,000 account in stock index and bond contracts in January, and had increased it to $200,000 by the end of March.

Williams went on to make over $1 million by the end of the contest, and won it by a country mile, his nearest challenger amassing a "paltry" $40,000. As soon as the contest ended, Robbins Trading Co. took out more full-page advertisements in *Futures*, this time featuring Larry Williams' portrait, and with this solicitation to prospective investors: "Managed accounts utilizing Larry Williams' World Cup Approach to Futures Trading." Simultaneously, commercials saying the same thing hit the airwaves on FNN, the then *Financial News Network*.

The National Futures Association was not amused. There were some bothersome omissions in the disclosure statements supporting the solicitations, and on August 10, 1988, the NFA issued a formal complaint against both Robbins Trading Co., and Larry Williams. It seems the NFA had got wind of some odd discrepancies between Williams' personal trading performance and the performance enjoyed by his investors during the period the World Cup contest was running.

Commodity Trading Advisors (CTAs) registered with the NFA are obliged to disclose their actual trading records to the NFA when soliciting public funds through promotions. A large part of the NFA's Complaint had to do with whether Williams ought to segregate the results of his personal trading from the results of the accounts he was handling for others. Williams claimed in his defense that the NFA's guidelines were unclear, and he may well have had a point. One disturbing fact, however, was not in dispute. During the first quarter of 1987, when his "contest" account was appreciating from $10,000 to over $200,000, Williams' managed accounts were losing, and losing big. From the *Findings and Conclusions* of the NFA:

> There is no question that Mr. Williams's personal trading accounts had a material effect upon his composite trading performance. The record reflects that for the first quarter of 1987, Mr. Williams's composite performance showed a loss of $6,122,281, while at the same time Mr. Williams's personal accounts experienced a gain of $902,599. The Panel finds that the fact that Mr. Williams was making significant gains while his managed customer accounts were suffering considerable losses would be a material fact which a potential customer would need to know in order to make a fully reasoned decision.

On December 19, 1989, the NFA imposed fines of $35,000 on both Williams and Robbins Trading Co. Both fines were appealed with some success. On June 8, 1990, RTC (Robbins Trading Company) consented to a finding that it had violated an NFA Compliance Rule governing risk disclosure in its promotional material and agreed to pay a reduced fine of $15,000. On the same date, the Appeals Committee agreed to make no findings against Williams, but imposed a $13,000 fine. With these minor slaps on the wrist, the affair seems to have rested—as far as the NFA is concerned.

The ongoing problems with the NFA did little to dampen the promotional hype surrounding Williams' World Cup Championship victory. In July 1988, the *Larry Williams Financial Strategy Fund* was launched, followed in March 1989 by the *World Cup Championship Fund*, managed by Larry Williams, Jake Bernstein, and two other members of the self-proclaimed World Cup Trading Team.

In October 1989, *Futures* magazine issued a terse announcement: the Larry Williams Financial Strategy Fund was no more. The heavyweight champion of futures trading, who had turned $10,000 into $1 million in 1987 trading his *own* real money, had found the going tougher when it came to trading *customers'* real money. In fact, he had suffered one of the fastest knockouts in commodity fund history, losing more than fifty percent of his clients' equity in barely one year. It was a virtuoso performance in consistency, with scarcely an uptick to interrupt a relentless string of losing months.

And what of the *World Cup Championship Fund*, launched with such ballyhoo in March 1989? After scarcely more than a year had passed, this fund, too, had lost more than half of its original equity. In May 1990 the bell tolled again, and World Cup Championship Fund slipped quietly beneath the waves to join its predecessor, *Larry Williams Financial Strategy*, on the ocean floor. No heralds marched. No horns sounded. No trumpets blared.

The silence was deafening.

Three years later, in the March 1993 issue of *Futures* magazine, a full-page advertisement for subscriptions to *Commodity Timing* appeared, with the header, "Legendary Larry Williams does it again and makes this special subscription offer for you." The copy reads:

> Yes, the 1992 tabulations are in and Larry Williams *Commodity Timing* sweeps the honors. Of all the major services whose every trade was monitored in 1992 by Commodity Traders Consumers reports, Larry Williams *Commodity Timing* was the clear winner. And, more importantly, the big winners were his subscribers who found out you really could make money trading commodities.

> Talk about consistency, and you'll talk about Larry Williams.

Hats off to Larry. You just can't keep a good man down.

3

MISCONCEPTIONS

Commodity Futures Basics

A doctor friend of mine—proficient enough in his own practice—once prevailed upon me to explain commodities to him. I gave him some commodity reports to read, and after a few weeks we sat down to talk about what he had learned. Expecting some penetrating questions, I was much taken by surprise when he opened: "How come pork bellies go up one day, down the next, back up the next, then down again? It's absurd. There's no sense to it!"

That's when I realized how dangerous it is to assume an audience will be familiar with notions that traders who have been around the market for some time take for granted. For instance, take the words *long* and *short*, two of the most common terms you will encounter in commodities. In trading circles these expressions have very definite meanings—everyone understands them completely. But elsewhere, *short* is jargon and will only be understood vaguely, if at all.

Selling short, which means contracting to deliver something one does not possess, appears at first sight to violate the code of fair play, if not common sense. Buying, or going long, is more readily understood because to speculate on something—be it a house, antiques, or baseball cards—you normally buy first then sell later—at a profit you hope. In commodities, however, buying and selling short are simply the necessary and opposite components of each transaction.

Think of a commodity trade as a simple bet—a straightforward wager between two individuals on the outcome of an uncertain event in the future. That event is the price of a commodity on a specified delivery date. To fully appreciate the versatility of the commodity futures contract, consider real estate, where no futures market exists. Suppose you correctly forecast a boom in real estate values; you capitalize on your correct judgment by buying property early and selling when you feel the market is peaking out. Suppose you are correct in identifying the peak and, therefore, the subsequent decline in prices. Can you profit from the price decline as well as the price rise? In real estate the answer is *no*. In commodities with actively traded futures markets, the answer is *yes*. If you believe gold, or pork bellies, or soybeans are overpriced, you can back up this judgment by selling short, expecting to deliver the goods later, after picking them up more cheaply.

Let's say sugar looks too high at 13 cents per pound. You would like to bet that three months from now, or three weeks from now, it will be lower in price. Who is going to bet against you? How do you find someone who wants to bet that sugar is going up just at the precise moment you want to bet the other way?

Well, you have the commodity futures exchange, and the sugar futures contract. Through your commission broker you will find a buyer to make a contract with you at a definite price agreed upon *now*. Between the two parties to the contract are interposed your commodity broker, the exchange, and the buyer's commodity broker. Nevertheless, anonymous though he or she may be, there, on the other end of your contract waits another speculator hoping that *you* are wrong and trying to take *your* money. Keep it in mind.

A commodity futures contract calls for delivery of a specific quantity of the commodity at a particular location and during a particular delivery period. Contracts are standardized as to amount and quality; they are indistinguishable from each other, and they may be transferred to third parties (after all, futures contracts are no more than obligations on paper). If you change your opinion about a position you have taken, you can transfer the obligation to someone else, via the exchange, where you will always find a trader willing to assume your obligation. The function of the exchange is to bring bettors together in such numbers that any buyer can always find a seller, and any seller can always find a buyer.

Whenever you close out a position in a contract (that is, when you sell one you have previously purchased, or when you buy one you have previously sold), your commission broker calculates the difference between the purchase price and the sale price, regardless of the order in which the transactions occurred, and credits or debits the cash balance in your account accordingly. In this way, cash flows back and forth among the players with no physical transactions whatsoever.

Reading the Financial Columns

Most large newspapers publish a daily summary of commodity trading. Take, for example, the daily numbers for COCOA, a commodity traded on the New York Cocoa Exchange (Table 3-1).

The size of the cocoa contract is ten metric tons, and prices are quoted in dollars per ton. On Friday, August 20, 1993, the September future closed at $979 per ton, or at a total contract value of $9,790. If *margin* is set at *five* percent of contract value, then one contract of September cocoa could be financed with approximately $500 (.05 x 9,790). This is the amount a commission broker would demand from his client as a security deposit against an adverse price change. It is the small security deposit, or margin, that creates the great leverage available to commodity traders. For example, an increase in the price of September cocoa from $979 per ton to $1,029 per ton is equivalent to a change in total contract value of $500. Therefore, a trader who is long during this price move (a price change of only five percent) will find his $500 investment doubling to $1,000; a trader who is short will find his $500 going to zero. Of course, traders need not finance their positions with such small amounts—and five percent *is* very close to legal minimum. As I will show you later, trading with equity close to minimum margin levels is a very dangerous practice.

Table 3-1 contains essential data on all contract months that were being traded on August 20, 1993, from the nearest delivery contract, *September 1993*, to the most distant contract, *May 1995*. Each delivery month is a distinct futures contract, independently variable from all the others and with its own set of statistics. Going across the page now, from left to right, and taking *December 1993* as an illustration, we have:

Sea Hi and Sea Low (1506, 919) The highest and lowest prices recorded since the contract began trading. (In cocoa, contracts begin trading 24 months before delivery comes due.)

Open (1018) The opening price—the price at which the first transaction of August 20 was completed.

High (1031) The highest price of the day.

Low (1012) The lowest price of the day.

Settle (1030) The last price of the day.

Change (+1) The change in the settlement price from the previous day.

Open Interest (36056) The number of outstanding contracts in the *December 1993* future.

TABLE 3-1

COCOA

SeaHi	SeaLow	Mth.	Open	High	Low	Settle	Chg.	OpInt
COCOA 10 tonnes, dollars per tonne								
1536		Sep93	970	980	965	979		676
1506	919	Dec93	1018	1031	1012	1030	+1	36056
1345	956	Mar94	1052	1067	1049	1065	+1	18034
1368	978	May94	1068	1068	1076	1084	+2	6361
1270	999	Jul94	1087			1104	+2	2210
1280	1022	Sep94	1115	1125	1115	1125	+4	4415
1185	1048	Dec94	1130			1153	+4	5227
1185	1085	Mar95	1160			1176	+4	4001
1185	1111	May95	1180			1196	+4	756

		Prv Sales		Prv Open Int				Chg.
		5466		77736				-584

From the bottom line, under COCOA, we also have:

Prv Sales (5466) Trading volume—the number of contracts traded the previous day.

Prv Open Int (77736) The open interest from the previous day. (Total for all contracts.)

Chg (-584) The change in open interest from the day before. This measures whether, on balance, players are entering or leaving the game.

When a new buyer enters into a futures contract, he may complete his transaction with a new seller who is going short. Or, he may complete his transaction with someone who was already long and wishes to sell out his position. In the latter case, the new buyer is *replacing* an existing buyer, and the number of contracts outstanding does not change as a result of the transaction—the open interest remains the same. However, if the buyer has encountered a new short-seller, the number of outstanding contracts must increase by one—open interest (+1). If two speculators, one long and one short, decide to flatten their positions simultaneously, and encounter each other's order on the trading floor, then an outstanding contract disappears and the open interest drops by one—open interest (-1).

On any given day, depending on the composition of transactions, the open interest may increase, decrease, or stay the same. If, on balance, new players are entering the market, the "interest" will be increasing, and the total open interest will rise. If players are leaving, the "interest" will be lessening and the open interest will drop. The volume of trading and the open interest are independently variable, and theoretically there is no limit to the open interest that may build up in a future. Typically, a future for a specific month starts with zero open interest, builds to a peak about two months before delivery, then declines until delivery day, when very few open contracts remain open (the vast majority having been offset through traders exiting the market). Those contracts that are left belong to commercial interests intending to make or take delivery. This pattern is reflected in the open interest statistics of Table 3-1. *December 1993* has the highest open interest, 36056 contracts; *September 1993*, approaching expiry, has 676 contracts outstanding; and *May 1995*, the farthest future on the board, has an open interest of 756 contracts.

A futures contract is a device of delightful simplicity. With an appreciation of these few basics, and with the occasional reference to the glossary when jargon pops up, all that follows should be accessible to the general reader.

Now it is time to turn from the delightful simplicity of the futures concept to the fearful complexity of its application.

Living with Uncertainty

A trader must learn to live with the unexpected, and learn to make difficult decisions under conditions of great uncertainty, and possibly—if he's not careful—under conditions of great pressure. Uncertainty surrounds any decision, of course, or there would be nothing to decide. A decision on whether to set out on the golf course under threatening skies, for example, does not take much soul-searching. If we call the game off and the sun comes out, we feel mildly cheated. If we play and get drenched, we say tough luck. But, whatever the outcome, we are not likely to dwell on the wisdom of the original decision; weather is highly unpredictable and accepted as such. If it turns foul, we don't waste time trying to *explain* why this happened. Nor do we use the experience to predict what will happen next time.

Uncertainty, then, is taken for granted in an environment with which we are familiar, and when the stakes are relatively minor. But when the ante is raised, when the adrenalin starts to flow as it inevitably does in trading, logical responses to uncertain outcomes may disappear, and people will start demanding "explanations for the weather." Credulity will increase, and, as Henry David Thoreau pointed out: "Men will believe in the bottomlessness of a pit without ever taking the trouble to sound it."

To be sure, randomness has little aesthetic appeal. A desire for order and predictability, and a preference for patterns over chaos is a normal enough human impulse. Since the majority of commodity traders are normal enough human beings, and since we know their collective fate, it follows that the exception, the successful trader, will have developed rather abnormal human responses. He will have trained himself to deal with uncertainty in a rather unusual way. In large part, what this book is about is conditioning—the cultivation of the abnormal response.

Chartists

The commodity price chart is a favorite mechanism traders use to impose order on the disorder endemic in the market. Chartists are traders who ignore economic determinants in coming to their trading decisions. They rely entirely on emerging chart formations, for it is their belief that the best way to forecast prices is to study recent patterns of daily highs, lows, and closes.

An imaginative chartist "sees" identifiable patterns among the jumble of prices—patterns he believes have predictive value: *head-and-shoulders* formations, *flags*, and *pennants*, to name but a few of the more popular. *Support* and *resistance* levels also mean a lot to chartists.

In the standard bar chart (Figure 3-1), time is measured along the horizontal axis; price (high, low, and close) is measured on the vertical axis. In chartist jargon, what we see at the extreme right of this chart is a market approaching a triple bottom. Such formations occur fairly regularly in all commodities. It is apparent that the price is close to a level where, in a *geometric* sense, it appears to have bounced *twice before*.

Chartists watching the action around time *A* may be bullish or bearish, depending largely on what they want to perceive. Although the chartist will claim that the chart formation itself will be the determinant of future price direction, so logically he ought to be unbiased, it is almost certain he will be favoring one side of the market. What the chartist really wants from his chart is support for his bias.

A chartist who is bullishly disposed will be looking to buy in area A. Impressed by the geometry of the chart, which does have a nonrandom look about it, he visualizes a support level. He perceives a "floor" under the market, and experience tells him that objects bounce off floors more often than fall through them. Therefore, in his estimation, a *long* position established in area A is a good bet. The bearishly inclined chartist also recognizes the support level. But for him, far from being solid ground, the "floor" consists of rotting planks about to cave in under the crushing weight of a falling chandelier. For him, any penetration of the support level will be a signal of an impending price collapse. Therefore, he is ready to go *short*.

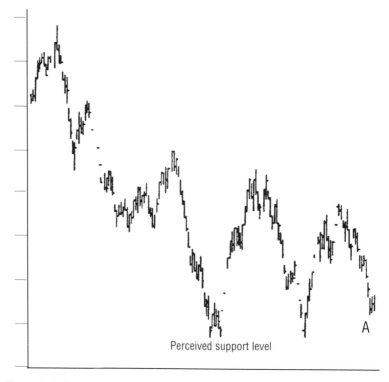

Perceived support level

Figure 3-1 Support and resistance levels

Who is right? Let's probe their thinking a little. The existence of support and resistance levels—the building blocks of chartism—would seem to imply coordinated efforts by groups of like-minded players to align themselves cooperatively. After all, an individual cannot support or resist a price all alone. Yet traders *are* individuals; they do *not* act in concert; they are adversaries, not only the longs against the shorts, for such is the fickle nature of the commodity trader that allegiances are constantly switching. In military analogy, the commodity pit is the most chaotic battleground imaginable, a conflict where everyone wants to be on the side that's winning. Loyalties do not exist. Traders are united only in the pursuit of self-interest; brothers-in-arms they are not. Why should there be support or resistance? Support for whom, by whom? Does the commodity care?

The reality of the price chart is that even a randomly produced set of numbers drawn in a bar chart will generate peaks, valleys, and areas of congestion, which *geometrically* appear to have meaning, though no meaning exists. Insofar as chartists are able, as a group, to identify potential areas of resistance and support—even if these be random occurrences, as I am suggesting—they may, in their efforts to outwit each other, succeed in increasing price volatility at certain times and price levels. The actions of chartists may therefore cause prices to stall temporarily, thus lending credence to the belief that support and resistance levels are real. Such self-fulfilling prophecies are most likely to be short-lived, unpredictable in their own way, and of no real consequence.

One prediction can be made with certainty: The price will eventually move substantially away, up or down, from any perceived support or resistance level; it has to, given enough time. In the case of a support level, if the price goes up, the bull chartist will be vindicated; his floor theory will have been proven correct. If, on the other hand, the price goes down, the bear will have seen *his* ideas confirmed. Fine, for whoever is correct. The winner will be doubly convinced of the significance of support levels in general, because it worked in this *particular* case—an error.

What will the loser read into his loss, though? Naturally, he will be disappointed at the outcome. But will he be disposed to review his beliefs? Will support lose credibility with *him*, in the way that it gained credibility with the winner? Not likely. Rather, the losing chartist will look for special conditions that account for the chart failure in this particular instance. Accordingly, the failed test of the theory will not be accorded its proper weight.

Harmless illusions like these…

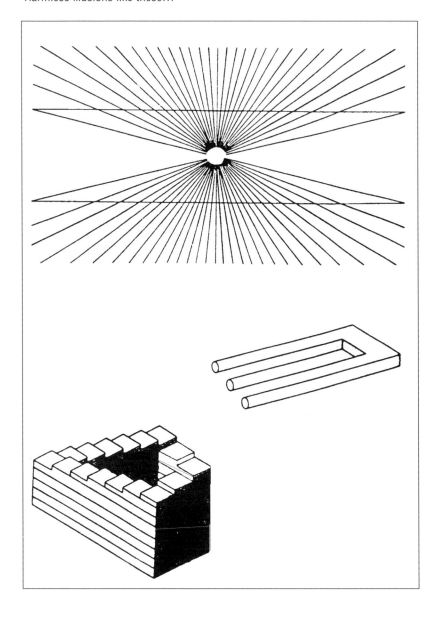

...Can lead to this

— Complex Head & Shoulders Bottom

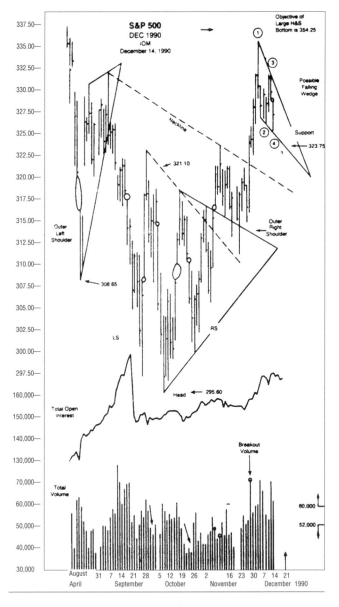

Figure 3-2 Who says the market is a random-walk? You can always "join the dots" and invent your own order. There's no one to pronounce you right or wrong. (From *Technical Analysis & Options Strategy* by K. H. Shaleen.)

Regardless of who wins, it will be a victory for chartism. It's not so surprising that people persistently read more into charts than is really there. Consider the capacity of the mind to perceive never-ending staircases, to see straight lines as curves, and to construct pictures from disconnected blobs. Such facilities, fascinating and adaptively useful as they may be, are a curse on the need to keep a clear head when trading. In price forecasting, the geometric illusion is a powerful one, and an illusion that must be resisted vigorously.

The desire to draw lines and triangles on bar charts may stem from a deeply rooted unwillingness in the human psyche to accept the existence of a cruel and dispassionate universe. The chart is a kinder, gentler creature when its intractable squiggles are neatly bound into nice orderly channels and wedges. Children get great satisfaction from connecting the numbered dots in a puzzle, and seeing a horse and rider appear from nowhere. It would be equally satisfying if the universe could be made to reveal its purpose simply through the drawing of neat little triangles on a commodity price chart. I'm sorry, commodity trading is strictly for adults, and if we want to make any sense of it, we really have to put away childish things.

Murphy's Law

There is no geometric interpretation of any chart that can withstand serious critical scrutiny. Take the simple *trendline*. This is a straight line superimposed on a chart, and drawn connecting (in the case of a down trend) the descending peaks on a daily or weekly bar chart. In chartist philosophy, if price breaks through an established *down* trend line to the *up* side, a reversal is considered to have taken place. The trendline-penetration school of thought has it that protracted bull and bear markets naturally proceed in straight-line fashion, and that when this pattern is violated, a major change in price direction will occur.

The trendline is born of a geometrically inspired desire; there is no *a priori* reason to suppose that a bull or bear market should proceed at a constant rate of increase or decrease. A path does not ascend from a plain to a mountain top at a steady rate of ascent; sometimes the path is steep, sometimes it is flat, and sometimes it goes down—all on the way up. It would be ludicrous to expect dips in the path to fall on a straight ascending line, and even more ludicrous to attempt to confirm this.

The trendline on a bar chart *can* look impressive, *after* it is drawn. Unfortunately, by the time the line can be drawn, it is too late to act upon it. During the Watergate hearings twenty years ago, a favorite question was asked of witnesses: "What did you know, and when did you know it?" These are questions the chartist might well reflect upon before running wild with his pencil and ruler.

The present day scion of technical trading is John J. Murphy, whose *Technical Analysis of the Futures Market* is perhaps the most popular of all books on technical analysis. Murphy appears regularly on a financial news network—where he interprets chart action on stocks and futures contracts and answers viewers' questions. He avoids making forecasts, wrapping his "interpretations" with so many layers of qualification that it is difficult to measure whether his remarks have any value or not. Some observations from his book, however, are most revealing.

Murphy is a strong advocate of the trendline as a means of determining when a trend has changed. In a bear trend, for example, he suggests drawing a line connecting rally highs. A line connecting *two* rally highs is considered a tentative trendline, while a trendline connecting *three* rally highs each one lower than the previous one suggests a *strongly established trendline* whose subsequent penetration on the up side is indicative of a change in market direction. These ideas are summarized, schematically, and succinctly, in Figure 3-3.

Let's see how this definition of a trendline plays out on an actual chart. Figure 3-4 is a commodity price chart which reproduces as accurately as possible trendlines drawn by Murphy in his book. I suggest the reader study Figures 3-3 and 3-4 carefully, before turning to Page 55. Can you spot the inconsistency between the author's definition and his interpretation?

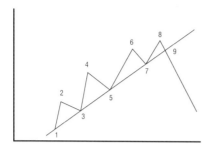

Chartists believe that once an upward trendline is established, subsequent dips near the line offer good buying opportunities. In this example, points 5 and 7 could be used to establish a long position. The violation of the trendline at point 9 signals a reversal of the trend and the point at which all longs should be liquidated.

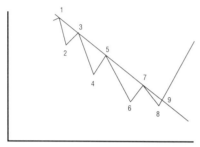

With a downward trendline in place, points 5 and 7 provide selling opportunities. An upside trend reversal is signaled by the violation of the trendline at point 9.

Figure 3-3 Trendline analysis, according to John J. Murphy. So far, so good. Problems, however, arise in its application (Figure 3-4).

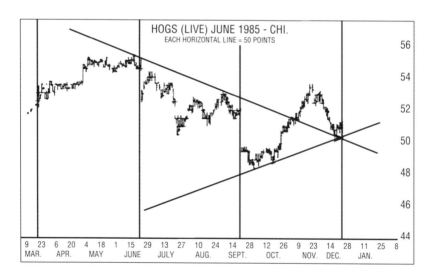

According to Murphy, the down trendline along the June/September highs became a support line in December, after it had broken through on the upside. In addition, says Murphy, the up trendline along the October lows checks the price decline in December.

Figure 3-4 Can you spot the inconsistencies between theory and application?

Now look at Figure 3-5, which is the same chart with the *true* trendline, which would have been established *given the information available on or around August 17*. In adding this line, I am using Murphy's exact criterion for establishing a down trendline: a line connecting two reaction highs successfully tested by a third reaction high. Note how this true trendline (by Murphy's definition, not mine) was penetrated decisively in early September, giving a trend reversal signal that failed. Of course, trendline penetrations that *don't* work are not what technical analysts are going to show you. I could also draw in another trendline, this time an *up* trendline connecting the reaction lows of July, August, and September. Do you see that if you were to play this up trendline according to Murphy's principle, you would have been buying just before the massive gap down in late September? Whenever you feel seduced by an attractive chart formation with a neat trendline, I suggest you take a hard look at Murphy's chart of June 85 Hogs. Not very clever stuff, I'm afraid. How could Murphy fail to see such a glaring anomaly? Simple. Chartists see what they want to see, not what is really there.

> The lesson? All examples of the alleged usefulness of trendlines, flags, pennants, etcetera, will, under scrutiny, be shown to be the product of hindsight, perceived *after* the occurrence of the events they are alleged to foresee.

Chart readers might also ponder the philosophical implications of forecasting by looking backward. The notion that prices evolve in predictive patterns is consistent with a deterministic view of the universe. Frankly, I doubt whether commodity prices are preordained. It is possible, I suppose, and what a joke that would be on all of us!

Chartists don't care much for orange juice in January (Figure 3-6) or coffee in July. Why? They hate surprises. The weather confounds and exposes the true bankruptcy of the philosophy. It is in the cold weather markets that the real forces behind price change reveal themselves with a vengeance. A hundred chart resistance points will not keep orange juice from going up when a deep freeze hits Orlando. Yet it would hardly occur to the chartist that the same market forces so dramatically evident in weather markets might be responsible, in subtler ways, for price movements in all markets.

Figure 3-5 The *true* trendlines, which ought to have been drawn according to the definition of Figure 3-3. A false upside breakout would have occurred at the end of August. Furthermore, a trendline follower would have been buying in mid-September and been left holding the bag when the market gapped limit down. Hindsight is the chartist's best friend. Unfortunately, we cannot trade hindsight.

I wonder why we can't be happy with orange juice at whatever price gloriously unpredictable nature decides? A chart is no more than a reflection of man's feeble attempt to guess at the road ahead by looking in the rearview mirror.

Turtles

Richard Dennis is something of a legendary figure around the commodity markets, where he is reputed to have turned several hundred dollars into several hundred million. In the early eighties, so the story goes, he took under his wing a select group of aspiring super-traders called *The Turtles*, the object being to create an exclusive trading club—a kind of Knight Templars society of the trading pits, if you will. Dennis wanted to dispense his market wisdom—but only to his turtles. The methods by which these super-trading turtles were supposed to succeed were kept secret. In due course, a number of "baby turtles" were selected, weaned, and trained by Dennis. The turtles were then sworn to secrecy and made to sign nondisclosure documents.

Larry Williams, who made a million dollars in 1974 and won the *World Cup of Futures Trading* without any assistance from the turtles, has become a latter-day convert to "turtlemania." This, of course, several years after the debacles following his world championship victory. Williams has teamed up with a Richard Sands, one of the original baby turtles whose nondisclosure agreement has expired, and together they have begun offering the turtle system to the public at large. When the news was announced, the now-mature turtles flapped and snapped at this assault on their exclusivity, but all to no avail. The secret is out. Well, not quite *out*. The latest batch of hatchlings are also required to sign nondisclosure documents, so the turtle system will remain something of a mystery. Larry Williams was certainly impressed with its performance:

> During the winter of 1983, legendary trader Richard Dennis taught his trading system to 14 people who became known as The Turtles. They made $175 million dollars in the next five years.

—from the Williams advertisement

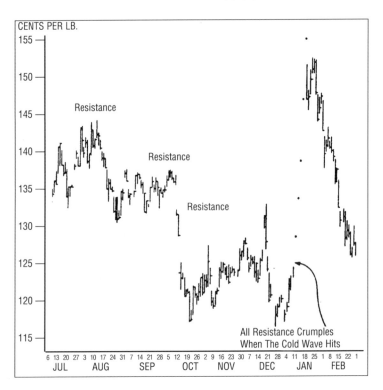

Figure 3-6 Orange juice after a freeze in Florida

That works out at over $10 million each. Surely Williams' offer must be a bargain when offered for only $2,500. Yet those who are forking out $2,500 each to hear the secrets of Dennis' success would do well to read an article in the July 1988 issue of *Futures* magazine:

> It is an understatement to say that legendary trader Richard Dennis is having a tough year. Two of Dennis's public commodity funds have stopped trading after losing more than 50% in April. He is no longer the trading advisor for Collins Future Fund II which dropped 75% in April. He had traded the fund since it started in 1984. He was also taken off the Collins III fund.
>
> ... From a high of more than $150 million under management, he is now trading $7 million in customer funds.
>
> ... Gone are the "turtles," the apprentices who managed in-house money. Gone is the marketing effort for his talents.

Shortly after this fiasco, Dennis announced his retirement and declared his intention to enter politics. That was back in 1988. Four years later, turtle-thought is back in vogue. Dennis is not around, but the promoters of his secret are trying very hard to capitalize on his legend. It looks like W. D. Gann all over again.

How could Dennis lose 75 percent of his fund's capital in one month? There is only one way to achieve such a result. You must massively overtrade your account, have a wanton disregard for risk, and be massively wrong. If you can get all three right at the same time, yes, it can be done. If you happen to be massively right, of course, you can make a fortune. Easy come, it seems, but just as easy go.

I am watching a turtle slowly make its way over some rocks on a small island. It moves irregularly without apparent purpose, sometimes pausing, sometimes backtracking, sometimes moving fast (for a turtle), sometimes hardly moving at all. It reminds me of the cocoa market. There is a flagpole in the middle of this island, providing a fixed reference from which to gauge the turtle's progress. I program my fancy watch to beep every two minutes, then fetch paper and pencil.

The turtle continues on its random walk, circling the flagpole, never getting really close, never straying very far. But then it begins to head straight for the water. If this keeps up, I'll be off the paper. Big question.

Is this the start of a trend, or just a "stochastic pop" leading nowhere? Now, if only I had that latest hand-held programmable software from ... It's a hot day and I have been working very late to finish this manuscript.

—Paul Myers

Seasonality and Other Myths

I already touched on seasonality when talking about the "sure-thing trading" of Larry Williams. Seasonality pops up regularly in various guises. For example, let's say that in eighteen of the last twenty-four years the price of live cattle has been higher on the first of December than on the first of November. Does that mean the strategy of buying on November 1 and holding the position for one month has a 75 percent chance of being successful? It certainly *has* been true. But did anyone suspect this twenty-four years ago? Will it pay to place *this* bet *this* year?

All commodities analyzed for seasonality will throw up what appear to be distinct patterns purely as a matter of chance. If chance were not the cause, and historical seasonal patterns had real predictive power, trading would simply be a case of placing bets and letting the probabilities do their stuff. But experience and common sense tells us, correctly, that the world is not like that. Presented with a seasonality claim, all one can do is apply common sense and judge from the evidence and from one's own experience whether chance or hidden order is the better explanation. Statistical inferences have to be assessed in relation to the available evidence, for there is no authority to pronounce them right or wrong.

One mustn't become pathologically skeptical, of course. Show me a pattern that has repeated for twenty-five years straight, and you'll definitely get my attention. You can show me plenty of eight out of tens, but so what? I could do that with a random number generator. Whenever you run into "sure things," or "How I made $864,000 last year starting with $50," there's a good chance that seasonality is behind it.

The seasonality fallacy *is* seductive. We are all inclined to put too much faith in the results of small samples and to overestimate grossly the repeatability of these results. People are notorious for predicting the outcome of an event as the result most common in previous trials, even when the process is suspected to be random.

It can be tricky, and common sense must always be applied. You shake a piggy bank and four pennies fall out. What are the chances that the next coin that falls out will also be a penny? Excellent. Many people collect pennies. Now you look at the dates on the coins. They are all the same. What is the likelihood that the next coin will bear the same date? Not so great. Few people collect coins of the same date in a piggy bank. Same evidence, different interpretation.

It's generally wiser to assume a process to be random, unless there is good reason to suppose it is not. Otherwise, you may fall into what psychologists call *the error of nonrepresentativeness*. This may be the most fallacious of all human intuitions, and an intuition that the successful trader must learn to resist. The myth of seasonality is a prime example of this error.

Even a *true* seasonal pattern is unlikely to reward anyone. For example, it is popularly believed that the stock market has a tendency to go up early in the new year; it's called the January effect, and they say it works most of the time. Perhaps it does. There might be a catch, though; the year that it *doesn't* work may balance all the years that it does.

Trading on Psychology

I have been dealing with attempts to read patterns into actual price history without considering the processes whereby the marketplace arrives at a price. I have argued that prices respond to events over which man has little control. (There are some exceptions, most notably, political interference.) Now, it is true that prices are expressed through interactions of buyers and sellers, so that it might be argued that people make prices. Except in the very short term, this is not so. But the perception is strong enough to spawn a school of commodity thinking with market psychology as its guiding principle.

Watch what the others are doing, says the market psychologist. Let's see who is long and who is short, how actively they are trading, and whether players on balance are entering or leaving the game. Hence the popularity of volume and open interest and various combinations of these statistics as forecasting tools. For example, many books will tell you that a price rise accompanied by an increase in trading volume is more bullish than a price rise accompanied by a decrease in volume.

But, let's say some crazy billionaire in Taiwan reads Larry Williams' book, finds a sure-thing seasonality trade, and buys ten thousand sugar contracts all on the same day. There you have your price rise, your increase in volume, and your increase in open interest. Is this bullish for the future? I'd be happy to bet against it. Using volume and open interest to forecast a commodity price is like forecasting the winner of a horse race by counting the number of people at the track.

Various *psychological indexes* are measured and published regularly by such organizations as the *Bullish Review* out of Minnesota, *Consensus Inc.* of Kansas City, and *Market Vane*. The latter two are basically polls purporting to measure which side of a market is favored by the majority of traders; the former tries to analyze the *composition* of traders on opposite sides of the market. To construct a psychological index, a pollster surveys brokerage firms each week for opinions on each commodity. When more than half favor buying, a *bullish consensus* reading for a commodity will be greater than 50 percent. If almost everyone interviewed wants to buy a commodity, the bullish consensus for that commodity will approach 100 percent.

There are no precise rules for trading using a bullish consensus reading. However, the philosophy behind it is most decidedly contrarian: Simply stated, when everyone thinks something is going up (*overbought* they call it), then it must be worth selling; and if everyone thinks something is going down (*oversold*), then it must be a good buy. The contrarian viewpoint is particularly attractive to the macho trader. He feels smart and brave—me against the world, so to speak. Moreover, a bullish consensus index is very easy to follow; commodities are ranked in order of bullishness, and it's basically a case of selling the bullish ones and buying the bearish ones. There's just one problem, though. The contrarian trader is always selling into rising markets, and buying into falling markets—guaranteeing that he will end up on the wrong end of major trends whenever these develop. Curiously, the bullish consensus is always high in a bull market.

It may seem odd that the measured consensus should always be in the same direction as the market has recently been moving, but there is a rather simple explanation. First, there is no such thing as a bullish consensus or a bearish consensus. At any point in time, the consensus in a futures market is 50 percent—exactly 50 percent. No more, no less. Long and short positions *must* balance at all times. Therefore, a bullish consensus of 80 percent, say, can mean only one thing: The longs have been eager to talk, while the majority of the shorts have either declined to express a point of view or have erroneously stated their true positions. Can you guess why a short-seller in a bull market might be less than candid—especially in hindsight? It's an old, old story; success has a thousand fathers, failure is an orphan.

Other popular variations on the mass-psychological approach to price forecasting make use of the *Commitments of Traders (COT)* report put out regularly by a government agency, The Commodity Futures Trading Commission. This report shows the composition of the open interest in each commodity, broken down into these categories: commercials, hedgers, large traders, and small traders. The COT report serves no obvious economic purpose other than to keep a staff of bureaucrats employed. However, its statistics are avidly awaited by analysts who believe the report reveals what "smart money" is doing.

Smart money may or may not exist. But there is no hard evidence that large traders or commercials, as a group, hold a significant trading edge over the small trader. Indeed, it would be very surprising if this were the case, for it would be too obvious a tip-off, and whatever edge momentarily existed would quickly be neutralized by traders shifting positions. The veracity of the COT report itself is also suspect, because the lines of demarcation between commercials, hedgers, and large speculators are fuzzy, to say the least. Some services go as far as to construct derivative indexes from the COT reports and will advance corroborating examples where trading decisions based on using such indexes have worked out. Examples of noncorroboration you don't hear so much about.

The notion of smart money is hardly new and has some credence. After all, most of us know people who are considerably smarter than ourselves. The smart money hypothesis, however, ought to be amenable to objective testing. But, to the best of my knowledge, no one has advanced any statistically sound test results to support it.

One advisory service catering to the contrarian community is *The Bullish Review*, which publishes an index called the COT Index—an arbitrary formula based on the numbers within groupings on the COT reports. The COT Index is supposed to identify where commercial funds are moving, the premise being that commercials are usually right. If we wish to test the hypothesis that *commercials know better*, it shouldn't be too difficult; there's plenty of historical data. Even if it can be shown that commercials are just a little bit smarter, that finding, in itself, would be significant.

Imagine, having set up the premise that commercial positions are synonymous with smart money, you discover that commercials do indeed have a significant edge over the small trader; in other words let's say the hypothesis is confirmed. Now suppose that on breaking down this edge by commodity, you find considerable variation—a positive edge in soybeans and cattle, say, but a negative edge in orange juice. What would you infer from this breakdown—as far as taking action in the future is concerned?

Would you, for example, deduce that betting with the smart money in soybeans and cattle has a positive expectation, while betting with the smart money in orange juice has a negative expectation? Because, if that is your conclusion, why not go one step further and deduce that trading *against* the smart money in orange juice is a positive play? Why not go for *all* the marbles?

> This [orange juice] is the exception that proves the rule. You cannot go too far wrong trading *opposite* Commercials in this market.
>
> —*The Bullish Review* on orange juice

Excuse me, Bullish Review. What rule? Your whole philosophy rests on the premise that commercials are the *smart* guys. Surely you are not asking us to swallow a mixed hypothesis? Now you are telling us we have two types of commercials: *smart* commercials and *dumb* commercials. But tell us, please, why you think orange juice commercials should be so dumb when commercials in other markets are so smart? Are you not just a *little* bit curious, yourself?

Well, let me give you the answer. Your rather feeble case against commercials in orange juice is that they were caught short before two of the biggest bull markets in recent years. But what you fail to appreciate is that these bull markets erupted suddenly—one from a freeze, the other the result of a surprise crop forecast—events that stunned commercials and small speculators alike. What's more, a little fundamental investigating on your part would have revealed the one fact that makes a mockery of your theory: *Commercials always have the big short position going into the winter, for the simple reason that small speculators are terrified to be short.* Commercials receive a hefty premium for taking the short (risky) side of the market, and simply because they are sometimes jammed by a freeze proves *absolutely nothing* about their acumen or their likelihood of being right or wrong in the future.

Trading off mass psychology has its attractions, of course. It's quick, simple, requires little input, and is great for the ego when it works—a wonderful crutch for the nonthinker. I wholeheartedly welcome devotees of mass psychology to the trading pits, for they will become regular contributors to the trading kitty and never take the trouble to find out why.

I do not reject the psychological approach totally out of hand. One cannot rule out the possibility of beating the market purely on the strength of intuition. A trader, I suppose, may develop "antennae" that sense short-term rallies or declines, and that put him in sync with the short-term waves of buying and selling pressure hitting the market. I wouldn't rule that out completely. On the other hand, I have never seen anyone succeed consistently on intuition alone. Some floor brokers—those who execute orders in the trading pits—claim to have a winning edge just from being close to the action. Whether this is true or not I cannot say, never having been that close to the action myself. Floor brokers do have the advantage of paying almost zero commission, a major cost to the rest of us trying to beat the market from outside the pit. But floor brokers, I imagine, have all the same bad habits as the trading public at large.

Shortly, I will be dealing with rational approaches to uncertainty—ways of thinking that do not occur naturally to most people. There are countless theories on how to beat the market, and it is easy to obtain confirmations or verifications for nearly every theory—if it is confirmations that are sought. The witch doctor who performs a sun dance at dawn may convince the faithful that he is bringing the sun up. But let him sleep late one morning and he may end up in the soup—literally. That the market may not be beatable at all should be retained as a hypothesis, even though we hope to find evidence to the contrary. And any theory that appears to yield net positive results should be regarded not only with interest but also with a healthy dose of skepticism.

Too many would-be gurus of the market look for evidence to support their preconceived notions, and invariably find such evidence. Pay attention to the man who tries to refute his own theory, for it is only when a theory is hard to refute that it has any real power.

The Zero-Sum Game

Profits in commodities do not fall as the gentle rain from heaven; your opponents have to pay for them. We know that trading in the aggregate is a losing proposition. Why? Because trading is a zero-sum game with a commission charge. Traders can only redistribute their own funds among themselves; there is no infusion of money from any other source. Not only do traders play with their own money, they must "pay the house," in the form of a commission, each time they make a trade. Therefore, each trader, regardless of ability, starts out with an unfavorable edge against him. Whether this edge is significant remains to be seen. Suffice it to say that the winner must beat the market with enough of a margin to at least cover his own commission overhead.

If the market is a random walk—another way of saying that prices evolve in a totally unpredictable manner—then every trader must expect to lose, if he plays long enough. Trading could then be compared to a game like roulette with the zero on the wheel representing the commission. We ought to retain the market-as-random-walk hypothesis as a possibility, even though there appears to be powerful evidence to the contrary. That there are big winners each year does not, in itself, refute the random-walk theory. We are dealing with hundreds of thousands of players, and chance will have its way. Random walk or not, the average trader's expectation is zero, minus whatever commission charges he accumulates over his trading career—a sobering reality.

Regression

A pure-chance process is governed by what statisticians call the law of regression. Failure to perceive regression in operation may result in erroneous conclusions about a situation governed by pure chance.

> The instructors in a flight-training school, on the advice of psychologists, adopted a policy of praising their students after each successful execution of a flight maneuver. After some experience with this approach, the instructors claimed that high praise for a well-executed maneuver typically caused a poorer performance on the next try. Failing to observe regression at work, the instructors abandoned praise and began responding with equal indifference to both good and bad performances.

A true story, I'm told. And the moral? Should excellence be punished while the substandard is rewarded? Of course not. What the instructors failed to realize was that chance was largely responsible for the variations in performance observed in the maneuvers, just as chance is largely responsible for the sequencing of winners and losers a trader encounters in his trading—something worth remembering in the flush of confidence that comes after a string of winners, and the despair that sets in after a string of losses. Sometimes we feel like geniuses; sometimes we feel like bums. Truth is, we are probably just pawns in the grand regressive scheme of things.

So much of the action in the market is random that even the best traders may experience long periods of regressive results. Just as regression indicates chance, so lack of regression indicates nonrandomness. Do the performances of winners and losers regress towards zero over the long haul? Is a winner one year just as likely to be a loser the next? The answer is most definitely, *no*. Over the long haul, a small number of winners win fairly consistently—though not quite as consistently as a large number of losers lose. Were chance alone responsible for market performance, the roster of winners and losers would be continually changing. But this is not so; there is a definite *lack of regression* to be found in trading performance. Exactly how this lopsided redistribution of funds occurs through trading behavior remains to be seen. Few would argue that redistribution is very lopsided indeed. Figures of 90 to 99 percent losers are regularly quoted. Winners—consistent winners—are rather a rare breed. But they are out there winning, and sometimes winning very large amounts.

Losers come at the market with consistent, identifiable modes of behavior. From personal observation, I can vouch for two behavioral patterns associated with losing in commodities. If I may stretch an astronomical analogy, I will call these losing paradigms the *big-bang exit* and the *steady-state erosion.*

The big-bang exit is the destiny of the player who *overtrades*, or finances too much commodity with too little money. Exchanges set minimum margin levels, and sometimes these are very low indeed. An account trading with minimum margin can be wiped out in *one* day, and players who finance their speculations this way cannot expect to survive for more than a few trades. Like the gambler who gambles everything on one spin of the roulette wheel, one wrong call and the overtrader is history. The person who overtrades does not give himself a chance. He is most likely a novice to the market who has not thought very much about the negative aspects of high *leverage*. Since he will not be around long enough to pay many commissions, the overtrader contributes more or less directly to the jackpot.

What is to be learned from observing the folly of overtrading? Actually, very little. One is tempted to say: Let's observe an overtrader in action and do the opposite. But this doesn't work. There is no counter-strategy to overtrading; the mirror-image of overtrading is still overtrading. And, since gamblers occasionally do win big amounts, why take the chance of being on the opposite end of a big gamble that pays off? About all we can learn from the overtrader is not to emulate him, and quietly and gratefully accept his donation to the general pool of cash from which the profits of the winners must be drawn.

There is a great deal more to be learned from observing the habits of the *steady* loser. Here we are looking at a player who has enough savvy to stay alive, but not enough savvy to stay away. Aware of the ever-present danger of being blown out through overtrading, the steady loser is conservative to the extent that, barring sudden crop catastrophes or currency devaluations, he will not be forced out of positions due to money problems. The steady-state loser supports his habit by regularly injecting fresh capital into his account to shore up its continuously eroding balance.

As I pointed out before, regression is not a major component in the redistribution of wealth among players. There is distinct nonrandomness in the way the kitty gets divided up. Losers tend to keep losing and, significantly, they *lose much faster than chance alone would account for*. If losing were a strict matter of chance, the losing rate would be determined by commission charges, since winning and losing trades would tend to balance. What I am suggesting is that the habitual loser possesses a *losing technique*, which ensures he will achieve results far worse than those he would achieve if he were to trade simply at random. Don't laugh. This is the irony confronting the vast majority of traders—they uncover a potent market weapon, but unwittingly point it directly at themselves. How do they manage this? By cultivating and perfecting a repertoire of bad habits.

Dr. Alex Elder, a psychiatrist and trader, has some fascinating insights into the psychology of the chronic losing trader whose romance with the market parallels the alcohol's addiction to booze. In Elder's view, a loser can only stop losing if he confronts his problem the way a reformed alcoholic confronts liquor.

> Every morning before trading I sit in front of the quote screen in my office and say: "Good morning, my name is Alex, and I am a loser. I have it in me to do serious financial damage to my account." This is like an AA meeting—it keeps my mind focused on the first principles. Even if I take thousands of dollars out of the market today, tomorrow I will say: "Good morning, my name is Alex, and I am a loser."

Could there be a way to harness the "losing power" of the chronic steady-state loser? Theoretically, yes. In practical terms, however, it would involve some extraordinarily perverse planning. Let's be perverse. Imagine we form a trading team from among the most consistently bad traders we know.

Now we ask this team to trade with the sole objective of losing money. Let's make this a trading contest—The World Cup for Losers—by promising a large reward to the one who can lose the most in a year. Will these chronic losers now be able to lose when they want to, in the same way they lost when they were trying to win?

Not a chance. They will win, simply because they are trying to lose. The reason for this apparent paradox is that, while the chronic loser's *objective* may be changed, his *behavior* in pursuit of that objective cannot be changed. Faced with the bizarre objective of trying to lose, the chronic loser will grab at losses quickly because taking losses will be instantly gratifying. Likewise, he will avoid taking profits on winners, since all his instincts will tell him to procrastinate.

For the trader trying to beat the market on pure technique alone, there could hardly be a better strategy (if it could be implemented) than that of simply *fading*, or opposing, all the trades of all the chronic losers. If you were to examine the accounts of the typical commodity brokerage firm, identify all the *open trade losses*, take the *opposite positions* in your own account, and hold these opposite positions until the clients closed them out, you would, in effect, be galvanizing the collective power of *losers anonymous*. And you would win, because you couldn't help but win!

The Crying Game

If taking a loss is such an unpleasant step to take, does it follow that a loser will usually hold a losing position until the contract runs out of trading time? Actually, no. Some traders *are* sufficiently stubborn that they will only quit a losing position when the contract expires. Most losses, however, are cashed in on a whim, when the trader loses patience or can no longer stand looking at the open trade losses on his brokerage slips. Ironically, chronic losing positions often get liquidated just as the market is turning in the losing trader's favor. If you have endured a losing position for some time and then find the market coming back your way, the temptation to break even or get out at a small profit may be overpowering. Needless to say, this is normally a bad move.

Even if a trader wants to get out of the market with a small loss, he will find it psychologically much easier to wait for a rally (if he is selling) or wait for a dip (if he is buying) than to use a stop in the first place. Shall I get out now, or shall I wait for the market to come back? Such quandaries bedevil all traders whenever they get careless. Traders who do not use stops risk becoming permanently hobbled by indecision. Trading without a plan can sap your energy and distract you from the real business at hand—looking for opportunities.

For the most part, traders detest stop orders. One of the reasons is that if the stop price turns out to be the extreme price of a minor move against the trader's position, insult is piled upon injury. Having a stop taken out by the market is rather like having a cavity filled by the dentist: The waiting is worse than the drilling. And it is definitely no fun *watching* a stop being hit—another good reason for keeping a respectable distance from the market.

You don't want to use stops? Well, sometimes you will be proven right and derive a satisfaction of sorts: the satisfaction of having toughed it out and prevailed. But this is not the way to win in commodities, where all "feel good" moves are bad for the health of your account. People are naturally optimistic, so the widespread reluctance to use stops is very understandable on psychological grounds. Deliberately preparing for a loss is perverse, pessimistic, unnatural, yet correct—the reason that the vast majority of traders can *never* win in commodities.

> A scorpion wants to cross a river, but he can't swim. He asks a frog, who can, if he can hitch a ride on the frog's back.
>
> "You'll sting me," says the frog.
>
> "It would not be in my interest to sting you," says the scorpion, "because then I would drown."
>
> The frog thinks about the scorpion's logic, finds it impeccable, agrees to take the scorpion on his back, then braves the waters. Half way across the river, the frog feels a burning spear in his side. The scorpion has stung him after all. As they both sink beneath the waves, the frog cries out.
>
> "Why did you sting me, Mr. Scorpion? For now we both will die."
>
> "I can't help it," replies the scorpion. "It's in my nature."
>
> —*The Crying Game* (Movie, 1992)

Fundamentals and Technicals

Winners and losers both pay the same commission charges, and these can be large, especially for frequent traders. Funds must flow from losers to winners at such a rate that winners overcome the commission edge against them with a good deal to spare. How does this come about?

It is still an open question whether winners beat the market with superior information or by employing superior technique. The terms *fundamental* and *technical* crop up repeatedly in commodity discussions, so we should be absolutely clear about the meaning of each. In practice, a trader may employ elements of both fundamental and technical analysis. However, these two philosophies of trading are grounded in radically different beliefs about the nature of price change.

The fundamental trader perceives the future to be essentially *independent* of the past, so that he is keenly interested in economics and current events, and not particularly interested in price charts. The technical trader sees the future as *highly dependent* upon the past and therefore best forecasted from recent price history and without regard to current economic realities. For a philosophical (though imperfect) analogy, we are talking *free-will* versus *determinism*.

Consider, first, what is meant by fundamentals. I think we can all agree that prices must ultimately reflect conditions of supply and demand—only a supply squeeze could make sugar go from 6 cents to 45 cents, as it has done twice in the last twenty years. But in what way, one might ask, did such bull markets evolve? Is it possible that the price of sugar advanced in highly irregular waves, so that the price chart still conformed, *technically*, to a random walk? Put another way, is it possible for a big price move to occur in a commodity in such a way that a technical trader will not be able to capitalize on it? Few would imagine such a possibility. I do. At least, I don't dismiss the idea. Remember, the technical trader ignores fundamentals; he must be prepared to go short just as easily as he is prepared to go long; he may be repeatedly *whipsawed*, even in a strongly trending market. I am not saying he *will* be whipsawed, only that it is conceivable.

Let's say a technical trader adopts a symmetrical strategy; he goes long after a set reversal amount off a market low price, holds long until a similar set reversal amount off a market high, then liquidates and goes short (Figure 3-7). Here is a disciplined attempt to trade with the market trend, but an attempt that loses because it is playing both sides. And this despite a sustained advance. A fundamental trader who calls the market direction correctly will be much less likely to lose; he may be stopped out occasionally, but he would still catch most of the move—and naturally he would never be short.

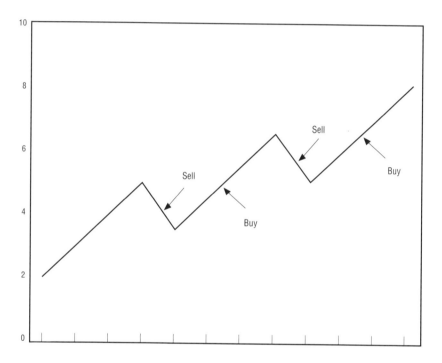

Figure 3-7 A market may respond to fundamentals, yet still confound technical traders.

Toss a regular six-sided cube repeatedly and tally the results. A completely "fair" cube will land 1, 2, 3, 4, 5, or 6 with equal probability, 1/6. If the result is 4, 5, or 6, mark a point higher on your paper by one unit. If the result is 1, 2, or 3, mark the point lower by one unit. Toss the cube until you have produced enough points to generate a chart. The result must be a random walk, for there is no way of influencing the outcome of a toss from what has gone before. But what if the dice are "loaded" so that the cube has a slightly increased chance of coming up 4, 5, or 6 than of coming up 1, 2, or 3. The result will no longer be a random walk. An objective observer, however, would be unlikely to detect the bias. To him, the result would still be a random walk—unless the bias were gross, and he would lack the information to bet with the bias in his favor.

To the player who is aware of the bias in the cube—that is, the player with fundamental information—the game is *not* a random walk. In time, he can capitalize on his knowledge by betting on the right side. Some academics argue that if stock and commodity prices *are* random walks, winning by any means is a matter of luck. From the analogy above, I believe that this is not necessarily the case. Randomness may reside in the blinkered eye of the beholder, and fundamental traders may profit amidst *apparent* price chaos—if they are fundamentally correct.

How might such traders acquire this fundamental information? Consider some possibilities. Perhaps there are soybean experts—marketing specialists, say—working for the big grain companies whose intelligence on upcoming export orders or on crop exports may give a decisive advantage in price forecasting. Perhaps there are pork belly specialists who skulk around cold-storage warehouses counting the bacon slabs, while the rest of us are munching on BLT sandwiches.

And maybe this pattern of "inside" advantage is true of all commodities— that is, each commodity with its own group of insiders habitually operating with an information edge over the general public. A plausible explanation, certainly: insiders beating outsiders. Plausible, but untrue, I believe. So-called insiders seem to fare no better than anyone else when it comes to playing the market. Farmers, for example, are notoriously poor judges of grain prices. Cattle ranchers are just as bad at beef. Foreign exchange traders are forever embarrassing the banks they work for by racking up losses in currency speculation. Working close to the physicals seems to breed an insider's bravado, which goes hand in hand with stubbornness and an inclination to hide losses under the pretence of hedging.

In *The Merchants of Grain*, an exposé of the machinations of the international grain companies, Dan Morgan agrees with the insider view of commodity trading:

The fact is that the places where grain is actually physically sold in huge quantities—Geneva, Winnipeg, Ottawa, Paris, London, and Moscow—are where prices are really made. What happens at the exchanges tells us about changes in the balance of supply and demand that usually have already occurred. The floor men have a more glamorous and exciting life than most, but it is the life of a mercenary sent into battle by generals who oversee the whole battlefield from some remote command post—from the wheat, corn, and soybean desks of Cargill, or from the map room of Continental far away in Switzerland.

This would be a depressing situation indeed—if it were true. Morgan wants us to believe that a privileged clique controls the price of grain and that the rest of us are merely drones playing a game where the outcome is a foregone conclusion—we lose, they win. Not true. Big winners in the grain market are often *outsiders*. The much talked about secret wheat sale to the Russians in 1972 is probably the only documented instance of insiders enjoying a significant advantage over outsiders. It's not that such plays won't ever happen again; they might. But they are so infrequent that for practical purposes they can be discounted.

The truth is that successful speculators are winners across the board; they win in all markets, though not all at the same time, of course. One year it may be soybeans, the next gold, the next wherever the action is. Winners suffer losses too, but their wins dwarf their losing trades. Successful speculation has little to do with specialized knowledge or insider information about particular commodities. It is rather a question of understanding how to interpret news differently from the crowd, a question, perhaps, of looking at the world from a different perspective. For example, a good trader learns to suffer, with equanimity, the slings and arrows of outrageous fortune—instead of getting angry and becoming impotent.

All the big winning plays I have seen in the market can be traced to a correct call on economic fundamentals. Big trades are not stumbled upon by accident. The trader who correctly identifies a prospective shortage of pork bellies, say, based on changes in sow breeding habits, must have an advantage over the technical trader who is forecasting belly prices from charts, because the fundamentalist will be correctly biased to the long side of the market. Two other factors will be in his favor. He will likely be concentrating a lot of fire power in that one position, because good fundamental ideas don't pop up every day. And he will be more inclined to persist with the position for some time, because fundamental developments take time to unfold.

It is one thing to predict a move and another to nail down a profit from it. The market may prove sluggish, and be slow to react to significant news. The market may exhaust the trader's patience and may even cause him to exit the position in frustration just before his judgment is confirmed.

What's more, the true state of supply and demand for a commodity can be obscured by forces beyond the trader's ken. Cocoa traders rely on crop forecasts from "pod-counters" who may be bribed, stoned, or just plain lazy and inaccurate. As a consequence, should traders avoid cocoa because of possible misinformation? I don't think so. One accepts inaccuracy as a natural hazard and plays the game accordingly. The way to counteract bad information—or incorrect analysis—is to back up all trading positions with technical trading discipline, so that no matter how wrong a forecast turns out to be, it cannot inflict a serious wound or result in premature ejection from the game. This means no careless selling of a rally without a stop; no giving the market "just one more day," which becomes one more week or one more month; no averaging against the trend in a show of futile bravado.

The technician believes that a price series is not a random walk at all. He has to, for there is no other justification for what he does. Circumstantially, there is support for this point of view. After all, if losers lose more than by chance alone—using no fundamental inputs—should it not be possible to win by doing the opposite? But the opposite of what? I already discussed the natural reluctance we all have to taking a loss and how losers always succumb to this reluctance.

Why a trader is prone to persist with a losing trade is rooted in the confirmation bias which creeps into his attitude *after* he has taken a position in the market. The brain accepts new information supporting a position more readily than it accepts new information tending to undermine a position, so that judgments become distorted, and traders will hold on to losing positions they would definitely reject as new trades. It's pretty safe to say that the average trader has no problem sticking with a trend—provided it is against him.

A habit common in losers is that of entering positions by buying dips and selling rallies—an innocuous tendency, superficially, since short-term price movements look very random, but dangerous, since it reveals a propensity in the trader to go against the trend. It may be comfortable to know that in buying today's price dip you got your cattle more cheaply than yesterday's buyers. Comforting, perhaps, but misleading, for today's dip may turn out to be the start of a major slide. Odds seem to slightly favor the continuation of *any* trend, even a short-term one. There is a widespread belief that it is somehow safer to wait for a dip before buying or a rally before selling, rather than go with the market and pay the prevailing price. People overestimate the success rate for the strategy of "buying cheap" and underestimate the success rate for the strategy of paying top dollar. This is one counter intuition that the good trader can oppose and exploit. Buying high and selling higher is difficult mentally and, therefore, very likely to be effective.

I would be happy to bet against almost any commodity account, sight unseen, simply on grounds of probability. A typical commodity account will contain, at any given time, positions with large *open trade losses* rather than large open trade profits. It may contain, as well, pseudo-hedges like long April silver (big loss) and short June silver (small profit), indicating a reluctance in the trader to accept a very real loss into the cash balance. A distinct preference for keeping losses open—the illusion being that a loss is not real until it is realized—is the hallmark of the chronic loser.

Since the opposite pattern—cashing in losses and keeping profits open— is much less common, it is indicative of a winning style. As usual, because it is so counterintuitive, trading with the trend is psychologically hard to deal with. Swallowing frequent cash losses while infrequently cashing in profits, even if these are large, is not a habit that comes easily. The trader who has endured a string of losers is particularly vulnerable to making a grab for a small profit just at the start of a big move. Why? Because it feels good at the time. The good feeling does not last, however, and in retrospect, the missing of a big move will hurt more than the pain of taking a series of small losses.

Since habitual losing arises from consistently trading against the trend and allowing losses to accumulate, it is remarkably systematic. And, being systematic, it may be directly opposed, more or less, by a counterstrategy. It is useful to remember that a surefire losing system is just as useful as a sure-fire winning system. All you have to do is reverse the rules. Reversing the rules means simply trading *with* the trend. But to estimate the possible returns from employing a pure trend-following system, extensive testing is required. You certainly aren't going to get this information by asking those who contributed to the kitty. Nor are you going to get it from fund operators claiming to be operating systems, since they will have their own special reasons for being less than forthcoming.

In summary, from the way the money pool gets redistributed, it does appear that funds flow steadily from a large group of losers to a much smaller group of winners, so that over the long term luck is not a big factor in trading performance. It also looks possible for prices to change radically, without necessarily yielding much return to pure trend followers. Really big profits may well be reserved for those who correctly call market fundamentals, and the biggest profits of all may go to fundamentalists who are not only correct, but who back up their positions with good technical discipline.

One way of assessing the returns from technical trading is to hypothesize a *system* that embodies, in reverse, all the anti-trend moves the typical losing trader might be expected to make, and then to test the effectiveness of that system over a broad enough spectrum of commodities and for a sufficient length of time to make a reasonable conclusion about its worth— and by implication, the worth of *any* system.

In the next chapter, I take up the subject of technical trading in detail, not because I particularly believe it is the way to trade, but because it is *the favored technique* of most money managers, of most commodity funds, and of most serious traders. Although I show how a system should be tested, I am not *recommending* this or any other system, but simply testing one that should be typical. The questions I hope to answer are How inherently profitable is systematic trading? and Are the returns commensurate with the risks involved? The reader should note that if systematic trading turns out to be significantly profitable, this finding alone will reject the random-walk hypothesis of price change.

4

EXPECTATIONS

Knowledge and Experience

As the reader will have gathered by now, I believe fundamental trading will outperform technical trading in the long run. Nevertheless, I am prepared to give technical trading its due, and I will deal with it in depth later in this chapter.

But first, a word on fundamentals: To trade fundamentally you need to have real knowledge about a particular market. And real knowledge about a market can only come from experience trading that market. So, how can a beginning trader, even if he is prepared to work, expect to have any success with his first trades? The answer is by concentrating on discipline rather than on insight.

Lacking experience, the trader new to the markets is well-advised to trade conservatively, to buy time, and to learn by doing what he cannot learn by any amount of theorizing or "papertrading." In this regard, aspects of the technical trader's systematic approach can prove very useful for the inexperienced trader. I say aspects, for I would not suggest that anyone begin with a purely mechanical technique for getting in and out of the market—it would be impossible to learn anything about fundamentals that way. Technical disciplines *are* useful in that they do incorporate rules that, properly observed, will make it difficult for the trader to lose in the long run— even a beginning trader who is trading blind to the fundamentals. Disciplines prevent carelessness, which can be something as simple as the taking of a position without thinking about how much to risk.

Technical trading is planned trading, unimaginative perhaps, but powerful in discipline because it is counterintuitive. In a sense, technical trading conquers emotional weakness by reducing trading to a pure numbers game. Later, I make the case that fundamental insight is the *sine qua non* of great trading. But we will put that argument on hold for now, give pure technique its due, and try to come up with an estimate of the return a pure technician can reasonably hope for. It would be desirable to corroborate statistically what has been observed behaviorally—that winners are trend *followers*, and losers are trend *fighters*.

Technical trades seldom last anywhere as long as fundamental trades. Within a major trend there will be lesser countertrends that will cause the technical trader—but not the fundamental trader—to reverse position. The technician is relying on method, not inspiration. What is crucial from the technical standpoint is the consistent application of a method or *system*. Over the course of time the system trader will execute a large number of trades, none of which, taken alone, will significantly affect his overall performance.

Previously, I said that chronic steady-state losers seem to lose faster than chance would suggest because they apply a powerful weapon in reverse— cutting profits while letting losses accumulate. Even chronic losers know in their heart of hearts that opposing the trend is a losing play. And few will admit to being consistently contrarian, even though the majority act this way. Are they blind to the discrepancy between what they do and what they claim to believe? Probably not. But intellect is one thing; emotion is quite another. Traders not only deny their bad habits, they delude themselves with their results. Don't expect a trader ever to accurately recount his commodity record. If a trader boasts about how well he did last year, chances are he just cleared commission. If he tells you he's breaking even, you can bet he dropped quite a bit. And if admits to a loss, it may be that he's close to being wiped out.

Technical Trading Systems—Design

I promised a trading system, incorporating all the behaviors of the chronic loser—but in reverse. To avoid repeated references to "the system" or "the method," I am going to call it simply, PLODDER (not out of disrespect, but as a reminder that like all technical trading systems it follows rather than leads).

The PLODDER system is dedicated to cutting losses and stretching profits, commonplace as that may sound. The notion may be commonplace, but translating the notion into a concrete plan of action is not. For example, the following questions must be addressed, as they would be of any system:

- What causes a position to be taken?

- What triggers the exit from a position?

- Are all signals acted upon?

- What mix of commodities is to be traded?

There are no absolute best answers to these questions, just as there is probably no master system that consistently outperforms all other systems. In designing a system, you must postulate trading rules that are as generally applicable as possible, so that any conclusions are broadly relevant—so that you can make some inference about system trading in general.

There are four requirements, I believe, that will make a system rigorous enough that some real meaning can be inferred from its test results. The first of these requirements (I am talking about long positions here—the reverse is true for shorts) is to buy on strength; long positions should only be initiated when strength is evident in a market.

REQUIREMENT ONE—*Go with direction*

A strong market is defined as one making some kind of new high, be it weekly, monthly, penetration of a moving average, whatever. And a long position in a strong market should always be put on just as a market is making a new high price on the day.

That gets the position on. Now we need a rule to define when a position should be closed out. Since a technical strategy is based on evolving price patterns, we must allow the *market* to decide when a position is to be closed. A logical consequence of allowing the market to dictate the exit point for a long position is to take that same exit point as the entry point for a new, opposite, and short position. If, technically, there is reason to get out of a long, there ought to be a technical reason to go short. And a weak market should be defined in exactly the same way as a strong market. This leads to the second system rule.

REQUIREMENT TWO—*Define symmetrical signals*

A long position will be held until the market shows weakness by the same objectively defined criterion that defined strength—weekly low, monthly low, or whatever. At this time the long will be liquidated, and a short position will be established.

A third requirement is for system universality in testing. PLODDER's rules ought to be applicable in all commodity markets. It is safer to assume that the same behavior is evident in all markets, rather than to assume that each market has its own profile or characteristic requiring its own modified rule. It is tempting, but completely unsound, to devise little sub-rules to handle perceived "idiosyncracies" in particular markets. Any valid conclusion about PLODDER as a predictor must come from its *general applicability* across a broad spectrum of futures markets. Too much latitude in the trading rules invites the creation of an *ad hoc* system with a high historical performance but a low predictive value. I want to avoid a hodgepodge of rules incorporating a ten-day moving average for cattle, a fifteen-day moving average for sugar, and an exponentially smoothed average for copper. Given enough latitude, I can come up with a rule to fit any price chart, random numbers included. Unless a rule embraces the whole spectrum of commodity markets, it is a waste of time to test it. One rule for all is mandatory.

REQUIREMENT THREE—*Universality*

The trading rule must be applicable to all markets, and it must be conceived without reference to the data it is to be tested upon.

A final requirement of a logical trading system is consistency of application. All trading signals must be acted upon; there can be no selectivity, no exceptions. A system is a system is a system, and technicians must take all or nothing. Large and profitable moves are bound to occur from time to time in all commodities, and technicians have to make sure that none of these are missed or rationalized away through any "precognition" on their part.

REQUIREMENT FOUR—*Consistency*

The trading rule must be operational in all markets (under study) all of the time.

A system can only be judged in a broad context, for it is so easy to produce nonrepresentative results from small samples—usually excessively favorable results. A common complaint about systems is that they work well in trending markets but are useless in choppy markets. This is true. But to make such a criticism is to fail to understand the nature of system trading. Naturally, a trend-following method will be profitable during big price moves and unprofitable when the markets are marking time. But we simply have no way of telling when a choppy market will turn into a trending market, because we have no idea of what the future will be like—except in a statistical sense.

Whether a system works or not depends on its net performance taking the favorable and the unfavorable periods together, and taking the performance of the system *averaged over all commodities*. For PLODDER to be judged a success, it must advance in the good times and hold its own or give ground grudgingly in the bad times. Trying to anticipate when it will work is pure guesswork, and probably lousy guesswork at that. How much of a positive expectation does PLODDER have at all times? That is the real question. Do the odds always favor its advancing in spite of its ups and downs? If this is not the case, there can be no reason to be in the market—ever. Even though PLODDER, or any system, can be expected to stagnate or retreat for lengthy periods, to be a viable proposition it should still have a steady *positive expectation*, in which case, as far as picking a date to start testing, one point in time is as good as any other.

Technical Trading Systems—Operation

For a demonstration of PLODDER in operation, let's look at an actual price sequence from the historical record (Table 4-1). The prices are for the *February 1980* pork belly futures contract, and cover the period October 8 to December 14, 1979. These same prices are also shown in standard bar chart form (Figure 4-1). There is nothing extraordinary about either this time period or this commodity. What we have is a sequence of prices laid out so that I can make clear the logical application of the now-to-be-defined trading rules.

Assuming an initial short position (we have to begin somewhere), that position will be maintained provided on any subsequent trading day the highest price of the *previous ten days* is not exceeded. When this condition *does* occur, the short position will be covered, and a long position will be taken. The long position will then be held as long as the low price on any day is not below the lowest price of the *previous ten days*. PLODDER's rule is therefore *trend-directional* and *symmetrical*, and ensures that a *position will be maintained in a commodity at all times*. The choice of ten days, rather than, say, nine, or twelve, is purely arbitrary—I'll return to this later. For now, I want to concentrate on the mechanics of PLODDER in operation.

	Open	High	Low	Close	
Oct 8	37.27	38.72	37.22	38.57	
Oct 9	39.12	39.55	36.57	36.67	
Oct 10	36.92	38.77	36.47	38.77	
Oct 11	38.67	38.87	37.67	38.52	
Oct 12	38.02	38.17	36.87	37.05	
Oct 15	36.37	37.57	35.42	37.42	
Oct 16	37.62	38.42	37.12	38.22	
Oct 17	38.22	38.62	37.22	38.17	
Oct 18	38.02	38.67	37.62	38.32	
Oct 19	38.02	38.37	37.22	37.97	
Oct 22	39.02	39.97	39.02	39.97 *	*Reverse short to
Oct 23	41.07	41.92	40.47	41.62	long @ 39.57
Oct 24	40.77	40.87	39.62	39.82	
Oct 25	40.22	41.67	40.22	41.62	
Oct 26	41.77	42.30	39.87	40.70	
Oct 29	40.97	42.57	40.80	41.77	
Oct 30	42.57	43.77	40.77	43.50	
Oct 31	43.32	44.67	42.52	42.85	
Nov 1	42.52	43.32	41.92	42.07	
Nov 2	42.07	43.07	41.67	42.97	
Nov 5	43.22	43.97	42.67	43.82	
Nov 6	43.97	44.45	43.32	44.27	
Nov 7	44.97	46.27	44.75	46.27	
Nov 8	47.07	47.17	45.57	45.65	
Nov 9	45.85	47.65	45.47	47.65	
Nov 12	47.97	49.65	47.57	49.65	
Nov 13	48.97	49.47	48.20	49.00	
Nov 14	49.97	51.00	49.97	51.00	
Nov 15	51.27	51.27	49.00	49.00	
Nov 16	48.57	48.72	47.27	48.00	
Nov 19	48.07	48.57	46.62	47.65	
Nov 20	48.17	49.65	48.12	49.65	
Nov 21	50.87	51.37	49.45	49.85	
Nov 23	49.37	49.72	48.82	49.25	
Nov 26	48.37	48.37	47.25	47.25	
Nov 27	46.57	48.62	46.47	48.02 *	*Reverse long to
Nov 28	47.87	48.22	46.02	46.02	short @ 46.57

	Open	High	Low	Close	
Nov 29	45.52	45.67	44.17	44.22	
Nov 30	44.47	44.92	43.57	43.67	
Dec 3	44.17	45.37	44.02	44.62	
Dec 4	44.37	44.37	43.20	42.20	
Dec 5	42.37	43.77	42.10	43.62	
Dec 6	44.17	44.37	42.12	42.30	
Dec 7	42.37	43.97	41.62	43.62	
Dec 10	43.57	43.77	42.65	43.17	
Dec 11	43.62	45.17	43.37	45.17	
Dec 12	45.27	47.17	44.67	47.02	
Dec 13	47.27	47.32	46.12	46.87 *	*Reverse short to
Dec 14	46.12	47.12	45.67	46.75	long @ 47.27

Table 4-1 The PLODDER trading system operating on pork belly data from October to December 1979. (The numbers are from a continuity series and may differ from actual prices by a small fixed displacement.)

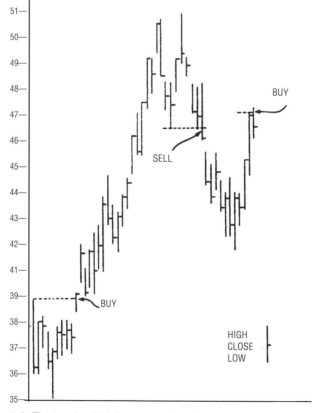

Figure 4-1 The ten-day high/low reversal system

Looking at the prices of Table 4-1 then, and assuming a starting short position on October 8, we see that nothing happens until October 22, when the price level, 39.55, is exceeded. Since the highest price of the previous ten days is 39.55 (October 9), we have the first reversal condition and must assume the short covered and a new long initiated at 39.57. In this instance, it is fair to take 39.57 as the *execution price* as well as the reversal price, since the opening price is *below* the reversal price. Had the opening price been higher than the reversal price, the execution price would have to be taken as the opening price.

If PLODDER were operating in real time, the order to the trading floor would have read: "October 22, 1979. BUY 2 FEBRUARY PORK BELLIES @ 39.57 STOP." One of these contracts is bought to cancel out the existing short position, the other is to initiate a long position. In practice, a *stop order* would be entered every day, even though most of these orders would expire at the close without being triggered. As a technical trader you never *want* a stop order to be filled, because at that particular moment the market will be going *against* your existing position.

Now that PLODDER is "long" pork bellies, daily low prices are the ones to be watched. Each day a stop-sell order is placed one tick (the minimum price change between trades) below the low price of the previous ten days. Finally, on November 27, a stop-sell at 46.60 is hit and the position is reversed. On this day, the opening price is *below* the reversal price and must be taken as the execution price.

Continuing then with the new short, we see the next reversal occurring on December 13. And so it goes, on and on, switching back and forth from long to short. Clearly, given sufficient time, PLODDER will generate a string of trading results that can be studied for net profitability and for variability.

I trust the reader agrees that PLODDER fulfills the four requirements I said were essential in a properly designed trading system. To recap:

> *Direction* Reversal points are on daily highs or daily lows so that trades are always initiated with positive market momentum.

> *Symmetry* Longs and shorts are initiated using identical criteria.

Universality The trading rule is derived without reference to any particular data base.

Consistency Positions are maintained at all times so that a large trend, when it develops, will not be missed.

That is the method. Now, the results. To draw any statistically valid conclusions about PLODDER, we will have to go far beyond one ten-week period in one pork belly contract. We need results over a much longer time period and over a broad range of independent commodities. So that results across the commodity spectrum can be directly compared, I propose to express all profit-and-loss figures as percentages of the approximate margin requirements prevailing at the time a position was initiated. This gets around several problems.

First, contracts in different commodities vary a great deal in total dollar value, making per contract comparisons rather meaningless. Second, using margin as a base, transactions in different commodities with different inherent volatilities become more directly comparable. It would not be appropriate, for example, to compare a transaction in sugar with a transaction in eurodollars on a percentage of contract value basis, because sugar will routinely vary by *four* percent of contract value each day, whereas a eurodollar contract will fluctuate by less than 1/20th of that amount, percentage-wise.

Although margin is a good base for expressing *comparisons*, it is not an appropriate base on which to project return on investment. As I will show later, trading anywhere near minimum margin levels is deadly.

Take the transactions in the February 1980 belly contract, for example, where the price is expressed in cents per pound. Contract size is 40,000 pounds, and the approximate margin is say, $1,500. The first PLODDER trade yields a dollar gain of:

$$(46.57 - 39.57) \times 400 = \$2,800$$

which, expressed as a percentage of margin equates to a return of:

$$2,800/1,500 = 187\%$$

Likewise, the second trade yields a loss of:

$$(46.57 - 47.27) \times 400 = \$280$$

equating to a return of: $\qquad 280/1,500 = -18.7\%$

In the ten-week demonstration period for bellies, only two transactions were completed, a rate of switching much lower than one might normally expect, this being a somewhat nonrepresentative period of mostly trending market. If I extend PLODDER to a much longer horizon, two and one-half years, say, I will find a much higher rate of switching.

Why two and one-half years? Only because the data base available to me covered this time period. The PLODDER study appeared in the first edition of *Winner Take All* and was carried out in 1982 when access to historical data was rather more difficult than it is now. Since PLODDER is designed to illustrate an enduring and general truth, deductions from this data base ought to be as valid now as they were then.

Hypothetical profits and losses, in the order in which they occurred, are listed in Table 4-2. When all is added up, the net gain is 691 percent, or 277 percent annualized. (This return looks most impressive—expressed, for the moment, on the basis of margin requirement.) For sure, PLODDER has been net profitable in pork bellies, albeit with a highly irregular pattern of profit accumulation; there are huge swings in equity, and strings of losses comparable in magnitude with the final net profit figure.

Transaction	Gain (%)	Gain to date	Transaction	Gain (%)	Gain to date
1	-21	-21	22	106	-282
2	130	109	23	-76	-358
3	-93	16	24	-81	-439
4	21	37	25	-67	-506
5	-95	-58	26	83	-423
6	-64	-122	27	-71	-494
7	24	-98	28	524	30
8	-72	-170	29	173	203
9	-97	-263	30	81	284
10	86	-177	31	257	541
11	-71	-248	32	-21	520
12	45	-203	33	-220	300
13	-21	-224	34	81	381
14	-35	-259	35	-161	220
15	94	-165	36	-62	158
16	-22	-187	37	-132	26
17	-56	-243	38	199	225
18	-88	-331	39	-155	70
19	-58	-389	40	41	101
20	44	-345	41	590	691
21	-43	-388			

Table 4-2 Gains and losses expressed as a percentage of margin requirements, trading the PLODDER system on pork bellies for a period of two and one-half years. Note the enormous equity swings comparable in size with the final net gain.

Now let's see what happens when PLODDER is applied to other commodities. Is the 277 percent annualized return for bellies repeated? The same analysis was carried out on ten of the most widely traded commodity markets (Table 4-3). The ten commodities studied are traditional nonfinancial ones, and include grains, meats, and tropical products. You will have to take my assurance that these *particular* ten commodities were not pre-selected to produce a result I wanted.

Pre-selection for a favorable result is a common error among researchers with a "big theory" they would like to see vindicated, so the reader should be wary of any such published results of the type I am giving you. I can simply remind you that I am not trying to sell a system, or any other formulaic tool, and consequently have no particular result I wish to establish in advance.

	Full contract value ($)	Margin ($)	Average annual gain ($)	Annual gain as % of margin
Pork bellies	18,000	1,500	4,150	277
Live hogs	10,000	750	2,770	307
Live cattle	30,000	700	30	4
Gold	40,000	2,500	10,550	432
Copper	25,000	1,000	7,000	700
Sugar	20,000	2,000	4,400	220
Cocoa	30,000	1,500	3,600	240
Coffee	60,000	4,000	42,300	1058
Soybeans	35,000	2,000	7,700	385
Wheat	18,000	750	1,260	168
		Average		385

Table 4-3 Average annual returns by commodity after testing the PLODDER system for two and one-half years. Average returns expressed as a percentage of margin are deceptively high—one of the reasons so many outrageous claims are promoted in the commodity press.

The PLODDER trading system turns out to be net profitable in all ten markets, albeit with a huge variation in performance—from a tiny 4 percent in cattle to an enormous 1,058 percent in coffee. But ten winners out of ten all the same. The average return per commodity (ARC) came out at 385 percent.

What about the spread of individual results? For sure, it would have been nice to have traded coffee and left out cattle, but that would be hindsight. And it would be incorrect to assume that PLODDER is inherently more suited to coffee trading than to cattle trading, for a big cattle trend may have been in the offing, and coffee may have been about to turn nasty just as the study period ended.

The PLODDER results are best looked at as a whole, without regard to which commodities the profit and losses came from. In other words, the results ought be viewed as coming from a *generalized commodity market*— with any conclusion then applicable to commodity markets in general.

The real question here is whether PLODDER's combined results are appreciably above the pure chance level. It is only when chance can be fairly ruled out as a possible explanation that a conclusion about a system's positive expectation has any value. A cautionary note: There can *never* be an absolute statement on whether a system "works" or not. That issue can only be answered in terms of probability. No laws of physics are involved here. Certainly, the greater a sample size, the more positive one can be about a conclusion. But there are limits to what can be practically tested. Endless data processing can be soul destroying. Furthermore, trades are hypothetical, and true execution prices are conjectural. Biases may also creep into a study despite all attempts to screen them out.

Imagine you wish to test a system on a portfolio that includes foreign currencies. You don't want to use all currencies, especially ones that tend to mirror each other's movements almost exactly. You wonder whether to use the Swiss franc or the D-mark. A rapid scan of historical price charts reveals a period of great whipsawing, which you know will wreak havoc on any trend-following system. But you notice slight differences between the franc and the mark, differences that make it clear that *your* system will fare much worse if you select the franc rather than the mark. Under these conditions, which currency will you choose for testing? If you want to be conservative with your results, as you should, you will include the franc. But more than likely you will choose the mark because your bias will be undetectable, quickly forgotten, and easy to rationalize. A bias like this may exist almost on a subconscious level, influencing your selection of markets, time periods for testing, and the very rules of the system itself.

During the stock market crash of 1987, commodity markets went haywire, producing very weird chart patterns with enormous whipsaws. It is no accident that so many "performance records" for systems mysteriously terminate in September 1987 or begin in November of 1987.

Technical Trading Systems—Evaluation

As we have seen, the average expected rate of return using PLODDER came out to be 385 percent per annum—based on margin requirements. And the expectation was positive in *all ten* commodities studied. Although this is a most encouraging finding, we don't yet know how much confidence to place in the result. In particular, we do not know how far removed from pure chance this result really is. A seemingly nonrandom result from an experiment is often tested by what statisticians call a *null hypothesis*: Assume chance to be the cause of a result unless there is powerful evidence to the contrary. How powerful is powerful? Ten to one against? One hundred to one against? Ultimately, system traders must decide for themselves.

The null hypothesis in terms of system testing is that commodity prices are random. If commodity price action is truly random, applying PLODDER repeatedly to ten random price sequences for two and one-half years would produce a distribution of average rate of return centered around zero, since each transaction would have an equal chance of being profitable or unprofitable. On the other hand, even with random inputs we would hardly expect the answer to come out *exactly* zero, any more than we would expect one hundred tosses of a coin to come out exactly fifty heads and fifty tails.

If the latter experiment (tossing a coin one hundred times) were repeated many times, we could produce a frequency distribution of results with an average value of fifty heads. We could record the number of heads on each trial of one hundred tosses and assemble the results in a relative frequency distribution (Figure 4-2)—a pictorial display of the relative frequency of all the possible outcomes of an event.

Before subjecting the PLODDER trading results to the null hypothesis, let's continue with the coin tossing analogy. Suppose we wish to know whether an *unknown* coin is a fair coin or whether it is biased either towards heads or tails, and that the only test allowed on this coin is to toss it a hundred times. We know in advance that the hypothesis about the coin can only be answered in terms of probability. If the result of the tossing is, say, within ten of the average value of fifty for a fair coin (heads and tails, equally likely), it would be logical, though not necessarily correct, to assume the unknown coin to be a fair coin.

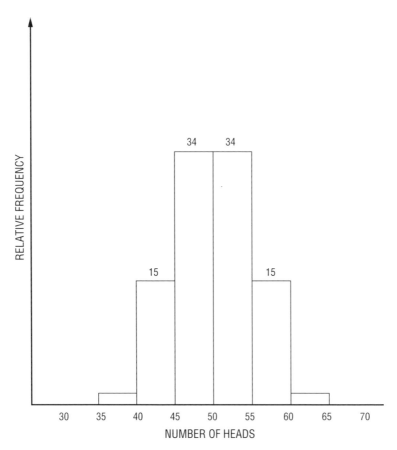

Figure 4-2 Tossing a coin one hundred times and recording the number of heads. There is only one chance in a thousand that more than sixty-five, or fewer than thirty-five heads will turn up.

What if the coin were to come up heads a hundred times out of a hundred? Such a result *is* possible from chance, but so unlikely that one could conclude the coin is almost certainly "bent." But what if the answer comes out to be sixty-five? Here a conclusion becomes difficult, because sixty-five is getting to the outer limits of what one might expect from a fair coin. The odds against getting sixty-five heads or sixty-five tails in a hundred tosses, are approaching one thousand to one against. At some point we are going to make an arbitrary judgment about the coin based solely on probabilities.

We are faced with an analogous problem when it comes to evaluating PLODDER. The system is the unknown coin, and we want to make a judgment on whether it is a normal coin or a special coin. Did PLODDER appreciably outperform chance, or is its actual result, 385 percent, within acceptable chance limits? To answer that question, PLODDER's average rate of return of must be compared with a relative frequency distribution of average rates of return from simulated trading using random commodity price sequences.

Fortunately, many random price series incorporating the same type of *daily* price fluctuations as are found in real commodity prices can be generated from a computer in an endless stream. By applying the rules of PLODDER to *ten* of these series over a two and one-half year period, and repeating the process over and over, we can generate a frequency distribution of rates of return with which to compare the *observed* 385 percent result. The pattern we are interested in is the frequency distribution of average rate of return (Figure 4-3), produced from multiple simulations of PLODDER applied to known random price sequences, and expressed on a base of margin.

As expected, the answers cluster around the value zero; *ninety-five* times out of a *hundred* the average return is within 250 percent of zero; and more than *ninety-nine* times out of a *hundred* it is within 375 percent of zero. Yet, on the test with real commodity data, a result of 385 percent was observed. Could it be chance? Yes, but with a very low level of probability. The observed value is so far outside the normal chance limits that with great confidence we can reject the null hypothesis in favor of a conclusion of nonrandomness. We can take it that the commodity price sequences would have been technically tradable for a profit.

Now, is it fair to jump one more step and deduce that commodity prices *in general* are nonrandom? The objections to such a conclusion would be that the particular commodities I selected for testing were nonrepresentative, *or* that the time period I selected for testing was nonrepresentative, perhaps more "trendy" than normal. There is no way to confirm or deny this. Unless one is prepared to cover every future that ever traded—a mind-boggling undertaking, *any* test result will always be nonrepresentative to a degree. Common sense has to tell you when enough is enough, or the process of testing could go on forever.

The reader might question why I selected *ten* as the number of "comparison days" for generating reversal signals. The reason I chose *ten* is the ease with which it allows price sequences to be scanned; these are often grouped by week in blocks of five. The number of days for comparison could just as easily have been *eight*, or *twelve*, or *fifteen*. I doubt the overall result would have been much different. It is the principle of objectively defining a consistent criterion for reversal that ensures a reliable result. PLODDER compares a daily price with the highest or lowest price of a certain number of previous days, but a system based on comparing a daily price with previous high *closing* prices would have a very similar expectation.

Two systems operating on the same data *may* give sharply contrasting results in the short run. Consider traders Jake and Larry, both using trend-following systems, but with different reversal criteria. Both are short gold. Larry has a reversal buy-stop at $400, while Jake has a reversal buy-stop at $405. The market rallies to $401, triggers Larry's stop order, then promptly collapses. Larry suffers a huge whipsaw loss (on both the short and the long), while Jake emerges from the potential whipsaw, unscathed and still holding his short. Short-term variances in performance balance out in the long run, just as heads balance out tails. But sometimes the long run can be longer than the trader imagines. My experiences with system trading results leads me to the following conclusion:

All trend-following systems have about the *same* long-run expectation.

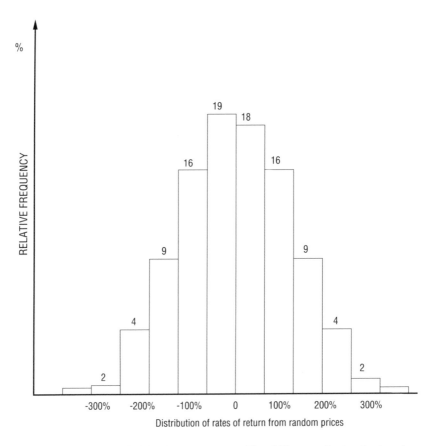

Distribution of rates of return from random prices

Figure 4-3 Could PLODDER have come up with a 385 percent rate of return by chance? Not likely, says the Null Hypothesis. The chance of getting such a result from a random commodity price universe is very low indeed.

If that is the case, there is little point in constructing an elaborate trading system, and even less point in being secretive about it. The principle difference between systems is not how reversals are generated, but how *often* reversals are generated. A system that compares *five* daily highs will trade a lot more often than a system that compares *fifteen* daily highs. Systems that trade a lot face both hefty commission charges and further profit erosion from unfavorably executed market orders.

Every commodity guru and promoter on the planet will disagree with what I am saying here; they have to. They need to convince you that only *their* systems are special. But there *are* no special systems; they are all pretty much the same because they all face the same degree of disorder in the information they are processing. There is no super-trading technique; there never has been; there never will be. All major league batters face the same quality of pitching. Can you imagine one batter hitting .600 when everyone else is hitting .350 or less? Claims for super systems arise from poor understanding rather than deception, though the two do go hand in hand. How do I know this? How can I be so sure that my result is representative of all technical systems? From observation and from common sense. These are pretty reliable guides.

Sure, I can alter any number of variables in my system until I find the very best result. But consider what I would have to sacrifice to achieve this. To perfect or optimize a technique, I have to alter it to make it *best fit the data* it is going to be forecasting. This results in an unrealistic measure of a system's ability to predict. It's oh-so-tempting, but very, very unsound.

Low-frequency trading systems are the ones most likely to succeed. They are not popular with operators or brokers because commission charges are low. An argument advanced in favor of high-frequency trading systems (i.e., systems sensitive to sudden price reversals) is that an eight-day moving average, say, will respond more quickly than a sixteen-day moving average, so that the maximum loss possible on any *one* trade is less with the eight-day moving average. True enough. But problems arise with strings of losses, not single losses, and in that respect a high-frequency trading system is just as exposed as a low-frequency trading system. You could drive yourself crazy trying to prove this point by testing system after system. However, the following example may help to clarify the issue.

Again, consider Jake and Larry, each with $2,000 to risk in the gold market. They both want to get long and hold for a big profit. We will assume that they are unusually disciplined—for commodity traders—in that they concede the possibility of being wrong about their beliefs and have planned from the outset for this contingency. Jake buys his gold contract, risking the full $2,000. The gold contract is for a hundred ounces, so should gold fall by $20 per ounce, he is out. Larry also buys a gold contract, but risks only $1,000. Should gold fall by $10 per ounce *he* is out. But he gets another chance; he may wait a few days and try again. Larry gets two shots, whereas Jake gets only one. True? Of course. But Jake will be stopped out twice as often in pursuit of his objective. In the long run, Jake and Larry will have exactly the same chance of succeeding, though chance will ensure that they will get there by very different paths.

Now that technical trading with PLODDER has been vindicated, so to speak, we have to examine the practical difficulties of employing it under real market conditions. At first pass, it looks as if the potential return is 385 percent per annum. But, as so often happens in commodities, just when you think you're on to something ...

5

VALIDATION

The Real Cost of Trading

Idle speculation and real speculation are very different activities. When you have discovered a mechanical trading system yielding upwards of 300 percent per year, it may seem your troubles are over. Promised rates of return of this magnitude—and rates much higher—are commonplace in the literature of promoters and vendors of systems. The bald truth, however, is that a growth rate of 300 percent per year is a rate of return that cannot be sustained for any length of time by anyone; fortunes from system trading are always on paper—never in fact.

Yet I have just demonstrated a system which appeared to yield such a return for *over two and one-half years*. In the previous chapter, I did not discuss the real cost of trading—the difference between theoretical results and the results achievable from real trading. My objective was to show whether systems work, even in theory. The conclusion was that they do; systems *are* theoretically profitable, possibly in a very big way.

Let's see what would have happened with the PLODDER system had we made reasonable allowance for some of the complications inevitable in an actual trading environment. There are two potential problems. One has to do with execution costs, which reduce the expected gain on each transaction. The other has to do with sequences of losing trades, which raise the amount of capital required to finance PLODDER, or any system, to a level way above exchange margin requirements.

First, execution costs. The most obvious execution cost is the broker's commission. This varies from broker to broker and is not constant by commodity either. I am picking $75 as an average commission for all commodities—a good estimation of what the trading public is likely to be paying, especially dealing with small lots. Another less obvious but very real cost is incurred whenever an order is not filled at exactly the price specified on a market stop order. Anyone who has used stop orders will be well-acquainted with this unfortunate cost. If the order is executed well away from the stop price, this is called a "bad fill." People who study trading systems and understand the practicalities of trading refer to this cost as *slippage*.

Sometimes the slippage on an execution is so large that you wonder whether your pit broker was asleep when the stop order was activated. A series of "bad fills" can induce paranoia in the most rational of minds. They are best accepted as a natural hazard of trading. If you approach trading thinking that the floor brokers are "out to get you," the quality of your decision-making will likely suffer.

We *all* get lousy fills from time to time. Admittedly, it is galling to be told that your 64.50 buy stop was filled at 65.25 when you know from the screen that it has traded at many prices in between (a good reason not to watch screens). But these things do happen, and the more often you trade, the more you will become aware of them.

A market may even zoom right through a stop and *lock at limit*. Let's say you have a sell stop at 59.25—close to limit down—in a market that is falling fast. The price ticks at 59.25, your stop, and sails right through to the limit at 59.15, say. There is no guarantee your order would be filled. But a hypothetical trading system operating on historical data would *assume* that your order was filled, because a system, poor hypothetical thing that it is, would have no way of knowing whether the trade could have been made or not. And there could be worse yet to come. Imagine that the next day the market opens down *another* limit. In reality, you are stuck with a long position you cannot get out of. But the system says that not only are you out of your long at yesterday's stop price, you are also short and holding a good profit on that short. It only takes one or two of these mistaken assumptions to seriously reduce the true profitability of *any* trend-following system. We had better make allowance for this before jumping to too many optimistic conclusions based on theoretical trading results.

A proper trend-following system has to work with stop orders; otherwise, it is trading against the trend. Whenever a stop is hit, that order becomes a *market order*, and the broker handling it must find someone in the pit to take the other side—at the best price available. For example, you have a buy stop that is touched, but it happens that there are few sellers around just at that time. Your broker must keep bidding at higher and higher prices until he finds a seller to sell to you. This is the broker's mandate, this is his job.

On a typical day, in a high-volume market, a stop order will be filled at close to the stop price. Occasionally, very occasionally, it will be filled at a *better* price than the one specified on the ticket. Accept these gratefully, but don't expect too many of them. Sometimes, if prices suddenly become volatile—due to surprise information hitting the floor during trading hours, the execution on a stop order will be distinctly unfavorable simply because everyone wants to do the same thing at the same time. Stops are not going to be filled, on average, where you want them to be filled. You just have to live with this, and you certainly must allow for it when "paper-trading" a system.

An alternative to the straight stop order is the *stop-limit* order, which instructs the broker to execute your order at a price equal to or better than your stop-limit price. In practice, you rarely get a better price, but you never get a worse price. The down side is that sometimes you don't get your order filled at all, and when that happens, it is almost always expensive. If the order is not filled on the day a stop-limit is triggered, it will have to be filled at a price well away from the stop-limit price, and most sensibly *at-the-market* at the next day's opening. The alternative is to wait for a rebound that may never come. Dithering over a missed stop order can seriously distract you. Better to pay up right away, and treat a missed stop-limit order like a very expensive parking ticket.

Whether it is better to use straight stop orders or stop-limit orders is hard to say; the long-run costs are probably about the same. It's a question of pay now or pay later. If you prefer your aggravation meted out in regular doses, use the stop. If you would rather have it all at once, maybe the stop-limit is the way to go. But stops of some sort should always be used.

Some systems operate on *market-on-close* orders. When you see a closing price in the newspaper recorded as 60.60, for example, it means that at the closing bell the bid price was 60.45, perhaps, and the offering price 60.75— with 60.60 representing the mid-range point. *Buy* market orders on close would have to pay 60.75, while *sell* market orders on close would get

60.45. It's rather like buying and selling currency at the airport, but with a much narrower spread. Market-on-close systems also have to contend with the limit situation where execution may be impossible.

Slippage occurs twice in each completed transaction—at both the buy and sell points. Costs are much higher than most traders believe. Having logged many hundreds of trades and measured the slippage on each, my best estimate of this cost is $160 per transaction. In bellies, for example, $160 is equivalent to forty points—twenty points each side of the trade. If this number seems high, remember, when a stop is hit, the market will be running in the direction the trader wants to trade. In a fast, unstable market, a fill could be as much as a hundred points away. It will take six trades, perfectly executed, to bring that average down to twenty points. And of course the $160 must also cover that nasty of nasties—the massive slippage incurred when a stop order is wrongly assumed to have been filled.

Combining commission costs ($75) with slippage ($160), we arrive at an estimated execution cost of $235 per trade. A trading system reversing about once per month—like PLODDER—will incur annual execution costs averaging around $3,000 per contract per commodity. This is considerably higher than the average margin requirement. The effect on previously estimated rates of return is profound (Table 5-1). The system estimated rate of return expressed over margin drops from 385 to 162 percent.

	Cost per trade	Trades per year	Annual cost of trading	gross gain	net ($)	gain (%)
Pork bellies	235	16.0	3,750	4,150	400	27
Live hogs	140	10.3	1,440	2,770	1,330	177
Live cattle	100	10.0	1,000	30	-970	-138
Gold	295	10.3	3,040	10,550	7,510	300
Copper	200	20.0	4,000	7,000	3,000	300
Sugar	220	16.0	3,500	4,400	900	45
Cocoa	270	19.0	5,100	3,600	-1,500	-100
Coffee	475	8.8	4,200	42,300	38,100	952
Soybeans	235	13.6	3,200	7,700	4,500	225
Wheat	180	14.0	2,500	1,260	-1,240	-165
					average =	162%

Table 5-1 Average rates of return from the PLODDER system drop sharply after allowing for commission and slippage. Note how in many cases the cost of trading is larger than the expected return. Nevertheless, even after adjustments the average expected rate of return is still 162 percent of average margin (final column).

Losing Streaks

One nagging question remains. Is it realistic to assume that PLODDER's trading could have been financed with minimum margin? There is nothing to prevent a trader from trading with the minimum margin in his account. Broker's margin will usually protect the trader from losing all his capital through being very wrong on *any one trade*, but it will certainly not protect the trader from being wrong on more than one trade.

Brokers set margins to protect themselves from traders, not to protect traders from themselves nor to advise them on how to finance their speculations. The margin demanded has no bearing on the true amount of capital a player needs to keep playing the game—never mind prosper. The trader whose equity is always margined to the hilt is in constant danger of succumbing to a short string of losing trades—an inevitability. And yet, ludicrous as it may seem, you will come across traders fussing, complaining, and threatening to change brokerage houses over trivial differences in margin requirements.

If it is incorrect to finance trading with basic margin demanded, how much is really needed? Hardly full contract value, because it is leverage that separates commodity trading from stock trading and makes it such a fantastic vehicle for speculation. It would be unproductive to tie up all one's capital in financing contracts at their total value. Some middle ground is needed, but what? Leverage has to be used to the extent that it is safe, and I mean safe in the sense that the chance of being wiped out by an unlucky string of losing trades is reduced to an acceptably small level.

What is acceptably small to one trader may not be acceptably small to another; the track can be made as fast as the trader wishes. Aiming for a high rate of return, of course, necessarily increases risk. What constitutes the optimum balance between risk and reward is a fascinating imponderable that has taxed the minds of many market theoreticians. (For an in-depth look at money-management, see Chapter 8.) The PLODDER test results are not comprehensive, but they do reveal something about the relationship between leverage and risk.

Perhaps the most interesting statistic to come out of the whole PLODDER study is the size of the *worst losing streak*, or *largest equity drawdown*, encountered in each commodity during the two and one-half year period the system was in operation. Once again, purely for convenience of comparison, largest equity drawdowns are expressed as percentages of contract margin (Table 5-2).

	($) gain in 2 1/2 years	largest equity drawdown in ($)	as % of margin
Pork Bellies	1,200	9,150	610
Live hogs	3,325	3,200	426
Live cattle	-2,425	9,200	1328
Gold	22,530	15,600	624
Copper	7,500	6,250	625
Sugar	2,250	6,800	340
Cocoa	-3,750	17,100	1140
Coffee	95,250	9,000	225
Soybeans	11,250	11,800	590
Wheat	-3,100	5,100	680

Table 5-2 Equity drawdowns, by commodity, trading just one contract on the PLODDER reversal system for two and one-half years. Final column expresses the largest equity drawdown as a percentage of margin required. Execution costs have been included.

The size of the largest equity drawdowns are astonishing: over $9,000 in cattle, over $15,000 in gold, and over $17,000 in cocoa—trading just one contract. And all this within a system that is overall net positive! For a graphic example of just how quickly a losing streak can build, consider the wicked action in pork bellies following the release of the September 1982 pig crop report (Figure 5-1). This vicious whipsaw would have cost virtually *all* trend-following systems 10 to 15 cents in less than ten days.

You won't find many books that publish the kind of charts I do. Most would rather show you benign formations corroborating the author's pet theory—whether it be a series of neatly descending tops that can be perfectly connected by a straight line or an elegant price breakout from a trading range. Nasty chart formations are rather common. Sorry, but it's true. And the trader who is not prepared to deal with this reality is in for a series of very nasty surprises. In the PLODDER test, largest equity drops ranged from a minimum of 200 percent of margin to over 1,300 percent of margin. Moreover, the period covered by the PLODDER test was only two and one-half years. Over longer periods *larger equity drops would have to be expected.*

Figure 5-1 The system trader's nightmare

If you accurately track equity change over time, you will be surprised at the insidious way equity drops mount up when sequences of losses are briefly interrupted by profitable trades. Two medium-sized losing strings interrupted by a winner can be much worse than a single large continuous string of losses. It is the equity drawdown from a *peak* value to the lowest subsequent *trough* that determines the true margin a system requires. The destructive aspects of bad runs are rarely explored in depth because the consequences for the system trader are so depressing. Since there is no advance warning of when a rotten streak is beginning, the system trader must allow for starting his system just at *the worst possible time*. Granted, this would be unlucky. But a trader must be prepared for bad luck, and a thoughtful trader will plan for his system to withstand his worst foreseeable losing streak right at the beginning of his trading.

Suppose a trader wanted to trade a system just on pork bellies. In the light of PLODDER's results, he would be well-advised to maintain upwards of $12,000 equity just to finance *one* contract. Who would trade bellies with $12,000 per contract? Almost no one. Most belly traders would want to buy three, four, or five contracts. Even with five contracts the trader would still be way above exchange margins. Most system traders are unaware of the extent of the bad runs they will encounter purely as a matter of chance. Like drunks staggering through a minefield, they head into the fray, sublimely ignorant of the inevitability of being blown into small pieces.

From the equity drawdown patterns of Table 5-2, it would appear prudent for a system trader to maintain upwards of *ten times* exchange margins per contract. This, just to give himself a reasonable long-run chance of capitalizing on whatever positive edge he may have in the market. The implications for return on investment are somber, because the apparent rate of return (Table 5-1) of 162 percent—expressed, remember, on a base of minimum margin—now shrinks to a *real expected rate of return on invested capital* of 16.2 percent, which, to say the least, is beginning to look a little ordinary.

Diversification, a Bonus

Fortunately, there is hope through diversification. If a trading account can be diversified across a number of more or less *independent* commodities, then the margin requirement for any given level of safety is going to be reduced. For example, if the ten commodities I studied were margined from a common financial pool, they would tend to reinforce each other because each would have independent good and bad streaks. Like ten men fording a raging stream holding onto a log, the group might struggle across, where any *one* man attempting it alone would be swept away.

In terms of potential equity drawdown, there is a world of difference between a portfolio comprised of *ten* contracts of bellies—either long or short—and a diversified portfolio with *one* contract in each of *ten* different commodities. With a ten-belly position on, an account's equity would swing wildly from day to day, while its long-run expectation would be *no greater or no less* than that of an account trading the much less volatile diversified portfolio. An account concentrating all its resources in a single commodity is extremely vulnerable to unfavorable chance occurrences. Of course, such an account also stands to gain much more from favorable chance occurrences. But the issue here is financing, not hitting on a big winner. We are interested in the financing requirements of technical trading, and there is no doubt that diversification allows leverage to be increased without compromising safety.

I will deal with the subject of diversification in depth in a later chapter. For the moment, I am tentatively suggesting ten times margin as the rock bottom financing requirement to trade one contract (undiversified) for two and one-half years. The implied rate of return (according to PLODDER) is around 16 percent on true invested capital. With broad diversification, capital requirements on a per contract basis do drop, perhaps enough to double or triple this expected rate of return. On the other hand, we looked at bad runs in a two and one-half year period. Most traders expect to trade for more than two and one-half years. Extending the trading period has the *opposite* effect of diversifying the commodity base because the longer you trade, the greater your chance of running into an extremely unfavorable losing sequence.

I am going to suggest that the most a system trader can expect to achieve in the long run—from *any* system—is around 40 percent per annum. The price data I used to test PLODDER came from a two and one-half year period in the early eighties and appeared in the first edition of this book. I saw no compelling reason to retest PLODDER on more recent data, since I would be bound to get a different result and would then be faced with deciding whether the difference between the two results was significant or not. Frankly, I don't think this is a topic worth pursuing to exhaustion.

Expected returns may well be falling, and there is evidence that a 40 percent rate of return is no longer attainable from technical trading—if indeed it ever was. I say this not only from personal observation of system traders but also from the published results achieved by professional money managers, almost all of whom claim to operate systems of one kind or another. The reason returns from system trading are declining may be that more and more people are playing the numbers crunching game—thereby defeating each other's purpose. Commodity trading remains a zero-sum game. If a 40 percent return was achievable a decade ago, probably no more than 25 percent is achievable now.

What's wrong with 25 percent? Nothing at all. Not perhaps the stuff of dreams, but still a large return by any standard. Curiously, *hardly anyone can achieve even that.* Any system trader who consistently doubles his money on an annual basis has achieved the financial equivalent of skiing to the North Pole in a bathing suit.

Optimization

When testing PLODDER, I arbitrarily chose *ten* as the number of highs or lows a price would have to exceed in order to trigger a reversal of position. Using ten as the *reversal number*—the only variable parameter in the whole PLODDER system—I came up with a theoretical maximum return (with diversification) of 40 percent. But what if I had used a reversal number of eight, or nine, or eleven, or fifteen—instead of ten? I know before testing that the final rate of return will be different each time I change this number.

Let's say the PLODDER tests were to be run over and over, and the rate of return for every reversal number between five and fifty tabulated. If I wished to "optimize" PLODDER, I would pick the reversal number giving the greatest return, and project future performance using that return. Regrettably, there is no evidence to suggest that varying a system parameter— such as number of reversal days—can make any difference to the system's performance. In other words, there is no tendency for one value of the parameter to be optimal. Here's Jack Schwager, whose numerous articles on futures are always worth reading:

> Perhaps the most critical error made by users of commodity trading systems is the assumption that the performance of the optimized parameter sets during the test period provides an approximation of the potential performance of those sets in the future. Such assumptions will lead to grossly overstated evaluations of a system's true potential. It must be understood that commodity prices are subject to a great deal of randomness. Thus, the ugly truth is that the question of which parameter sets will perform best during any given period is largely a matter of chance. The laws of probability indicate that if enough parameter sets are tested, even a meaningless trading system will yield some sets with favorable past performance. Evaluating a system based on the optimized parameter sets (i.e., the best performing sets during the survey period) would best be described as fitting the system to the past results, rather than testing the system.

If, for example, I were to find that the reversal number of twelve was optimal, and that the system performance fell away rapidly on *either side* of that number, I would be pretty sure there was something very special about twelve. But that does not happen. It would be very nice if it did, but it doesn't. And surely, when one considers the random, chaotic forces that go into the making of a price, it would be astonishing if an optimal value were found to exist. A clear optimal value of a system parameter would impute order to a process that everyday experience tells us cannot possibly contain such order. Beware of results at odds with common sense. Whenever an unlikely hypothesis appears to be confirmed, it's worth pausing and asking whether the wish may have been father to the thought.

The attempt to optimize a system can be carried to ludicrous extremes. The more closely a system is constrained to fit its test data, the higher its apparent performance may be pushed. In deciding whether to optimize or not, it's worth considering the consequences of making an incorrect call. If optimization really *is* possible and *not* employed, the trader may be pleasantly surprised with his results. But, if optimization is a *fiction*, the optimizer is in a dark room looking for a black hat that isn't there. He will be forever wondering why his actual trading results never come close to his projected results. In short, he may be in for a lot of frustration.

With optimization producing such favorable paper-trading results, it is fertile ground for computer research. A company called Pardo Corporation markets a number of optimizable systems for traders, including a package called *Swing Trader*. If you are interested in finding the best way to trade last year's pork bellies, I am sure they have the answer. Pardo dismisses all doubters with a defiant zeal:

> Whether or not there are those who believe in optimization, I will continue to optimize my various *Swing Trader* models, and I will continue to let my optimized models produce winning trades. We will develop even more powerful programs and optimizable systems, and we will continue to sell *Swing Trader* to satisfied customers who are laughing all the way to the bank.
>
> —*The Dow Jones-Irwin Guide to Trading Systems* (1987)

I've no doubt *someone's* laughing all the way to the bank.

Why Systems Fail

If trend-following systems have positive expectations—and the evidence is that they do, why then do systems fail? I don't mean fail to live up to their advance billings; I mean fail, as in fall apart. For that's what becomes of most of them. Is it just a matter of underfinancing, aiming too high and getting caught in a bad streak?

Wittingly or unwittingly most systems operators will be aiming higher than is safe. But psychological pressures, too, are working inexorably against the system trader. Boredom is a constant danger, because the workings of a system are purely mechanical; there is no creativity outside of the initial design. The bored trader looks for excuses to modify his system. In his day-to-day contact with the market, he spots system trades that feel instinctively bad to him, for he is not *completely* isolated from the real world of fundamentals.

The process of system disintegration follows a pattern. The trader begins to select his trades, acting on those he likes, avoiding those he doesn't like, but still rationalizing to himself, and others, that he is operating a system. If he is trading for other people who know a little bit about the market, he will be bombarded with fatuous advice, always when the system is not performing well and he is most vulnerable to criticism. Furthermore, at the back of the system trader's mind there persists a nagging doubt that the future may not be like the past after all, that the rules have been changed, and that his best-laid plans may be doomed. Such doubts intensify under duress, and the temptation to quit can become overpowering.

Consider the case of an operator who has just lost 50 percent of his capital (a normal enough occurrence), trying to rationalize this reality to himself or his clients. Unless he is totally convinced of the statistical validity of what he is doing, unless he has gone through the exercise I have gone through here, his belief in his system will likely crack. Systems take "years of research" to develop, but they disappear in a flash—usually without explanation. Federal law insists that a caveat be placed on any prospectus soliciting funds and advertising theoretical performance. You may need a magnifying glass to read the type, but the words you read are among the truest you will ever come across:

> There is no guarantee that this system, if traded, will perform in accordance with the historical results.

Astrologers scan the commodity universe searching for nonexistent cycles. But the only cycle I have seen repeat with any regularity is the birth/death cycle of the system. It is as old as the first futures contract, and begins with *the discovery*: a mechanical trading rule that yields amazing results when tested over a few highly trending historical price series. The rule, once formulated, is then found to work much less well in "choppy" markets. This leads to *the modification*, which reduces the gains in the good markets but minimizes the losses in the bad markets.

People who discover these wonderful trading rules are usually long on time and short on money. Therefore, investors must be found. So, next comes *the packaging* and shortly thereafter *the promotion*.

When the first few trades with real money in a model account are shown to be profitable—and this can be arranged with judicious timing—people sit up and take notice. Money pours in; *the bandwagon* is rolling. Inevitably, a serious losing streak occurs. Investors become nervous and express doubts. As *the drawdown* becomes larger, pressure mounts on the system trader to modify the rules. After a particularly bad whipsaw, *the emergency meeting* is called. Someone notices that the system always seems to do badly at this time of the year. The trader resists the criticisms, but nagging doubts have been sown. After another nasty hit, a reason is found to *temporarily withdraw* from the market. (Perhaps the yen is yawing uncontrollably because of unprecedented bank interventions.) Now the system is *sidelined* just as major trends emerge. Poor system, left out just as the party is getting under way.

No one feels much like talking; we have *the silence*. After a *period of hibernation*, signs of life appear. Meanwhile, the old investors have slunk off, and new ones must be targeted. Finally, we have *the rebirth*. A new system arises from the ashes of the old, with new rules that accommodate and make profitable *the very sequences that led to the demise of the old system*. The "new improved" system will then be marketed under a new name, and traded by the same trader at a new brokerage firm. The cycle is complete.

I want to impress upon the reader that I am not knocking systems per se, only the human frailty that renders them inoperable. Systems *ought to work*; the numbers say so. The system I tested, PLODDER, had a very simple trading rule based on the previous ten days' prices. PLODDER's very simplicity is the source of its power. There are many other trading rules, or *algorithms*, one can construct to capitalize on trends. There are systems based on penetration of moving averages, systems based on momentum or rate of change of price, systems based on percentage reversals off highs or lows. There is no reason to favor any one of these systems over any other. Others disagree.

Dog Eats Dog

Bruce Babcock Jr., who publishes the *Commodity Trader Consumer's Report*, conducted a comprehensive study of many different types of systems, operating on the same data over a five-year period commencing in 1982. He summarized his findings in the *Dow Jones-Irwin Guide to Trading Systems*. The bizarre premise behind Babcock's report is that commodity trading systems can be consumer tested—like toasters, VCRs, or rubber tires. Babcock tested over sixty trend-following systems, a programming exercise (if it was rigorously followed) of surely unimaginable tedium.

After this prodigious feat of data processing, Babcock came up with an astonishing result: The net expectation from *the average of all the systems* was barely positive at all. In fact, had he used a proper slippage amount of $200 per trade, instead of $100, the overall net expectation would have been slightly negative. To repeat, I find this result astonishing, and I'm sure the authors of these systems find the result astonishing, too. The scope of the study was comprehensive—ten commodities, five years, and over *sixty* different systems. If ever there was a study corroborating the thesis that the markets are random walks this is it! On the surface, it is curious that Babcock would wish to broadcast such a result, for he is a dyed-in-the-wool champion of technical trading.

> To be successful as a speculator, you must follow rather than try to anticipate trends. Therefore, to determine whether to buy or sell, you need not make inspired predictions about future supply and demand. You do not have to anticipate the market's reaction to the latest political news. All you have to do is determine the current price trend and position yourself accordingly.

It is impossible to predict trend changes with a reliability that is better than chance. In order words, you might as well just flip a coin. Fortunately, it is not necessary to predict the markets to be successful as a commodity trader. You just have to determine the trend and follow it.

How do we know Babcock programmed his computer correctly? How much credence can we put in his result? It contradicts my own analysis. It contradicts, I'm sure, the analyses of the people who operate the systems Babcock is testing. And it contradicts Babcock's own belief in the nonrandomness of the market. I wouldn't suggest anyone waste time trying to refute or confirm his result. I'd rather look for the smoking gun. Could Babcock have gone over the top simply to glorify his own product?

Sure enough, Bruce Babcock himself has designed the one technical trading system that makes a mockery of the sixty others. He calls it the *Babcock Long-Term System with $2,500 Stop*. While everyone else's system stumbles and sputters for five years, *his* system sails along yielding profits that dwarf the wretched returns achieved by all the others.

Did Babcock ever trade his system after its discovery? Apparently he did, but only on paper, and long after all the contracts had expired. Babcock prefers to muse on what *might* have happened:

> You may be wondering how it [Babcock's long-term system] did in the succeeding year [1987–1988]. Although the table [not included here] shows losses, the system would probably have been profitable for anyone who actually traded it. The biggest loss was a $28,225 hit in the S & P 500, which occurred on October 22, 1987. The system was flat going into the October 19 crash [One wonders why. If ever there was a clear downtrend, this was it], but then flashed a buy signal on October 21. In that incredibly volatile environment, it would not have been prudent to take the signal. The excessive loss over the $2,500 stop resulted from an immense gap down on the next day's opening. That kind of unpredictable price action is precisely the reason to stay out of the market during such periods. Without that one huge S & P loss and without including the cattle market, which no one should trade with the system, the overall profit was $9,196, a respectable $340 per trade.

Yes indeed. And if the Titanic hadn't hit an iceberg, it probably wouldn't have sunk. What do you take us for, Babcock? Having promised to educate your audience on misinformation about systems (and having done so rather well for 120 pages), from out of the blue you produce your own proprietary trend-following system—a hodge-podge of curve-fitted nonsense violating every statistically sound principle you have been espousing.

THE BABCOCK LONG-TERM SYSTEM

by Bruce Babcock Jr., publisher of *Commodity Traders Consumer Report*. (According to Babcock, this system averaged a profit per trade of $848, while the average for all other systems tested was $58.)

> The *Babcock Long-Term System* takes action only after the market makes a 130-day high or low. That is the equivalent in market days of six months. It means that today's high is the highest price of the last 130 market days, or today's low is the lowest price of the last 130 days in that market. If that is the case, take the following steps to trade the system:
>
> 1. Wait until after the close the next day (the day after the 130-day high or low).
> 2. Measure the distance between the highest high of the last 20 market days and the lowest low of the last 20 market days.
> 3. Add the distance calculated in Step 2 to today's close (the day after the 130-day high or low). This point will be your buying threshold.
> 4. Subtract the distance calculated in Step 2 from today's close (the day after the 130-day high or low). This point will be your selling threshold.
> 5. Wait for the market to touch either the buying or selling threshold point. If the market hits your buying threshold point first, buy on the close that day. Keep the selling threshold point as a reversing stop. If the market hits your selling threshold point first, sell on the close that day. Keep the buying threshold as a reversing stop.
>
> If the market makes a new 130-day high before it reaches either of the initial threshold points, repeat steps 1, 2, 3, and 4. Replace the previous threshold point with the new one if it is higher than the previous one. Replace the buying threshold point if it is lower than the previous one. Otherwise, maintain the current buying and selling threshold points.
>
> If the market makes a new 130-day low before the market reaches either of the initial threshold points, repeat steps 1, 2, 3, and 4. Replace the previous buying threshold point with the new one if it is lower than the previous one. Replace the previous ...

And so it rambles on ... *ad infinitum, ad nauseam,* qualifiers heaped on qualifiers. Sound irresistible? Readers wishing the full story are referred to the *Dow Jones-Irwin Guide to Trading Systems*, page 120. Guaranteed to stop you cold. Shame on you, Babcock. You really do know better than this, I'm sure.

To distance *his* product from the pack, what Babcock did was hypothesize a system that trades with absurd infrequency; on average he changes position in a commodity only *twice* per year. By severely restricting the number of trades, and by introducing numerous qualifiers, Babcock was able to isolate the big long-cycle trends and tailor his signals to take advantage of these trends. Reducing the number of sample points increases the number of creative ways you can curve-fit a system to produce a nonrepresentative result. Mathematicians call this *reducing the number of degrees of freedom* of a system, and any academic worth his salt would verify that Babcock's projection, made from such a small sample, is statistically worthless.

It is with some regret that I make these points. I was not aware of Bruce Babcock Jr., when I wrote the first edition of *Winner Take All*, and made no reference to him. In the meantime, *he* has said some very nice things about my first edition. Somehow, I doubt he will say the same thing about the second. I confess to feeling rather sheepish about tearing a strip off Babcock's hide. Sorry, Bruce, my duty is to my readers. You are what you write, and I must tell it like it is.

Along with Larry Williams and J. Welles Wilder, Bruce Babcock is one of the more conspicuous promoters around. A vicious and rather comical feud has developed recently between Babcock and Wilder, who now devote much of their energies to squabbling in the commodity press, where they challenge, ridicule, and threaten each other. While Babcock hides behind the cover of *Consumer Reports*, Wilder has marshaled the backing of another putative watchdog publication called *Futures Truth*. Wilder and *Futures Truth* both operate out of the same town in North Carolina.

In another bout of data processing lunacy, *Futures Truth* claims to have tested every Babcock system and proved that over the years these systems have generated huge losses. This raises a bit of a critical conundrum whose irony seems lost on Wilder and company. The most effective criticism of a system is that it just breaks even. Babcock was astute enough to come up with this answer when he tested other peoples' systems. If you show that a system generates large losses, you are inadvertently recommending it, because a trader can always *fade* a system, by doing exactly the opposite of what the system calls for. *Futures Truth*, in its efforts to discredit Babcock, have elevated him to the status of *idiot savant;* they make his systems look so bad that these same systems become very attractive propositions in reverse.

The crowning irony appears in the November 1992 issue of *Futures Magazine*. Which claims to test and rank one hundred different active trading systems, lists two of Babcock's systems in its top ten list of the most successful systems of the previous twelve months! C'mon, chaps, make up your mind.

I don't know who fired the first shot, but at one point Wilder demanded Babcock retract all his systems claims—or *Futures Truth* would publish all its negative dope on him. Babcock, naturally, declined to recant. *Futures Truth* is now publishing a book devoted exclusively to exposing the untruths of Bruce Babcock—as if anyone cares. We are reminded that the book is being produced at a loss, and is being *marketed in the public interest*. What a hoot! Send $35.00 or—get this—supply a receipt supporting a donation to the Salvation Army and get the book free! The commodity soap opera continues. Stay tuned.

Sheep

People hand over their trading decisions to others for different reasons. Some think they are getting expert guidance; some lack the confidence to try for themselves; some have tried for themselves and failed. But they are all guilty of the same error: They are expecting something for nothing. Having no personal involvement in trading and no understanding of how their funds are being handled, they can only sit and hope. And that means they will swing excessively between optimism and pessimism depending on the latest results. In the end, most of them will lose most of their investment and never understand what happened.

Why are people so readily persuaded to entrust their funds to neophytes without any real knowledge? Part of the answer lies in the aggressive promotion of unproven "systems" by brokerage firms, where "production" is the paramount consideration. A few good results can work wonders for a broker, and a broker who sticks it out long enough is bound to look good once in a while.

In commodities, where bad news is the norm, good news can travel fast, and a rolling bandwagon will find plenty ready to jump aboard. A system operator who is experiencing a good run in the market is inclined to see himself as a guru rather than as a mechanic—an image fostered by secrecy and the trappings of high technology. To the uninitiated he may seem like a wizard, particularly if his system is encased in impenetrable mathematics.

For burnt-out salesman, the guru may indeed by a godsend. Fellow brokers may "prospect" clients, not for themselves, but for the system operator who will handle the new accounts and split the commissions with the funds raiser. Sometimes layers of personnel will be in on the action, all expecting a take for their part in attracting the "johns," and all with their hopes riding on the operator's continuing performance. (Not only are these johns guaranteed a royal screwing, they also have to pay a hierarchy of pimps for the privilege.)

Commodity brokers are out to make commissions. This is their *raison d'etre*, and the reason the firms they work for exist. The ability to attract money is much more important than the ability to make money, and truth is a debased currency. Prospecting the public is the name of the game, and, since the public is in love with diamonds, why not "salt the claim" by dropping a few phony carats where these will most easily be found?

If I harbor such jaundiced views about trading systems and the people who operate and market them, why did I go to such lengths to test whether systems work? It's simple. I felt it necessary to investigate the random-walk theory, and *that* leads one, inevitably, to the study of technical trading systems. The trading public, for the most part, believes technical trading to be the whole story. I do not, but I have to recognize that other people do. To demonstrate, objectively, the existence of nonrandomness in the market I had to show that it was possible to trade systematically and make a profit. I believe I accomplished this with the PLODDER study. Nevertheless, I stopped short of advocating the use of PLODDER, or any other system, as a way to trade the markets.

A rejection of the random-walk theory is a natural conclusion from a cursory fiddling with old commodity charts—especially nice trending ones. PLODDER's positive performance is also a strike against the random-walk hypothesis, but a more objective and therefore stronger refutation. But, to be realistic, while we may have cast considerable doubt on the random-walk theory, there's hardly a lot to shout about.

"That's sheep for you. One does something, they all do."

Commodity Funds

A great deal of managed money flows into commodity mutual funds run by "trading experts" of various stripes and variable talents. The guiding principles by which funds operate are pretty much the same: find trends and stick with these trends until they reverse.

Commodity funds are proliferating in numbers and growing in size, as more and more luckless individuals cast their lot with the professionals. With technical trading the dominant *modus operandi*—with everyone scrutinizing everyone else for clues to market direction—it is no surprise that communal navel gazing has led, in recent years, to a general *increase in short-term price instability.*

In the long run, the actions of technical traders can have *no* effect on prices; fundamental forces of supply and demand will eventually assert themselves in the marketplace. In the short and medium terms, however, increased price volatility is probably here to stay. The technical trader's knee-jerk impulse to jump into a market because others are doing so will inevitably lead to sharp false breakouts that go nowhere. We may truly be entering the age of the one- or two-day-wonder chart formation.

Because of this new instability in the market, it's possible that the returns available to system traders have been dropping in recent years—a pattern that may continue in the future because of convergent trading behaviors. The returns from system trading may eventually approach absolute zero, as every pattern of self-induced chaotic behavior is wrung dry of every conceivable scrap of tradable information that was ever encoded into it. The computer may have created the ultimate random walk.

A decade ago, I looked at the actual returns achieved by large commodity funds. On average, funds then were yielding just over 10 percent per annum—not much above the high rate of inflation at that time, nor much above the returns available on short-term money. Since then, the number of funds available for the public to invest in has grown from thirty-five to one hundred and five. Of the thirty-five funds listed in 1982, fourteen have disappeared (no prizes for guessing why) or have been reorganized under other names.

Would it have made sense to bet on those funds that have beaten the pack? Possibly, if you could have identified them early. But that would not have been easy. Fund performance, year to year, is highly regressive. I argued earlier that if expertise in the market were a big factor in performance, there ought to be a clear tendency for those funds that performed well one year to perform well the next. But no such pattern was evident (Figure 5-2 on next page). Regression was dominant, for there was no correlation in performance, year to year. What was observed was a random scattering with a predictability factor of zero (coefficient of correlation, -0.07).

The regressive nature of fund results is supportive of the thesis that *the expected long-term returns from any trend-following system will be about the same*. Funds achieve divergent results simply because some market conditions favor one system over another. But market conditions are constantly changing, so things average out. Occasionally, all funds do rather well in the same year because, once in a while, most commodities will experience benign trends at the same time. A rising tide raises all ships.

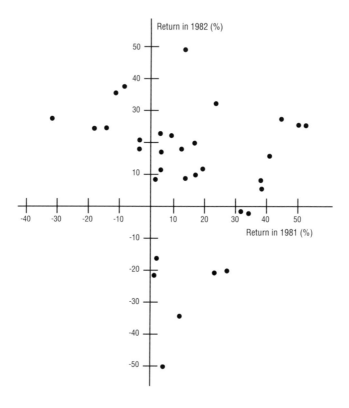

Figure 5-2 Commodity fund performance—zero correlation, year to year

Unfortunately for the fund investor, the average ship has not risen very much lately (Figure 5-3). Over the last ten years, the average performance of all commodity funds has been a return of less than 6 percent a year—and this in a period of mostly high inflation. The 6 percent return is also inflated by omissions—negative results from funds that have disappeared off the radar screen.

Why do funds achieve results so far below the level indicated by the PLODDER tests? How can it be that the smartest MBAs in Harvard, aided by the most sophisticated computational devices available, have managed to consistently underperform a checking account? Funds do have substantial management costs, it's true, but could there be more at work here than a simple skimming by the suits? Could it be that with funds, as with individuals, actions may contradict professed beliefs?

At this level of performance, it is remarkable that commodity funds continue to attract new investors. Or, perhaps it's not so remarkable; money continues to flow into stock market mutual funds with the Dow Jones at over 3600. So, commodity funds may well continue to prosper. Hope truly does spring eternal. My guess is that the age of the funds is passing—not that they ever really enjoyed a heyday. It would be nice to see them go in style. Could we be headed for a dinosaurian encounter in the S & P pit; two giant trading funds lock into a mutually destructive trading dance, triggering each other's stop until both collapse from commission exhaustion? What a marvelous end to an era *that* would be!

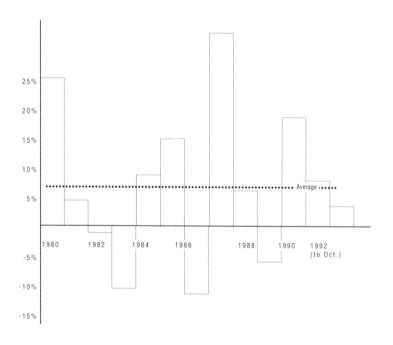

Figure 5-3 Average rate of return achieved by commodity funds since 1980. (Source: *Futures* magazine) The long-term average is 6 percent and is dropping. The average is also inflated by omission; casualties are not counted.

Artificial Intelligence

A computer sitting in the corner of a currency dealing room in the City of London was given $10 million yesterday and has started to play the market. Tests indicate it should make at least an 18 percent return in the first year—a profit of $1.8 million, and possibly much more.

It will accomplish this feat by using neural-network pattern recognition techniques. The subject of an explosion of theoretical research publications in the artificial-intelligence community over the past four years, neural networks are now emerging into the workplace.

—The Guardian News Service, London

Neural networks are cellular models that biologists and physiologists construct to understand how the human brain processes stimuli and issues responses. Science, I'm told, has yet to divine the true functioning of the nerve cells that give rise to what we perceive as intelligence. It *is* known that the brain consists of cells—called neurons, connected together in complicated networks. These neural networks have the odd ability that they can "learn" by experience. The way the network learns is by restructuring its internal neural connections every time it gets a desired result from a given set of inputs. Through repeated testing, the network will come to recognize patterns of inputs that demand certain outputs.

This is pretty cerebral stuff and not at all easy to grasp. Recognizing someone's handwriting at a glance is an example of your own neural networks in operation. You can't say *how* you know, you just know.

The biological response model holds out the promise of training a machine to perform tasks involving complex pattern recognition. I do not know whether neural network research will shed light on the workings of the human brain, but I am certainly prepared to believe it. However, I am not so sure last week's soybean prices can be "trained" to predict what this week's soybeans are going to do. Others are convinced.

If we are to believe the advocates of artificial intelligence in finance, the same kind of relationship exists between proximal prices on a soybean chart as exists between proximal neurons in the brain. If the learning process can be simulated at the physiological level, why not stretch the analogy and try to "teach" soybean prices to predict themselves?

So move over conventional analysis. Clear a path. The "talented" soybean has arrived, heralding the imminent triumph of artificial intelligence over the judicious application of common sense. Brace yourself for the wave of the future; artificial intelligence, we're told, is on the brink of unlocking the secret code of the historical price series. Forget the weather, forget the news, toss your economics books out the window. Fundamentals are obsolete. The future, long-known to be encoded in the past, has been exposed at last.

Or has it? I have a question that no one seems to want to answer. How can the evolution of prices in a commodity market—a system comprised of the whimsical actions of diverse and mostly irrational human beings—be in any way analogous to the processes at work in the individual brain cell?

I'm truly sorry for being such a party pooper, but really, somebody has to blow the whistle. Because, when you strip away all the verbal technobabble and straighten out all the algebraic contortions, you will discover behind this impressive exterior a methodology most inferior. Stripped naked, the artificial neural network (ANN) reveals itself to be nothing more than "optimization gone bananas." To construct a so-called ANN, you postulate every conceivable connection between every conceivable piece of historical price data, massage the data into submission, and come up with a model trained to recognize patterns and make forecasts based on these patterns.

Of course, phony optimization is hardly new. What is new is the massive amount of cheap, abundant computer power that allows this kind of "research" to be carried out. My guess is that the bulk of the papers written on financial ANNs comes from recently graduated math students who have never traded and whose resistance to optimization is therefore virtually nonexistent. The public hunger for the ultimate system is insatiable. If you can convince the public of your academic credentials, the more complicated and inaccessible you make your research the more attention you will get. What your audience is interested in is the bottom line—nothing else. Close your paper with an outlandish claim, find an uncritical editor to sanction and publish your work, and suddenly you are an authority on artificial intelligence. No one will question you, and your fancy is free to fly where it will; when you are trading ethereal dollars, the sky's the limit. Is it any wonder so many third-rate mathematicians are attracted to ANN research? As a proposition, what could be more seductive? But what could be more ludicrous?

One wonders what artificial intelligence would have made of events of October 19, 1987, when the Dow Jones Industrial Average plunged over 500 points, a singularity in the market never before witnessed and never witnessed since. Would an ANN have been a good student of the market crash? Would an ANN have "learned" the lesson? What could that lesson be anyway? Never be long the stock market if soybeans are over $6.00 a bushel? Always be short the stock market if bonds have had a four-day rally followed by a two-day decline?

Would a clever ANN learn never to be on the wrong end of a similar plunge in the future? One has to ask how it would achieve this feat, having a sample of precisely *one* to work with. (A sample of one is not considered too statistically significant.) You won't see many ANN tests applied to a data set that includes the month of October 1987. Can you guess why?

For those interested in the incredible returns available from trading "artificial" dollars, *Neural Networks in Finance and Investing,* edited by Robert Trippi and Efraim Turban, contains perhaps the most extraordinary claim for a system I have ever seen. The essay is by W. E. Borsage Jr. and is called *Adaptive Processes to Exploit the Nonlinear Structure of Financial Markets.* Traders who have wrestled with the often intractable S & P stock index future will be most disappointed to find out that had they traded with Borsage's neural network model *Frontier,* they would have been realizing profits of over $250,000 per year per contract—an amount greater than the full value of the contract and a rate of return of 1,000 percent, based on a margin of $20,000 (Figure 5-4).

According to the author, over $1 million has been spent developing this model on the Rice University mainframe computer. With this kind of backing, and with the kind of performance it is achieving, *Frontier,* we're told, is attracting the attention of some very big players.

Results from Combining Technologies: *Frontier's* Adaptive Indicators Combined with Neural Network Technology. S & P 500 Futures

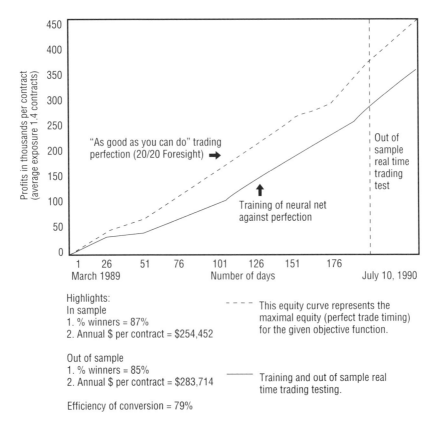

Highlights:
In sample
1. % winners = 87%
2. Annual $ per contract = $254,452

– – – – This equity curve represents the maximal equity (perfect trade timing) for the given objective function.

Out of sample
1. % winners = 85%
2. Annual $ per contract = $283,714

———— Training and out of sample real time trading testing.

Efficiency of conversion = 79%

Figure 5-4 Traders who have wrestled with the S & P futures contract will be chagrined to hear that a neural network is able to make $250,000 per year trading just one contract. *Frontier,* who made this claim in 1990, must surely have taken over the world by now. Anyone hear from them, lately?

Chart reprinted from Trippi and Turban, eds., *Neural Networks in Finance and Investing* Chicago: Probus, 1992.

To achieve its phenomenal results, *Frontier* employs not just the methods of artificial intelligence, but subjects these "intelligences" to the forces of evolution:

We diversify by building a number of models which we allow to compete. We have built a Darwinian selector (an elementary genetic selector) that selects the winning individual models from over a dozen neural network models. For example, we build one model from our historical indicators, and others from different classes of various real-time indicators. All of these models can be used to develop a customized output and a technology signal service for our worldwide client base of banks and international oil companies.

Pompous naivety on this scale is, of course, laughable. But although I have described the most ridiculous of the genre, this level of scholarship is in many ways typical of that found in the literature on artificial intelligence. Most of the articles on technical analysis appearing in *Neural Networks in Finance and Investing* are no more than childish wish lists overlain with a veneer of academic snobbery. There are, however, more sober voices. In a scholarly but lucid article from the same volume, *Economic Prediction using Neural Networks*, Halbert White describes testing a neural network on the price of IBM stock over a period of 5,000 days. He used the first 1,000 days to "train" his neural network to recognize the most predictive price patterns. He *then* tested the model on the remaining prices that had *not* been used to generate the model. White had no preconceived notions:

> Despite the strength of the simple efficient markets hypothesis (random-walk), it is still only a theory, and any theory can be refuted with appropriate evidence. It may be that techniques capable of finding such evidence have not been applied.

> Against the optimistic hope that neural network methods can unlock the mysteries of the market is the pessimistic received wisdom (at least among academics) of the 'efficient markets hypothesis.' In its simplest form, this hypothesis asserts that prices follow a random walk. The justification for the absence of predictability is akin to the reason that there are so few $100 bills lying on the ground. Apart from the fact that they are not often dropped, they tend to be picked up rather rapidly.

After studying 5,000 days (twenty years) of IBM price history, White could find *no* evidence that the neural network had uncovered *any* nonrandomness in the market.

Expect the ballyhoo over artificial intelligence to build for a few years then gradually diminish, as dismal real trading results confirm its irrelevance. I predict that in twenty years the neural network in price forecasting will be a mere historical curiosity, and that artificial intelligence will be developed by natural scientists—*not* financial analysts.

Expect an explosion of advertising in the commodity press in close proximity to articles shrouded in impenetrable math claiming "phenomenal results" from artificial intelligence. The strongest appeal of artificial intelligence will always be to those lacking the natural variety. Give it a wide berth and save yourself a lot of energy.

"I understand they're working on artificial intelligence."

6

FUNDAMENTALS

The Fundamental Edge

I'll admit to having been rather scathing with some of my criticisms, but I have had good reason. Having exposed half-baked theories for what they truly are, I hope to cast the positive things I have to say about the market in that much sharper relief.

I strongly recommend trading almost exclusively on fundamentals (supply and demand), but using technical disciplines to back up fundamental judgments. In market terminology I am a *fundamentalist*—a curious word for a trader, with its associations to Bible-thumping, puffed-up disciples of mindlessness and repressed intellect. A creative fundamentalist (in the market sense) has a heightened, not a deadened imagination. It is the technical trader who is closer, spiritually and behaviorally, to the evangelical drone. The technical trader wishes to get through the day with as little dynamic thinking as possible. That's fine, but there is a price to be paid for not thinking—for deliberately going into a fight with one hand tied behind your back.

The system trader can hardly complain about being consistently outperformed by the fundamentalist who is prepared to think for himself. I try to beat the market with fundamental knowledge on purely practical grounds— because it works better for me. Although the thought of programming a computer to tell me what to do each day does not excite me, I wouldn't reject this approach out of hand. Being as crassly motivated as the next person, if I thought there was a better edge, technically, that's probably the way I would trade. Fundamentalists and technicians have the same basic desires—to make money for themselves. My objective is to give the reader the essence of both approaches, but I have to try to influence the reader in the fundamental direction because that's what I believe in myself.

Do fundamental traders and technical traders perform the same economic function? Surely, the market couldn't care less how or why any particular trader comes to any particular decision. True. But an argument can be made that although all traders are acting blatantly in their own self-interest, fundamental traders perform a different economic function from technical traders. How so? If futures markets exist to facilitate commerce, not to satisfy the speculating needs of the public, does it not follow that the more quickly prices respond to upcoming shortages or surpluses the less volatile prices will be in the long run?

The fundamental trader has reason to take a position in a future only when he feels the price is too low or too high. By trading from this motivation, the fundamental trader is essentially voting to restore equilibrium to the market. The technical trader, on the other hand, acting solely on what the past portends for the future, is not registering a vote for equilibrium. If anything, he is voting to exacerbate an existing disequilibrium, a small philosophical distinction perhaps, but pertinent to an understanding of the increased short-term price volatility we seem to be seeing in a lot of markets these days.

Fundamental traders are particularly concerned with *value*; it is value that grounds prices in reality. The harder it is to estimate the true value of a commodity, the harder it is for the fundamental trader to gain an edge on the technical trader. Can anyone put a value (as opposed to a price) on an ounce of gold? I don't think so. In the last twenty-five years it has gone from $35 to over $800 and back to $300. Placing a value on a pound of bacon is a lot more straightforward; at 99 cents, bacon is historically cheap, while at $2.99 it is historically expensive. If bacon gets cheap people will eat more. In reaction to low prices, hog farmers will eventually cut back on hog production, thereby setting in motion forces that will drive the price of pork bellies back towards its normal average *value*—and probably, for a while, well past that value.

Many technical traders shy away from the pork belly market on the grounds that it is too unpredictable. Lacking any understanding of what makes bellies run, technical traders cannot appreciate the inherent price volatility of the market. They feel, wrongly, that the market is "rigged" because it defies technical analysis. The belly market is difficult for technicians precisely because it is the market most amenable to fundamental forecasting—hence the market offering the greatest edge to fundamental traders. In contrast, gold is probably the market with the smallest fundamentalist's edge. I'd stop short of suggesting that fundamentals don't exist in gold, though. It could be that they are just more difficult to fathom.

The Right Stuff

The commodities market provides a means for expressing an economic conviction in the boldest possible way. If a call is correct, it will be rewarded; otherwise, it will be censured where it matters most—in the pocket. It is true that the market is brutal to most of the people who challenge it. But so is Mount Everest, and that shouldn't—and doesn't—stop people from trying to reach the top. What is expected of a mountain or a market is only that it have no favorites—that it treat all challengers as equals. The commodity market achieves this goal in a remarkably efficient way. (The same cannot be said of the stock market, where the public is at a distinct disadvantage due to insider trading.)

For the fundamental trader who appreciates the subtlety of the game he is playing, commodity trading can be an intellectual stimulation, as well as a way to make money. Played well, it demands skills of the highest order, and skills the trader must work very hard to acquire. A well-conceived and -executed transaction is a thing of beauty, to be experienced, enjoyed, and remembered. It should have an essence transcending monetary reward. A piece of each trade should stay with you, forever, because the memory is important. This applies equally to unsuccessful trades, of which there will be many. Even getting out of a bad position, expeditiously, should provide satisfaction, not irritation.

There's not a whole lot of satisfaction in trading the market technically, especially when you close out a loser. Nor is there anything to be learned from a technical trade. The technician, of course, is not interested in learning from the market, so he is not likely to complain. And maybe he shouldn't. With good discipline, he *should* get a respectable return. But there is a price to pay for being complacent; he can expect mediocre performance at best and he must be prepared to endure boredom. Such are the rewards for aspiring to be an artisan when you might have been an artist.

To be a good artist does not require that you be undisciplined. A good fundamental trader knows the value of trading with stops and sticking with the trend. But the artistic trader is keen to participate, to be selective, to act on his dynamic judgment. He will try to avoid markets stuck in trading ranges, where supply and demand are in balance, as they often are. At times he may not care to be in *any* position—though he should always be on the lookout for opportunities.

Unlike art, trading is a form of warfare. Wars may be won by attrition, but more often they are won by a show of force in the right place at the right time. Tactical mistakes can be tolerated, if a strategy has been planned in advance. The shrewd trader will be mindful that his first concern is survival, so that he must always be prepared to back off, if necessary. Indeed, a trader attempting to establish a commodity position of a size commensurate with his resources must expect to have to *retreat* from time to time. What the trader must abhor above all is a reckless squandering of resources defending lost causes, or any temptation to exact revenge from a market for a trade gone sour.

Some aspects of campaigning are predictable. Discipline should be a habit, and money management should be organizational rather than inspirational. Approached rationally, such tactical skills may be learned; these skills are a necessary, but not a sufficient, prerequisite for success. For the absolute prerequisite, a trader must look into his own soul and seriously ask himself whether he has the right stuff.

The right stuff is imagination.

Inspiration or Perspiration?

Although any trader can learn the principles of fundamental analysis through dedication and hard work, I am not certain every trader can learn to use his imagination. The true art of trading lies in the ability to juggle conflicting pieces of evidence and come up with a balanced judgment, superior on average to the collective judgment already rendered in the marketplace. Can one *learn* to predict the future better than others? Or is the ability to predict an instinctive skill, acquired subliminally through accumulated experiences? You cannot forecast prices simply from following the news; price forecasting involves *anticipating* news as well as analyzing its probable impact, because a *liquid* commodity market is efficient in adjusting to breaking news. The instantaneous price level in a commodity reflects the consensus at that moment. And that consensus comes from players with access to exactly the same information.

If information on soybean fundamentals—in the form of a government crop forecast, say—is released after the soybean market has closed for the day, that news will be absorbed immediately at the opening of the next day's trading session. An unexpectedly bearish report (measured against traders' expectations) will cause the market to open lower, preventing anyone from profiting simply from *reading* the crop report and *acting upon* it. Those who were already short the soybean market before the release of the report will profit; those who were already long will suffer. Some of those who were short may have anticipated the bearish news—with various degrees of conviction. Some may have "guessed" correctly. Some will be short by pure happenstance, blissfully unaware that a major report was even coming out. If the market has been trending down in the days preceding the report, technical traders will most likely be short; if the market has been trending up, they will be long. If the report is a major bearish surprise, the market may open limit down, *regardless of previous trends*, sending chartists, Elliott Wavemen, Gannophiles, and devotees of the bullish consensus into apoplectic seizures—and triggering complex neuroses in "artificial intelligences" that have just issued buy signals.

How does a trader know if he has any forecasting skills or not? It would be hard to prove, true or not. If you correctly forecast a price move based on fundamentals, it is tempting to think you can readily repeat the process. You cannot. To forecast both the *direction* and the *timing* of a big move is a rare feat (even for the best of traders).

It will take some time for a trader to discover if he truly has an edge in the markets. The learning process is interactive; you pore over data, you make a forecast, and you enter a position. The market responds. You win, you lose, but you remember, or you'd do well to remember. After each trade some of the experience sticks with you, teaching you a little bit about yourself, about your strengths and about your weaknesses—and about your ability to forecast prices.

Forecasts, if they are worth analyzing as forecasts, must be made and acted upon *before the fact.*

"The bonds look like shit," says one trader just after the opening.

"Didn't I tell you?" says the same trader after the market has dropped sharply near the close.

"So how many contracts did you short?" I ask, knowing the answer is none.

A forecast has to be backed up with action, or else it is just so much hot air. And a forecast should not be confused with a desire. Many so-called forecasts are actually stubbornly held political viewpoints or opinions rooted in prejudice. Occasionally, one of these will be correct, but a broken clock will also show the correct time, twice a day.

I often run across the chronic loser with the unshakable belief. You find him a lot in gold and silver, almost always long. His strong belief works against him by never permitting his imagination to explore both sides of a market. If a trader is convinced that governments have lost control of their monetary systems, that hyper-inflation will eventually reappear, and that consequently gold has to go to $5,000, he is likely to dismiss any evidence of deflation, because acceptance would cause him to modify his prejudiced viewpoint. In the first edition of *Winner Take All* (1983), I described the gold bug thus:

> With his views as immutable as the metal he covets, he will be excluded from half of all the trading opportunities in his market. He may endure protracted bear markets within an over-all bullish trend. He may sit for years as carrying charges work relentlessly against him.

I had no idea that this scenario would be the one to actually play out. Since 1983, we have had almost ten years of solid bear market in gold, and anyone playing gold from the long side must have had a truly miserable decade. I do not claim to have forecasted the great gold bear market of the eighties; I was simply cognizant of the possibility. Gold bugs ought to have been cognizant, too. It's one thing to trade with conviction in one's forecast, quite another to trade with an inflexible viewpoint.

Bullish, Bearish, or Balanced?

We'd all love to be bulls in a rising market and bears in a falling market. Mostly, we won't. Whether a market is rising, falling, about to turn, or about to do nothing, will only be apparent in hindsight. The terms bullish and bearish are used, rather loosely, to describe what markets *have been doing* rather than what they are *about to do*. Strictly speaking, a freely trading market cannot be described as being either bullish or bearish—unless locked at limit. Buying and selling pressure equalizes via price, keeping the outcome of the contest between bulls and bears always in doubt. As information becomes available to traders, the balance point may shift; a commodity price may fluctuate from instant to instant yet always remain in instantaneous equilibrium. In certain kinds of markets, traders may be beneficiaries, or victims, of natural forces whose sudden occurrence is almost impossible to predict.

For example, orange juice traders hear about a winter storm building in the Rocky Mountains. Although it is a long way from Colorado to Miami, and although nineteen times out of twenty a winter storm will pass, harmlessly, north of Florida, the market will assess an element of threat to the orange crop. As a result of the gathering storm clouds, both buyers and sellers will perceive a slightly increased chance of weather damage and through their interactions in the trading pit agree on a slightly higher price for orange juice futures.

As the storm tracks east, the price of orange juice will mirror the ever-changing probability that the storm will damage the orange groves. Should the storm increase in severity, and, particularly, should the storm veer to the south, orange juice futures may take off. Although the price may be moving sharply and irregularly, it will still be in balance at all times—provided the market is open and a limit condition has not been reached.

News that develops overnight or on weekends can cause a sudden sharp change in price at a market opening. If the news is surprising enough, it may induce a string of limit moves—almost always advances in the case of a weather-dependent commodity like orange juice. Orange juice is perhaps *the* most consistently dramatic weather market. But a grain market, like soybeans, where the United States is a dominant world supplier, can also experience sudden large "weather" moves. At this time of writing (summer

1993), soybeans are trading at $7.60, after rising $1.50 in the past two weeks alone. A major flood in the US Midwest has delayed planting, making much of the crop vulnerable to an early frost. There is no question that the outlook for soybean supplies is considerably tighter now than it was just two weeks ago. Whether this perceived tightness is worth a $1.50 rally is something we will not know for some time yet.

But consider how this rally in soybeans has evolved. Years from now, a new generation of market seers will discover that the soybean advance of 1993 was the fifth crest of an Elliott wave. But old-timers will remember that it was caused by rain, a very great deal of rain. Heavy rain is not *that* uncommon in June and is usually welcome news to farmers. But heavy rain that won't stop *is* unusual. At what point did farmers start wishing for the rain to stop? And at what point did the meteorologists start thinking flood?

The transition from welcome to unwelcome conditions was not a sudden event, and soybeans did not suddenly jump from $6.00 to $7.50; the rise was steep, but there were setbacks, and there were few price gaps. At any point during the two-week downpour, the rain *might* have stopped, leaving the fields anywhere from slightly wetter than normal to totally waterlogged, and leaving the price of soybeans parked somewhere between $6.00 to $7.50. No one knew for sure when the rain would stop, or where the market would stop. It was a case of a market responding to fundamentals that kept evolving in favor of the buyers, but responding so as to keep prospective returns to both buyers and sellers *equal at all times.*

The odds-maker equalizes the odds in a football match (for the punters) via the point spread. The punter who bets a team handicapped in this way is registering his disagreement with the declared 50/50 odds, just as the trader taking a position in the futures market is registering his disagreement with the market's 50/50 assessment of a fair price. A trader must have cause to disagree either with the market's estimate of supply or the market's estimate of consumption at the prevailing price. Otherwise, he has no reason to trade.

With a crop, a trader will have few occasions to disagree with the consensus on supply—unless he is conducting his own crop survey. But a trader may have good reason to disagree with a market's estimate of consumption at the prevailing price level. This is where the fundamentalist looks for an edge in the market; here, experience and a knowledge of history can put the odds in the fundamental trader's favor.

The Eternal Triangle

A bull move based on weather is almost impossible to forecast, and no one need kick himself for missing such a move, at least the first leg of the move. With crops, supply prospects can change rather quickly, and prices will begin to respond before the relevant news is widely disseminated or its impact properly understood. Forecasting crop supplies during the growing season is very much a guessing game. With animals, supply prospects change rather more slowly—because of the breeding cycles involved. A forecast of livestock supplies is therefore less likely to be rendered invalid by a sudden unexpected shift in the fundamentals.

Other than during periods of weather scare, supply in a grain market will be fairly accurately known. Supply in a nonagricultural market, however, can be much harder to pin down. What, for example, is the supply of gold, or the supply of stock index futures, and how should a fundamental trader approach a market where supply is unknown or unknowable?

Let us for the moment stick with traditional agricultural commodities where the elements of supply and demand are readily identifiable. The United States Department of Agriculture (USDA) issues regular reports on grain stocks, on crop conditions, and on animal herds and breeding patterns. These reports are compiled by professional agronomists and statisticians working for the government. It is unlikely that any private speculator can have better figures than the official estimates, so it makes a lot of sense for the trader to take government supply estimates as *given inputs*, rather than to second-guess these estimates.

USDA statistics are released to all players at the same time—small traders and large commercial operations alike. All traders, therefore, have access to the same information. Where they part company is in assessing what a change in known supply will mean for price and consumption. The trader who gives serious consideration to the dynamics of the eternal triangle—supply, price, and consumption—will be betting on a reasoned fundamental judgment, and, if his judgment is just a little bit better than the crowd's, he will be trading with a winning edge.

To better understand how supply, price, and consumption are interrelated, let's consider the soybean market, where good accurate fundamental statistics are published with regularity. The domestic (US) supply of soybeans at any given time is the amount held in storage plus the amount expected to be harvested from the next crop. Every year, physical stock levels follow the same pattern—minimum levels at the end of August building rapidly to a peak with the harvesting of the crop in the fall, then steadily dropping as supplies are consumed. Because of this large annual variation in *visible* supplies, price forecasts are normally made on the basis of *projecting the level of carryover stocks* that will remain at the end of the crop year, *after* the crop in the ground is harvested and consumed.

TABLE 6-1

US SOYBEAN SUPPLY/PRICE/CONSUMPTION
SEPTEMBER/AUGUST CROP YEAR
(MILLIONS OF BUSHELS)

	Carryover	+	New crop	=	Total supply	Price/bushel*	Usage	Carryover
1981–82	313	+	1989	=	2302	$6.04	2048	254
1982–83	254	+	2190	=	2444	$5.65	2099	345
1983–84	345	+	1636	=	1981	$7.83	1805	176
1984–85	176	+	1861	=	2037	$5.84	1721	316
1985–86	316	+	2099	=	2415	$5.05	1879	536
1986–87	536	+	1943	=	2479	$4.78	2042	437
1987–88	437	+	1918	=	2375	$5.88	2073	302
1988–89	302	+	1553	=	1855	$7.42	1673	182
1989–90	182	+	1927	=	2109	$5.70	1870	239
1990–91	239	+	1928	=	2167	$5.75	1838	329
1991–92	329	+	1990	=	2319	$5.60	2041	278
1992–93	278	+	2199	=	2477	$6.10	2167	310

* Average price received by US farmers (1992–93 price is estimated.)

Source: USDA

By studying soybean statistics (Table 6-1), a trader can see, historically and in broad terms, how major changes in supply have affected the price of soybeans. This is the necessary base of knowledge from which to infer whether the *current* price in relation to *current* estimated supplies is overvalued, undervalued, or fairly priced. Fundamental comparisons with historical parallels provide the trader with a *frame of reference* from which to determine if a position in a futures market is warranted.

As one would expect, years of *low* supply correspond with *high* prices, *reduced* consumption, and *small* carryover stock levels—with the reverse situation holding in years of large supply. The correlation is rough at times, but it is there, and it certainly suggests a good first approximation of what a major change in supply is likely to do to the *average price level.*

A stronger supply/price correlation will be apparent when we look at the *true supply horizon,* because the market will always be looking a little bit further down the road than the end of its current crop year. For example, in the summer of 1988 (which is still the 1987–88 crop year) the price of soybeans—cash and futures—rose swiftly in response to drought conditions affecting the *1988–89 crop*—a crop that was still in the ground and would not be harvested for several months.

During the growing season, harvest markets will be estimating what carryover stocks are likely to be *more than one full year away.* Traders must also be aware that there is a *delay effect* in the consumption response to changing prices and that this effect is not symmetrical. A sharp rise in price will cut into consumption much faster than a sharp fall in price will stimulate consumption. The stick, as always, has a more immediate effect than the carrot.

Soybean prices are considerably more volatile than the figures in Table 6-1 might suggest. Prices quoted there are averages. In the summer of 1988, for example, soybean futures actually topped $10.00 per bushel; the average price for the 1988–89 crop year was only $7.42 per bushel.

Any commodity that can be stored—grains, fibers, base metals, sugar, pork bellies, and tropical crops—can be analyzed, fundamentally, in a similar way. Not, however, live animal markets, precious metals, or financials; these require a rather different kind of analysis.

The trader genuinely interested in pursuing commodity fundamentals must develop his own critical eye—must get to know what is important and what is irrelevant. I wonder if it is really my business to instruct the reader much further on what he has to learn to feel for himself. I could, after all, be injecting my own biases into someone else's thinking. Moreover, I cannot claim to be privy to any knowledge not readily accessible to the public at large.

And markets will change, while the contents of this book will not. What was important this year or last year may not be so important in the future. In the hope that what I am writing will be of enduring value, I want to avoid any dogmatic price predictions based on present fundamentals. For most commodities, these comments would be passé by the time the book is in print. So, it is with considerable caution that I include the following observations on specific commodity fundamentals.

Soybeans and Products

In percentage terms, soybeans experience the greatest price swings of all the grains. The United States produces about half of the world's soybeans and is the dominant exporter. US soybean production is still expanding, year to year, but mostly through increased yields on the same planted acreage. In 1992–93, after a very high yield harvest, production came in at a record 2,147 million bushels. Significantly, this large crop was absorbed *without adding appreciably* to carryover stocks.

If soybean acreage is pushing its limit, and production gains are coming only from better yields, the supply side looks vulnerable; one bad crop can push beans sharply higher at any time. On the other hand, soybean production continues to expand elsewhere—especially South America, which could place a long-term damper on prices.

As the price of soybeans rises, significant rationing takes place; beans have always had trouble holding above $8.00 for any length of time. In a roaring bull market you may see deferred contracts trading several dollars below the spot price. This is the market's way of making sure no one profits from something everyone knows to be true—that soybeans usually fall back quickly to their normal trading range.

The end products of the soybean—oil and meal—compete in the marketplace with other oils and feeds, so they can easily price themselves out of the market. A sharp rise in the price of beans will cut into consumption quickly; whereas, a sharp drop in price will take some time to stimulate more consumption.

Bull markets usually erupt from drought conditions. In 1993, however, a bull market erupted from a period of unusually heavy rain. A myth persists that the price of silver and the price of soybeans move together. There is little evidence to support this theory other than some tendency for them to move together during general panic market conditions.

Corn

Corn is the main feed grain for hog production and cannot easily be substituted by other products. Most corn is consumed domestically; about one quarter of the crop is exported, and demand is pretty constant. Annual variations in supply are the big price movers, and when the crop is bad it can be very bad. Extremely short crops were harvested in 1983 and 1988 (Table 6-2). Fortunately for the consumer (though not the speculator), on both these occasions carryover stocks from the previous harvest were very large, thus cushioning the blow from the poor crop.

In recent years, corn stocks have been hovering at historically low levels. Should a bad crop coincide with a low carryover, there's no telling where corn might go—$3.50 would certainly look cheap.

TABLE 6-2

US CORN SUPPLY/PRICE/CONSUMPTION
SEPTEMBER/AUGUST CROP YEAR
(MILLION BUSHELS)

	Carryover		New crop	=	Total supply	Price/ bushel*	Usage	Carryover
1983–84	3523	+	4176	=	7699	$3.46	6693	1006
1984–85	1006	+	7674	=	8680	$2.79	7032	1648
1985–86	1648	+	8885	=	10534	$2.22	6494	4040
1986–87	4040	+	8228	=	12267	$1.51	7385	4882
1987–88	4882	+	7134	=	12016	$2.04	7757	4259
1988–89	4259	+	4932	=	9191	$2.57	7260	1930
1989–90	1930	+	7527	=	9458	$2.46	8113	1344
1990–91	1344	+	7937	=	9282	$2.33	7761	1521
1991–92	1521	+	7495	=	9016	$2.40	7916	1100
1992–93	1100	+	9483	=	10583	$2.15	8470	2113

* Year average, No. 2 Yellow Corn in Central Illinois (1992–93 price is estimated.)
Source: USDA

Wheat

In contrast to corn and soybeans, of which the United States produces almost half of the world crop, global wheat production dwarfs US domestic production by a ratio of ten to one. Making price forecasts based solely on domestic statistics is therefore dangerous because the price of wheat correlates much better with world statistics (Tables 6-3 and 6-4).

This truth was hammered home in the spring of 1992, when the United States faced one of its lowest wheat carryovers of all time, and wheat futures rallied to over $4.50 per bushel—a price that was to prove unsustainable in light of the *world* supply situation. American wheat priced itself out of the international market, and its rapid price spiral was followed by an even more rapid collapse. In 1993 the situation has reversed. The United States has a big crop, price is low, and the world situation is a little tighter than it was last year.

More than one half of the US crop is exported, so it's worth keeping tabs on the weekly export inspections figure (released every Monday afternoon) to see if the government's export forecasts look like they're being achieved. (This is also applicable to corn and soybean exports—released weekly, along with the wheat numbers.)

TABLE 6-3

US WHEAT SUPPLY/PRICE/CONSUMPTION
JUNE/MAY CROP YEAR
(MILLION BUSHELS)

	Carryover		New crop	=	Total supply	Price/ bushel*	Usage	Carryover
1984–85	1398	+	2594	=	4003	$3.51	2578	1425
1985–86	1425	+	2441	=	3866	$3.22	1961	1905
1986–87	1905	+	2112	=	4017	$2.76	2196	1821
1987–88	1821	+	2124	=	3945	$2.89	2684	1261
1988–89	1261	+	1835	=	3096	$4.00	2394	702
1989–90	702	+	2060	=	2762	$3.92	2225	538
1990–91	538	+	2773	=	3309	$2.73	2444	866
1991–92	866	+	2022	=	2888	$3.49	2416	472
1992–93	472	+	2534	=	3003	$3.25	2503	500

* Year average, No. 2 Soft Red Winter Wheat, Chicago
  (1992–93 price is estimated.)
Source: USDA

In the long term, grain traders will have to watch developments in the republics of the former Soviet Union. There, the potential exists to produce wheat in enormous quantities. On the other hand, the potential also exists for chaos—and very little production of anything. In the meantime, carryover stocks of wheat in the US remain near historically low levels. The current price of $3.00 per bushel is low-average, so wheat could move up smartly if problems develop elsewhere on the globe.

TABLE 6-4

**COMPARATIVE WHEAT STOCKS
AT END OF CROP YEAR**

(IN MILLIONS OF METRIC TONS)

	US stocks	World stocks	Price/bushel
1983–84	42.8	145.1	$3.56
1984–85	38.7	164.0	$3.51
1985–86	51.8	168.3	$3.22
1986–87	49.5	177.6	$2.76
1987–88	34.3	148.4	$2.89
1988–89	19.1	118.0	$4.00
1989–90	14.6	120.9	$3.92
1990–91	23.5	143.9	$2.73
1991–92	12.8	129.5	$3.49
1992–93	13.6 (est)	137.8 (est)	$3.25 (est)

Source: USDA

Cocoa

What's being eaten faster than it can grow, yet keeps falling in price? In recent years, cocoa has proven a disaster for the poor countries that harvest it as a cash crop. Cocoa has endured one of the greatest protracted bear markets in commodity history and now fetches less than one fifth the price it commanded in the seventies. Why? Too much cocoa, of course. Unlike a grain, cocoa is a pod harvested from trees. Low prices, therefore, do *not* discourage production in the short run.

TABLE 6-5

COCOA SUPPLY/PRICE/CONSUMPTION

CROP YEAR OCTOBER/SEPTEMBER

(THOUSANDS OF METRIC TONS)

	Carryover	New crop	Total supply	Usage	Carryover	Price/ton
1976–77	394	1330	1724	1438	286	$3313
1977–78	286	1500	1786	1394	391	$3304
1978–79	391	1480	1871	1457	415	$3064
1979–80	415	1618	2031	1471	561	$2547
1980–81	561	1664	2225	1583	642	$1815
1981–82	642	1712	2354	1606	747	$1605
1982–83	747	1533	2290	1635	645	$1687
1983–84	645	1525	2170	1719	450	$2133
1984–85	450	1921	2371	1857	513	$1961
1985–86	513	1942	2455	1875	580	$1850
1986–87	580	1969	2549	1896	652	$1762
1987–88	652	2168	2820	1998	822	$1486
1988–89	822	2436	3258	2124	1134	$1275
1989–90	1134	2391	3525	2226	1299	$1035
1990–91	1299	2493	3811	2354	1437	$1015
1991–92	1437	2228	3665	2312	1353	$972
1992–93	1353	2320	3673	2444	1229	$930 (est)

Source: E. D. & F. Man Cocoa Ltd.

The cocoa market is still feeling the effects of a rapid expansion in tree acreage over the last fifteen years, the result of a number of new producers—like Malaysia—jumping on the production band wagon. Cocoa stocks have built up steadily for almost a decade, but are now beginning to decline, as steadily increasing demand has finally outstripped production (Table 6-5). A number of marginal producers, ground down by the miserable returns they have been getting, are finally throwing in the towel.

Cocoa trees don't last forever; when a declining production trend sets in, it will be hard to reverse. All of which suggests a major bull market in the nineties. The problem is, when? Because of the very large stock overhang (almost eight months' worth of annual consumption) even two years of declining stock levels has failed to trigger a rally.

There's nothing particularly prescient about forecasting an upcoming major bull market in cocoa. There are a lot of frustrated fundamentalists out there who have been predicting a turnaround for years—and losing.

Nevertheless, if I had to predict which commodity will make the greatest percentage advance between now and the end of the century, I would have to pick cocoa. Just don't ask me when the move will finally get under way.

Sugar

A sleeping giant that occasionally springs to life with a manic energy, sugar is usually in surplus supply and spends most of its time at a price below the cost of production. When occasional shortages surface, the price can advance in multiples. I have twice seen sugar go from almost nothing to 50 cents and back.

TABLE 6-6
WORLD SUGAR SUPPLY/PRICE/CONSUMPTION
(IN MILLIONS OF METRIC TONS)
CROP YEAR SEPTEMBER/AUGUST
(* WORLD RAW SUGAR IN CENTS/POUND)

	Carryover	New crop	Total supply	Implied usage	Carryover	Average price*
1977–78	25.1	91.2	116.3	85.8	30.5	11.65
1978–79	30.5	91.0	121.5	89.9	31.6	13.22
1979–80	31.6	85.1	116.7	90.7	26.0	21.03
1980–81	26.0	88.7	114.7	89.1	25.6	24.80
1981–82	25.6	100.9	126.5	92.7	33.8	10.42
1982–83	33.8	100.6	134.4	94.2	40.2	7.58
1983–84	40.2	98.0	138.2	97.2	41.0	6.74
1984–85	41.0	100.4	141.4	99.8	41.6	3.67
1985–86	41.6	98.7	140.3	101.3	39.0	5.99
1986–87	39.0	104.1	143.1	106.9	36.2	6.19
1987–88	36.2	104.7	140.9	107.2	33.2	8.95
1988–89	33.2	104.4	137.6	106.4	31.2	11.58
1989–90	31.2	109.2	140.2	109.3	30.9	13.94
1990–91	30.9	115.2	146.1	111.9	34.2	9.45
1991–92	34.2	116.3	150.5	112.5	38.0	9.42
1992–93	38.0	113.6	151.6	114.3	37.3	10.26(est)

Source: F. O. Licht

Sugar is a very tricky market to trade—a market characterized by huge whipsaws within an overall trend. When you're right, sit tight, for the market will do everything to persuade you you're wrong. Sugar holds incredible pyramiding possibilities for the truly courageous. Note (Table 6-6) the sensitivity of the price of sugar to rather moderate decreases in production and stock levels.

Cuba and the former Soviet Union are the wild cards. Cuba is a major supplier and an increasingly unreliable one, but it is still a force in the world sugar market, and developments there must be watched carefully. On the demand side, a great question mark hangs over the recently disintegrated communist bloc and its ability to pay for imports.

Most of the consumption increases in recent years have come from the underdeveloped world, which could mean that rationing in the future will be accomplished with *less drastic price advances* than in the past. This is bad news for speculators. (Every commodity trader, I suppose, dreams of one day catching sugar at 3 cents and riding it to 60 cents, pyramiding profits all the way.) If not the high-flyer it once was, sugar will remain an intriguing guessing game in the years to come. Too many imponderables, no prediction.

Cattle

Cattle has plenty of reports, information, and statistics, but is sometimes a difficult market to read. It's infamous for reacting perversely to government reports. Beef is not a popular storage item, so the supply (fresh kill) has to be consumed pretty much as it becomes available. For this reason, you will find different futures months trading at quite different prices.

The basic report is the USDA Cattle-on-Feed Report, a monthly summary of cattle movements in and out of feedlots. Since there are large numbers of range cattle as well as feedlot cattle, a small number of cattle moving into feedlots need not presage a shortage of finished cattle; the cattle may simply be grazing. Slaughter weights can vary, and a heavier-than-normal cattle slaughter at lighter-than-normal weights can actually mean a shortage of beef. This is a market where I am happy to take cues from trade "insiders," provided their reasoning makes sense. For my money, the best cattle analyst is Les Messinger, who writes a weekly column for *Barnes Brokerage Co.* Here's Messinger after the February 1993 cattle report:

It is true that the USDA numbers indicate a major increase in cattle-on-feed numbers, but nowhere in these numbers is there proper indication of the tightness of cattle for the next 60 days. Note that one of the numbers considered to be very bearish was the placement figure of 103 percent during this past January. While this number was 3 percent above the very low placement figure of 1992, note that it was 6 percent under the placements of 1991 and 16 percent under placements in 1990. I think it is important to note that these numbers bear out my previous opinion that we will not see a major increase in cattle numbers until June.

Many people (trading the futures) are of the mistaken opinion that a few weeks of moderate weather will allow cattle (severely stressed by excessive winter weather) to completely recover. Nothing could be further from the truth. As we progress more towards April and the weather thaws, I expect mud to become as big a problem as the cold and snow are today. Most of the cattle closed out during the March-April period have spent their entire feedlot lives in extremely difficult feeding conditions. This will continue to be reflected in lower weights. Note that our average dressed carcass weight this past week was 690 pounds compared with 709 pounds last year.

April futures made a new contract high price today of $80.50 before retracing slightly to settle at $80.12. I believe we will be shortest of beef supplies during the March-April period when we should see increases in both exports and domestic beef demand. I continue to believe we will see April futures surpass the record high price recently made in February of $83.75.

> —excerpted from "VIEW FROM THE PIT" by Les Messinger, as printed in *Consensus*, Feb 26, 1993.

And he was right. No charts, no trendlines, no bullshit. Just the facts.

Pork Bellies

Synonymous with commodities as a whole, pork bellies can elicit laughs or wry smiles from the uninitiated. In truth, this is the purest commodity of them all, with a remarkably consistent long-term price/supply correlation. A lot of information is available on bellies on a very regular basis, and it pays to keep track of it. It's one of the few markets where the trader can take a reasonable shot at an independent forecast of supply (by keeping tabs on sow breeding figures and extrapolating these into future supplies).

A major report, the USDA Hogs and Pigs Report, is released quarterly. This report provides information from which to project hog slaughter up to a year in advance. Each hog realizes about twenty-five pounds of pork belly—the source of fatty bacon. Bellies can be frozen and stored—but not forever. In terms of projecting supply, the forecasting horizon is limited to the end of each summer. Most available pork bellies come from fresh hog slaughter, but this production is augmented in the summer by frozen bellies stored from seasonal excess production in the spring. Biggest price moves tend to occur in the summer, as the market attempts to find the price that will clear the bellies from the freezers by the end of September.

It pays to watch hog slaughter weights (weekly). If these are increasing, it indicates hog marketings are not current, and the upcoming supply may be greater than the market anticipates. It also pays to check the slaughter (weekly) to see if there is any discrepancy between the kill rate and the kill rate implied by the government's inventory numbers.

Due to the wealth of fundamental information available, pork bellies are generally despised by technical traders; it is in this market that technicians are at their greatest disadvantage vis à vis fundamentalists. Money flows more or less continuously from a parade of technical traders and assorted crapshooters to a small number of pros who study hog basics. The price of pork bellies never remains out of kilter from the fundamentals for very long. Of course, if it *never* were to move out of kilter, there would be no trading opportunities. So, it behooves the prudent trader to use stops and to persevere.

In the spring of 1993, hog slaughter began coming in much lighter than expected based on the December inventory. When this trend persisted for several weeks, traders woke up to the possibility that hog numbers had been overestimated. The market staged a sharp rally from 35 to 55 cents. This was not an especially easy call to make because it was never clear whether the hogs had been miscounted or had just been delayed in marketing.

Given the light winter slaughter, traders were now primed to expect revised and reduced inventory numbers in the Hog and Pig Report of March 31, 1993. At 55 cents, however, the price of pork bellies had already discounted, or factored in, this expectation of reduced inventory numbers. Consequently, any surprises in the report were *likely to be on the bearish side.* And so it transpired; inventory numbers were revised downward, but not by as much as the market was anticipating. Bellies subsequently retreated and finally made new contract lows.

A savvy trader will always be on the lookout for this kind of trading opportunity—where the outcome is uncertain, but where a surprise is likely to occur on only one side of the market.

Precious Metals

After a decade of decline, gold and silver have recently shown signs of reviving. (As of July, 1993, gold is trading at $390, up from a low of $325; silver at $5.00, up from a low of $3.50.) With precious metals, supply and consumption are slippery concepts at best. Unlike things that are grown, most of the supplies of gold and silver already exist in bullion or fabricated form; fresh mine production is not a large part of the supply.

No one knows the true supply situation. Potential supply exists in the form of jewelry. An unknown horde is squirreled away in safety deposit boxes and hidden under mattresses in Kuwait. Demand for gold—and silver to a lesser extent—is whatever speculators wish to make it. Huge orders to buy may suddenly appear from nowhere, and former ready sellers may just as suddenly withdraw from the market.

The psychologists' market really. Anticipating mass psychology is more important than looking at any economic statistics. One school of thought maintains that gold will boom again when inflation returns, and a fashionable number to watch now is the Consumer Price Index (CPI). Many traders buy into gold whenever the CPI goes up. Historically, however, there has been little correlation; gold, after all, has declined from $800 to $350 over the past decade, while the CPI has continued its inexorable rise.

There was a time when an international crisis would trigger a rise in the price of gold. But, like the boy who cried wolf, this scenario has been played out too many times. Now, in anticipation of the reaction to the reaction, a crisis is more likely to produce *selling* in gold. Even that scenario is becoming overworked, so perhaps the next crisis will produce a "logical" response in gold. I wonder what the neural networks, poor babies, can possibly make of it all.

Interest Rate Futures

These are hardly commodities at all, but extremely popular with jumpy traders who look for trading possibilities in every rumor. Traders are inundated with a welter of daily statistics that are supposed to affect the bond market—housing starts; the consumer and producer price indexes; business inventories; the trade balance; and the latest fad, the number of people filing for unemployment insurance.

A number of years ago, traders would swarm round the newswire on a Friday afternoon to try and get a jump on the market with the weekly money supply numbers, M1 and M2. If there was ever any meaningful short-term correlation between money supply and interest rates, it has long since been wrung out of the system. Money supply is now virtually ignored as an input.

Doubtless, there are long-term fundamental traders who can call major turns in interest rates. Regrettably, I am not one of them. Remember the good old eighties, when you could get a 7 percent yield on short-term money, and 10 percent on a bond; when real estate was booming in the face of 12 percent mortgage rates? Now, Treasury Bills will get you less than 3 percent, thirty-year T-Bonds are at 6 percent, and the real estate market is moribund with the lowest mortgage rates since the Great Depression.

In the face of the so-called economic recovery of 1992 and 1993, the stubborn refusal of interest yields to budge from their abnormally low levels is puzzling to many observers. Some believe this indicates a decade of depression. Can interest rates go still lower? Bond buyers seem to think so. Corporations apparently do not and are issuing paper as fast as they can print it up to a public seemingly anxious to lock itself into low yields.

The most recent leg up in the bond market (1993) seems in some way to be connected with the Clinton administration's avowed intention of eliminating the federal deficit. Strange that the market should pay attention to Clinton, while it ignored Reagan, Bush, and all the rest; they all made the same promise when they took office, and they all failed to deliver.

One might think that a ballooning national debt would be bearish for bonds because of the demands made on the public to accept government paper. Not so. While the debt soared in the eighties, bonds moved generally higher. So, even a reduction in the deficit or the debt could, perversely, be accompanied by rising interest rates. It has been several years since there has been even one uptick in the discount rate. When this finally happens, all hell could break loose because it will stem from real pressure, rather than from considered policy, and real pressure that won't easily go away. I would have trouble restraining myself from shorting interest rate futures on the first stirrings of upward rate pressure in the cash markets. Interest rate futures look high and vulnerable—but they keep going up.

Stock Index Futures

After the market crash of October 1987, the Dow Jones Industrial Index stood at just over 1800. Five years later, most surprisingly, it stands at almost double that number. It used to be believed that the stock market was a strong leading indicator of economic activity. Recent events, however, have not borne this out. The crash of 1987 was *not* followed by a recession (in fact, it was followed by a real estate boom), while the recession of the early nineties has been accompanied by a generally *rising* stock market.

At this time of writing (summer 1993), stock market bears rightly point out that earnings and dividends in relation to stock prices are at historically low levels. Meanwhile, the market edges laboriously higher, as money continues to pour into stocks, money that has become fed up with the low yields available on fixed-interest investments. If one thing has become clearer in the last five years, it is the strong link between interest rates and stock prices. Any rise in interest rates from current low levels could cause stock market bulls to stampede for the exits.

Stock prices reflect public attitudes towards money and investments, even though, logically, stock prices ought to be related to company asset values. Even if the economy *does* recover with some vigor, there is no guarantee that stock prices will go up from here. Indeed, given the general perversity of the market, no one should be surprised to see an economic boom greeted by a bear in the stock market. Major surprises look like being on the down side. Hardly an original thought, I know.

Currencies

If reliable fundamentals exist for the forecasting of currency features, they are a well-kept secret, indeed. Currencies are rumor driven; they respond, unpredictably, to asinine statements by politicians and finance ministers. With many random inputs and few solid fundamentals to go on, currencies are a favorite trading vehicle for technicians, artificial intelligences, and computer geeks in general.

Currency traders do watch interest rates carefully. If interest rates rise in the United States, say, currency wisdom has it that money will flow from Europe to the United States (to benefit from the higher yields) and thereby *strengthen* the US dollar. A rise in the dollar would be the typical short-term response to a rise in domestic interest rates. There is, however, a fallacy both in this line of reasoning and in this response. It is an inflating currency that drives interest rates higher, and an inflating currency *ought to depreciate* relative to a noninflating currency. If a country could strengthen its currency simply by raising its domestic interest rates, why hasn't Argentina had the strongest currency in the world?

The one convincing fundamental move that has taken place in a currency is the steady rise in the Japanese yen, a result of the massive trade imbalance Nippon enjoys with the rest of the world. On a cost-of-living basis, the yen is now monstrously overvalued. If, or when, the Japanese trade surplus is eliminated, it could be a long way down for the yen. It's my candidate for the bear market of the decade.

Sources

The fundamentalist is always on the lookout for imbalances in supply/price relationships. Mostly, a commodity price will fairly reflect the prevailing economic realities, or the imbalance in price will be too slight to warrant the taking of a position. The rational trader, therefore, will try to keep abreast of the entire commodity spectrum, since there is no telling where or when an interesting proposition may arise. All commodity markets at all times are potential candidates for trading.

Some trading opportunities may suggest themselves to the trader with a good awareness of world events but no specific knowledge of statistics on supply and demand—I'm thinking particularly of opportunities in financial futures. In general, however, opportunities will not be obvious to the casual observer; the trader has to discover these for himself. Economic data is widely available, but it does take some effort to dig it out and keep oneself adequately informed.

Unfortunately, there is no authority to pronounce which data are relevant and which are not. Only experience can teach the trader *that*. The aspiring fundamental trader may be pleasantly surprised, though, at how critical he can become in a short space of time. And it does not matter if, at first, many fundamental predictions turn out to be incorrect; trading discipline should minimize losses during "drought" periods.

As for getting at *historical* fundamentals, there is the redoubtable *Knight-Ridder CRB Commodity Yearbook*. Here you will find detailed supply, consumption, and price statistics for all the actively traded commodities, along with articles on how to interpret these numbers. This publication used to be published as the *Commodity Yearbook* by the Commodity Research Bureau. It formerly contained a great many errors, and some of the earlier manuals cannot be trusted. The latest manual has been considerably cleaned up, but still contains a number of inexcusable mistakes.

For daily commodity news as it breaks, brokerage houses have access to all the major newswire services, both on computer display and on hard copy.

Probably the most useful source of information for the speculator is *Consensus*, a weekly commodity newspaper that summarizes all the important commodity numbers (striking about the right balance between timeliness and the need for reflection before action). *Consensus* also publishes, by commodity, abstracts from the market letters of the leading brokerage firms. Reading these abstracts is an excellent way to become familiar with the economics of each commodity. Moreover, a regular reading of the columns will give you an understanding of how "experts" come up with very different interpretations from the same set of facts—a most useful exercise for cultivating an informed opinion of your own.

Links and Linkages

If you become familiar with a commodity's fundamentals, your judgments may not always be correct, but they will always be logically based. Don't, however, expect a logical response from the market. But trade. You cannot remain passive and wait for a guaranteed winner. No one is going to do your research for you, or present you with winners on a silver plate. As I have stressed repeatedly, expertise cannot be bought. A winning attitude must come from within. Get the imagination working. If you can't, then don't trade.

There are intelligent, diligent, and dedicated students of the market who understand full-well the nature of the game—the risks, the rewards, and the need for discipline. Yet they cannot apply what they know, and they never make it. A vigorous imagination is, I believe, a prerequisite for success. If you cannot get the right juices flowing, you are not likely to win. It would be deceitful of me to pretend otherwise.

A winning commodity game and a fine golf swing have a lot in common. Both are unnatural, hard to perfect, and even harder to teach.

> Before you hit any shot, imagine everything about it. The feel of the club in your hand as you grip it; the backswing and the downswing, impact. Then imagine the ball flying to your target and finishing exactly as planned.
>
> Visualizing the shot from start to finish helps activate your muscle memory for playing the shot you want to play. It's especially helpful in a pressure situation. Visualizing the result you want also blocks out negative thoughts.
>
> I know that I'd rather miss with a confident stroke than make a weak attempt that never had a chance. Indecision inevitably erodes confidence. Have faith in the 'read' and go for it.
>
> *Mastering the Fundamentals of Your Game*
> Arnold Palmer

7

EXECUTION

Being Right and Being There

Getting into a trade, any trade, is delightfully simple. Getting out of a trade, especially a winning trade, can be problematic unless you are trading a mechanical system; history will show you either stayed in too long or got out too early. If you happen to get out exactly at the top or the bottom, frame the chart and hang it on the wall. But put a note on the chart that you were trading *against the trend* when you got out of the position.

If you are fundamentally correct about a market, you want to get the most from your trade. But you know, or you will find out from experience, that the end of a bull or bear market can be a ragged, messy affair, with the peak or trough only apparent many weeks after it has occurred. You will also find that when you are correct, fundamentally, the market will *overreact in your favor*; prices will rise or fall farther than you would anticipate strictly from the fundamentals. Naturally, you wish to take advantage of any excesses the market cares to offer you. Since you will not be able to correlate fundamentals with price action near the end of a big move, the logical way out of a fundamental trade is through *some sort of technical signal* you have determined in advance. Thinking your way out of a winning trade might seem like a challenge you will be happy to face anytime, anywhere. This is deceptive; a lot is riding on how well you cope with "successes." To be right in your forecast and then to fail to capitalize on that forecast is the unkindest cut of all in a business that can be very unkind indeed.

"I got in at the start of the big move, but I got blown out on the first downdraft," groans one trader.

"They took out my stop on the very day the major trend got under way," moans another.

You hear complaints like this all the time, people blaming the market for their own shortcomings. *All* traders are faced with the same problems, but it is the trader who is aware of the problem and has a plan to deal with it who will finally separate himself from the pack. A strategy has to be so designed that a trade does not get abandoned because of contrary market behavior, or because a trader puts himself in the position of having to make a crucial decision when he is least able to think rationally.

A correctly called big price move can fail to deliver for any number of reasons. The trader may become discouraged after being stopped out—perhaps more than once. The trader may fall in love with a winning position and hold it too long. The trader may cash in his winnings then give them back, trying to repeat his initial trade after the trend has turned against him. Or, the trader may fail to pull the trigger and take a position he believes in, because he is distracted by other positions he already has in the market, or because he is preoccupied by problems elsewhere.

Take my friend George, who, between ministrations to the sick and dying, has been known to make the occasional call to a commodity broker. George likes straightforward trades that appeal to his linear world view—like buying orange juice in December and hoping for a deep freeze to strike Florida the following week.

George has tried this play several times, but the ice and snow have never come when he is long, or have come *before* he's got himself psyched up to take a position. On occasions he has watched long positions steadily erode through winter and into spring as every cold front has swept harmlessly along the Georgia border. He called me a few years ago, just before Christmas, to tell me *this* was the year of the ultimate freeze.

"Don't ask me why," he said, "I just *know* it."

I didn't ask him why, but he told me in any case, citing various weather abnormalities developing in the Rocky Mountains. I had heard this kind of story before and wasn't impressed. George was convinced, but he wanted an ally.

"Look," I said, "you know I don't trade weather markets. But, if *you* believe in it, go for it."

"I'm going for it," he said, "I'm calling Peter right now."

"Just give him the order," I said, "Don't talk to him."

"Why not?"

"You know why not."

"No, tell me."

"He'll tell you to go long cocoa instead."

"I'm buying orange juice."

"When?"

"Now."

"At the market?"

"More or less."

"What does more or less mean?"

"The market's up 2 cents; I'll catch the first dip."

"What if there *is* no dip?"

"I'll go market-on-close. Look, there's a line building in my waiting room. I'll talk to you when I get back."

"Where are you going?" I asked.

"Florida, didn't I tell you?"

"No."

"See, this time I'm hedging by bets."

"How do you mean?"

"If the weather's lousy, at least I'll make a fortune."

George put his buy order in all right, but all day the market hovered just out of range. Just before the orange juice close, someone was rushed into emergency with a pencil stuck in his ear, and George never got around to changing his order and never did buy any contracts.

The following week, a massive cold front swept into Florida; for the first time in decades it snowed in Miami. George spent his vacation huddled in a blanket, watching CNBC, while orange juice traded up the limit for eleven consecutive days. He drinks grapefruit juice now. Come to think of it, I haven't seen him touch chocolate in a long time either.

Commodity trading can be a highly stressful pursuit. Indeed, it is an inherently stressful pursuit—witness the tortured, concentrated looks on the faces of traders as they stare at the dancing numbers on the quotation machines. Let's be frank. You cannot hope to trade commodities without experiencing some degree of stress. But that's all right; other stimulating pursuits are highly stressful, and should not be avoided for that reason. Still, in the trading of commodities, *decisions* made under severe duress are to be avoided, for they will likely be bad ones—whether these are decisions to take losses or to cash in profits. A tolerable level of stress is one that sharpens the senses without dulling the reason.

Stress would be acceptable if, at all times, the mind were capable of painstakingly searching for relevant information, assimilating that information in an unbiased manner, and evaluating alternatives logically. But it's difficult to think clearly while staring at a quote machine, and with a big position on. We may think differently depending on whether we are winning or losing, but in neither case do we think as well as we could, given pause to reflect on our positions.

When a position is going against us, we look for ways to avoid making a decision—through procrastination or through selective inattention to news we do not like. We hear what we want to hear, and what we want to hear are reasons to stay with the losers—perfectly understandable, and perfectly wrong. On the other hand, when the market is going our way, we seek relief from the emotional excitement, and look for excuses to cash in profits. Market banalities like: "You can't go broke taking a profit" spring easily to mind, though we know very well that cashing in winners prematurely is one of the surest ways to go broke.

For these reasons, it makes sense to place *action points* around each new position taken on. These action points are arbitrarily chosen *risk* and *minimum profit* target levels, and until one of them is touched, nothing has to be done. The decision to go for a fundamental trade should not be taken lightly. So, it is highly unlikely that within the time it would take for one of the action points to be activated, a trader would want to abandon the position for fundamental reasons.

One of the action points will eventually be touched. Until that happens, the trader is free to concentrate on other possible trades without being distracted by the open position he already has taken in the market. (On a personal level, I would confess that my biggest failing as a trader has been missing trades I wanted to make because I had problems elsewhere in the market.)

After a position is taken and a stop-loss entered—and I mean entered, not filed away as a "mental" stop, it's not a bad idea to consider the money risked on the trade to be already lost—for it may well be lost. It is certainly not money available to back up other positions. (If "lost" sounds excessively pessimistic, perhaps "temporarily sequestered" will suffice.) There is nothing negative about this way of thinking. Having mentally accepted the loss, and knowing you can stand it with equanimity, the future can only be brighter than this scenario. And it can be significantly brighter, perhaps incandescently so.

The use of action points is a particularly valuable discipline for the trader who wishes to specify his stop-loss point in advance. However, an equally valid discipline involves allowing the market to dictate a *variable* stop-loss point, based on a previously established reversal criterion—like the one I specified in the PLODDER system.

Building Blocks

Suppose you spot a price imbalance and would like to back up this judgment with a position in the futures market. You expect your position to be profitable, of course, but you are not sure how best to realize your objectives. You are faced with such practical considerations as these:

- How much of a price move to try for

- How to proceed if this objective is met

- How much to risk in the first instance

- How to persist if stopped out

Naturally, it is simpler to take a position hoping it develops favorably and that the way out will somehow become clear. Ordinarily, it won't. It's better to have a clear understanding of your objectives at the outset; you will not likely discover them on the way. There are so many ways to get sidetracked in a market—even with a correct forecast—that without the framework of a trading plan you can easily botch the trade.

Once you have taken the plunge and have your position on, it would be oh-so-nice if the market were to proceed in an orderly fashion to exactly where you have predicted it ought to go and then allow you to close out your contract and stash away the profit. We probably see, in our mind's eye, all trades working out that way. But we know it's rarely going to happen that way; suffering at some point in a trade—even a winning trade—is almost inevitable.

Consider the possible outcomes after you have taken a *long* position in a futures contract. First, and simplest, if the price hits your stop, you are out of the market and the trade is over—at least temporarily. Not what you wanted, but not necessarily a disaster. With a plan you are mentally prepared for this outcome and you know what to do. Without a plan, you may be tempted to curse this commodity and look elsewhere. If you're mad enough, you may even go short the commodity—out of sheer spite.

Let's stick with the scenario where you are stopped out of the market, but you have no fundamental reason to change your mind. What do you do next? It is really in the hands of the market. If the price of the commodity continues to decline well beyond your stop point, you will be wise to re-evaluate your fundamentals; consider your judgment to be suspect, at least for the moment; and look for opportunities elsewhere.

Suppose, however, that *after* your long position is stopped out, the market moves higher again (Figure 7-1). If the market works back to your initial buy price and goes higher, you will be caught on the horns of a potentially nasty dilemma because, unless you take immediate action, you face the prospect of watching ruefully from the sidelines while the market confirms your fundamental prediction. Your alternative to being a spectator is to re-enter the market, possibly above your original buy price, and with no assurance that you will not be stopped out a second time. (Since the consequences of being totally wrong about the direction of a market are so dire, the use of a stop-loss has to be considered essential.)

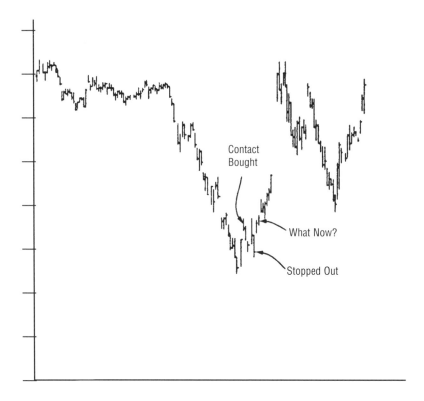

Figure 7-1 On the horns of a nasty dilemma

There is no reason to alter one's market viewpoint just because the market acts contrarily and takes out a stop order. Therefore, mentally difficult as it may be, the only logical strategy to pursue is one that continually reinstates a position after it has been stopped out—if it looks as if the market is going to confirm an original call. Eventually, this aggravation will come to an end because eventually the price will move away from the "combat zone" where the stops are being hit.

That's the dark side of the moon. Now let's look at the brighter side: The long position is successful; the stop-loss is *not* elected, and the price begins to trend in your favor. It is not a one-way street, though; there are setbacks, and each time a setback occurs you will be wondering whether to chuck it or tough it out. In the end you *will* get out of the position, of course.

(An attraction of commodities, as opposed to stocks, for example, is that commodity futures contracts have expiry dates, which force decisions upon the most stubborn of wills.)

Every major price move contains within it minor moves in the opposite direction. These minor moves are only identifiable as such in hindsight. While they are in progress, they look, for all the world, like major reversals. One of them *will* be a major reversal, but you have no way of telling which one at the time. All minor reversals have to be treated as potential major reversals.

How do you balance the need to stay with a trend with the need to protect yourself from a major reversal? You will discover that selling out a winning position into a rising market is usually a mistake, for the chances of picking a market top or bottom are slim. The solution is to use some sort of trailing stop order to get you out. This is not a complete solution, but it is part of the solution.

As soon as you close out a position, you become a spectator, for the dance goes on. You may get back on the floor at any time, of course. Imagine you have been stopped out of a long position with a profit, and now see the bull market continuing without you. Now you have another dilemma—whether to get back in or not.

I don't want to belabor the obvious, but I do want to stress that the successful execution of a fundamental futures trade needs a bit of forethought and a dynamic plan. Few traders will go beyond thinking about an initial stop-loss point. Few traders, indeed, will do even *that*. Yet, it is by planning for contingencies early that you will largely control the success of your venture. The strategy behind any fundamental plan is based on pushing hard for every advantage when the price forecast you have made is correct, while conserving resources when this forecast is incorrect. I intend to look at different fundamental strategies, at how they may be applied, and at how they would have performed in retrospect.

Trading is a balancing act—high leverage balanced against high risk; the desire to ride the wave as long as possible, balanced by the need to get off before it smashes on shore. A way of handling this balancing act is to formulate a trading strategy that satisfies the following conditions:

Condition One Establish a stop-loss price, and place a stop-loss order as soon as a position is put on. Obvious, yes, but easy to overlook in a flush of overconfidence. If you don't like stop orders, use stop-limit orders—but enter them! Then you will be free to look elsewhere on the board for other opportunities.

Condition Two Establish a re-entry mechanism; this is essential, if a major move is not to be missed. Painful too, since it will come hard on the heels of a loss—from a previous stop out. Being able to re-enter the same position after being stopped out is the hallmark of the true professional. Amateurs whine about the cussedness of the market and tend to give up; professionals take it in stride and treat each trade independently.

Condition Three Decide how you will get out at a profit. At some point the move will be over and the trade should be considered closed. Being able to walk away from a winning trade and move on to another market is also the hallmark of the professional. An amateur who has a good trade may delude himself into believing he possesses expert knowledge in a market and may have trouble leaving it alone. He is prone to play both sides of a market after a win and will often give back all of his profit and then some.

Many strategies may be devised satisfying conditions one, two, and three. But any strategy that fails to recognize any one of these conditions is, in my opinion, deeply flawed.

Retrospective investigation of a fundamental strategy only makes sense if we freeze a point in time, hypothesize a bullish or a bearish bias at that time, and assume that bias to be unchanging during the time of the investigation. This hypothesis is somewhat unrealistic, admittedly, since it implies a constancy of opinion over a considerable period of time. Under real market conditions, a trader will be constantly shifting in his degree of conviction as fundamentals shift. But usually, the conditions which prompted his taking a position are not going to change suddenly. Moreover, if the trader is disciplined, he will have designed a plan to see his trade through to completion, mindful that the temptation to find an excuse to cash in profits is ever present.

Since a fundamental trade involves judgment on where to enter, its hypothetical execution may not be simulated as accurately as a "system" trade (which has zero judgmental input). Nevertheless, it is legitimate to pick any point in historical time and pose the question: "If I were bullishly (or bearishly) inclined here, what plan could I reasonably have come up with so as not to miss a big move?"

Whether a trade is to last six days, six weeks, or six months, it will need a plan. The simplest of all strategies when you are bullish on a market is to *buy and hold*; you buy, you hold, and you hope it goes up. If it doesn't go up, you wait. Sometimes, that can seem like forever. I mention the buy and hold strategy not entirely facetiously as it is the dominant strategy in the stock market, where there are few short sellers. It is also a common strategy in the commodity market, not by design, but by default. Traders who cannot accept small losses on long positions have defaulted into the buy and hold strategy. Not surprisingly, the buy and hold strategy satisfies *none* of the conditions I suggested as mandatory in a logical trading plan. Let me restate the essentials of these conditions:

- *Condition One* The stop-loss order
- *Condition Two* The market re-entry mechanism
- *Condition Three* The market withdrawal mechanism

Perhaps the reader has already anticipated a strategy fulfilling these conditions. The one I intend to examine is simply a modified version of the PLODDER strategy I tested rather thoroughly in Chapters 4 and 5. It is as good a strategy as any and with minor modification can be made to fulfill conditions one, two, and three, above.

To demonstrate how this modified PLODDER system (whose parameters, incidentally, were specified more than a decade ago) can be employed to execute a *fundamental* trade, I need a data base from an actual market. Whenever one presumes to test a strategy on historical commodity price data, one is open to the charge that the market may have been pre-selected to make a pet theory look good. It is a fair criticism, and one that an author cannot truly counter other than by clearly stating his motivation. What I want to test with this data is not a forecast, but the execution of a strategy to take advantage of a forecast.

The market I have chosen to examine is the Japanese yen contract, covering the period commencing August 1, 1992, and ending July 30, 1993

(Figure 7-2). This is a time period spanning exactly one year, and is about as recent a set of data as I can come up with. Why the yen? For one thing, it's been a very active market. It is also a market with *strong contradictory fundamentals*, and that makes it eminently suitable for hypothesizing a trading strategy from both the bullish and bearish point of view. Let me stress that I am concerned here only with the *execution* of a trade—be it long or short, and not with the fundamental *wisdom* of being long or short.

In July 1992 the yen was close to its all-time high value against the dollar. Yen bulls could point to Japan's seemingly endless string of trade surpluses as justification for the yen to go still higher. Yen bears could justifiably point out that a cup of coffee costs $8 in Tokyo and argue that the yen was absurdly overvalued on a cost-of-living basis.

How to Execute a Trade

Previously, I described the workings of a pure technical trading system that I rather disparagingly termed, PLODDER. The system operated on a simple ten-day high/low reversal principle. Consider PLODDER applied now to the yen market over a period of one year (Figure 7-2). PLODDER is a reversal system; whenever it covers a short, it puts on a long. Over the course of the year, PLODDER would have completed eleven reversal transactions (the final transaction is an open position).

Taking *all* signals—long and shorts together, PLODDER would have yielded a cumulative net profit, after slippage, of 949 points (Table 7-1). The yen is a very small unit of currency, but there are a hell of a lot of them out there, and 949 points in a yen contract translates into $11,863—the per contract return an unbiased technical trader would have received using PLODDER.

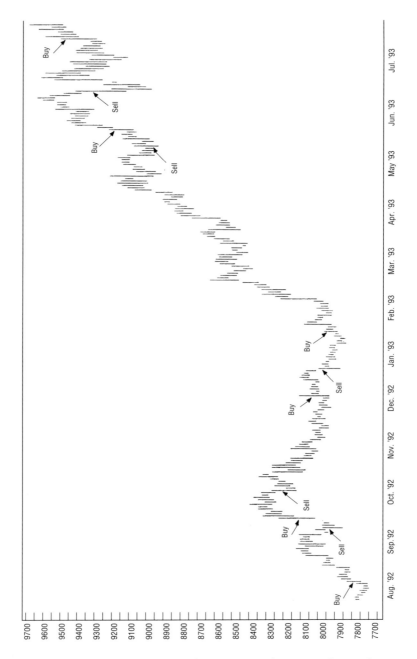

Figure 7-2 Ten-day high/low reversal system operating on yen futures for one year (prices adjusted for continuity)

	Buy price	Sell price	Position	Gain/ loss	After costs	Cumulative points	($)
1	7881	7860	short	-11	-31	-31	-387
2	7881	8005	long	134	114	83	1038
3	8162	8005	short	-157	-177	-94	-1174
4	8162	8246	long	84	64	-30	-374
5	8092	8246	short	154	134	104	1301
6	8092	8053	long	-39	-59	45	562
7	8007	8053	short	46	26	71	887
8	8007	8924	long	917	897	968	12100
9	9098	8924	short	-174	-194	774	9675
10	9098	9259	long	161	141	915	11437
11	9368	9259	short	-109	-129	786	9825
12	9368	9555	long	183	163	949	11863

Table 7-1 Trades generated by applying the PLODDER ten-day reversal system to one contract of Japanese yen for one year. Twelve reversal signals were triggered. Profits and losses are shown in terms of both points (1 point = $12.50) and dollars. Transaction costs (slippage + commission) are assumed to be 20 points ($250) per round turn.

How could a *fundamental* trader who thought the yen was going up have made use of PLODDER to execute a strategy? Simple. By following all the buy signals and ignoring all the short selling signals (Table 7-2). If only the buy signals are taken, the profit per contract improves to $16,500. This is to be expected, of course, since the yen was in an overall bull market; a trader correctly biased to the long side ought to have done better than the trader trading both sides. Over the year, the yen advanced from 7900 to 9500—a significant percentage increase for a currency. PLODDER, trading only long-side signals (there were six of these) managed to capture about 80 percent of this of the total move—$16,500 out of a theoretical $20,000 possible.

An obvious question to raise at this juncture is How much equity would have been needed to capture this $16,500 profit? An obvious question with no obvious answer. A simplistic answer is the legal minimum, the *margin* set by the exchange (around $3,000 for the yen). Although $3,000 would have sufficed in this particular example, in practice, $3,000 is much too small an amount with which to finance one contract of yen. With the yen at its present level of volatility, we are certainly looking at $10,000 per contract—

and that's still leverage of almost ten to one! Commodity financing requirements vary with contract size, with volatility, and with the degree of diversification in an account. (I will be treating the whole subject of money management in detail in the next chapter.)

	Buy price	Sell price	Position	Gain/ loss	After costs	Cumulative points	($)
1	7881	7860					
2	7881	8005	long	134	114	114	1425
3	8162	8005					
4	8162	8246	long	84	64	178	2225
5	8092	8246					
6	8092	8053	long	-39	-59	119	1487
7	8007	8053					
8	8007	8924	long	917	897	1016	12700
9	9098	8924					
10	9098	9259	long	161	141	1157	14462
11	9368	9259					
12	9368	9555	long	183	163	1320	16500

Table 7-2 Results of applying the ten-day reversal system to the Japanese yen—selecting only *long* signals.

So much for the bull side of the market. What would have happened to a trader who was fundamentally biased to the short side? Naturally, this trader would only take PLODDER's short signals (Table 7-3). In so doing, he would have racked up a loss of 371 points ($4,637). The strategy clearly lost money. But if you are fundamentally wrong, you must expect to lose money. Did PLODDER contain these losses effectively? That is the real issue.

It's arguable. No one could be happy with losing $5,000 per contract on anything. In comparison, however, the sell and hold strategy would have been catastrophic. To lose just 371 points out of a possible 1,600 points represents containment of a sort. The short-side trader could argue that when the yen finally turns he will be short at a much higher level than he was on his first attempt—and that when he catches a bear market he will be in profits at a much higher level too. True enough. But can he be sure there *will* be a major bear move any time soon? The cumulative loss on successively *higher-entry* short positions points out a weakness in the modified PLODDER technique as it currently stands—a weakness that will be exposed on the long side too, when the yen finally *does* top out.

	Buy price	Sell price	Position	Gain/ loss	After costs	Cumulative points	($)
1	7871	7860	short	-11	-31	-31	-387
2	7871	8005					
3	8162	8005	short	-157	-177	-208	-2600
4	8162	8246					
5	8092	8246	short	154	134	-74	-925
6	8092	8053					
7	8007	8053	short	46	26	-48	-600
8	8007	8924					
9	9098	8924	short	-174	-194	-242	-3025
10	9098	9259					
11	9368	9259	short	-109	-129	-371	-4637
12	9368	9555					

Table 7-3 Results of applying the ten-day reversal system to the Japanese yen—selecting only *short* signals

Something is missing. Let's return for a moment to the three conditions I said must be satisfied if a strategy is to cover all the bases.

- *Condition One* The stop-loss
- *Condition Two* The re-entry
- *Condition Three* The withdrawal

The selective trading using PLODDER signals observes the *first two* conditions, even though stop-loss points and re-entry levels are not set at fixed prices, but are dictated by market action. The problem lies with the *third* condition: There is no withdrawal mechanism, no way of terminating the trade, no way of saying stop, enough is enough. For the trader who has been fundamentally bullish, PLODDER's buy signals have been rather profitable. But any system will likely yield positive buy signals in a bull market. What happens when the bull market is over?

The bull market in the yen is still intact at this writing. If it should enter a major bear phase, there will be intermediate rallies that will cause PLODDER to issue buy signals. Most likely these buy signals will result in losses, and as a result some of the profits from the bull market will be given back, unless there is an override.

To clarify the absolute necessity for a withdrawal mechanism, we have to go back to the first buy signal on the yen, in August 1992. At *that* time, we have to probe the thinking of a bull and a bear who had arrived at opposite conclusions about the fundamental value of the yen—priced, as it was then, around the 7900 level. The bull thought 7900 too low; the bear felt 7900 too high. If the bull takes the first buy signal at 7871 and is stopped out, he would do well to ignore any subsequent buy signal that is not *above* 7871. And this logic applies to all subsequent stop-outs and potential re-entries.

Simply stated, the override rejects any buy signal unless it is at a price *higher* than the highest signal *already acted upon*. Only by restricting his trades to progressively higher entry points can the trader be sure that he is not just *buying rallies in a bear market*. With such a withdrawal mechanism in place, the hypothetical long yen positions must be modified slightly (Table 7-4). The effect of the withdrawal mechanism is minimal. Only one long trade would have been omitted because, of course, the yen has been in a sustained bull market. The withdrawal mechanism will kick in after a bear market begins in earnest. Then its *true protective power* will become apparent.

	Buy price	Sell price	Position	Gain/ loss	After costs	Cumulative points	($)
1	7881	7860					
2	7881	8005	long	134	114	114	1425
3	8162	8005					
4	8162	8246	long	84	64	178	2225
5	8092	8246					
6	8092	8053	omit				
7	8007	8053					
8	8163	8924	long	761	741	919	11487
9	9098	8924					
10	9098	9259	long	161	141	1060	13250
11	9368	9259					
12	9368	9555	long	183	163	1223	15287

Table 7-4 Results of applying the ten-day reversal system to the Japanese yen—selecting *only* long signals and re-entering only at progressively higher levels.

If we now look at the withdrawal mechanism from the short seller's point of view, we see that after the initial short position was covered at 7871, there *were* no signals to sell lower, and strictly speaking, no short position would have been taken—precisely what a bear wants in a bull market.

Am I saying there is no case for *ever* shorting the yen above 7871? Not at all. But the strategies I am exploring are relevant to executing a particular fundamental judgment made at a particular point in time. I am certainly not making a case *against* selling the yen short at 8500, 9000, or 9500. I am only dealing with the judgment that at 7900 the yen was overvalued, and the ways a trader who believed this could have formed a logical strategy. The fact that the yen subsequently soared to 9500 is irrelevant.

The need to include a withdrawal mechanism in a trading plan should be clearer now, for without this mechanism a trade could be endless. The PLODDER reversal system, then, modified by the override, looks like a valid technique for the fundamental trader wishing to nail down a decent profit from his correct judgment, yet contain his loss from an incorrect call. In the case of the yen, PLODDER would have kept the bullish trader long while the bull market prevailed, and also kept the bear's losses manageable.

Not too much should be read into the distribution of winners and losers resulting from PLODDER's trading. These were generated by a ten-day high/low reversal signal operating on a relatively small sample of data. (One year's worth of prices on one commodity *is* a small sample.) My guess is that *any* non-curve-fitted technical trading method, modified to accommodate fundamentals, would yield similar results over the long haul.

The PLODDER high/low reversal technique seems to work well in long-term bull or bear markets—such as the yen, which has been advancing irregularly for several years. In a peaky, blow-off type of bull market, a high/low reversal system can be expected to work much *less well*; here, a percentage reversal system would probably fare a lot better. It's very much a case of gaining on the roundabout what you lose on the swings. Let's face it, whatever you try, luck will be a big factor on any one trade. You just never known what kind of market you are going to be hit with.

No patents are pending on PLODDER. Feel free to use it, and consider it a bargain. People have paid thousands for a lot less.

Expanding a Position

What if a market starts to go in a trader's favor in a big way. Wouldn't he be advised to press his advantage by expanding the size of his position, using open-trade profits as margin for additional contracts? Yes, he would, but he'd better be pretty damned careful. This kind of play is attractive for the trader with a small account, the trader who likes to concentrate on just one market at a time.

If you are trading a small account, the temptation to expand a position can be overwhelming when the market is running your way. Problem is, on any setback you will be trading at your maximum level of exposure, and you had better be prepared to retreat quickly if things go sour—easier said than done. In the next chapter I deal with money management in detail. Suffice it to say, for now, that a trader should always be conscious of his exposure level in the market, and should be careful not to increase it through too rapid an expansion in the size of his position relative to his equity.

Traders who maintain positions in several commodities at the same time are less likely to want to expand the position base in any one commodity just because that commodity is performing well. In theory, with tight discipline it is possible to turn a small account into a large account by expanding the size of a position using open trade profits. However, I have seen so many disastrous attempts that I cannot honestly recommend expanding a position as a strategy; the markets are leveraged enough as it is.

The power of leverage is enormous. I just showed how a technical trading system could have taken $15,000 per contract out of the yen market. The margin requirements for one contract of yen are probably no more than $3,000 (not that I suggest anyone trade with such a high level of leverage). If you make your fortune trading, it will not be through harnessing the power of leverage; it will be through good price forecasting.

Opportunities abound in the commodity market. In twenty years of trading, I have seen soybeans go from $4.00 to $13,00, pork bellies from 20 cents to $1.05, silver from $2.00 to $50.00, and sugar from 2 cents to 66 cents. There is no reason to suppose that equally large moves will not occur in the future; that we fail to capitalize on them (and most of us must fail) will be a fault in ourselves, not in our stars.

Two for One

Although I believe a trader should always be searching for that elusive big move, most of a speculator's trades, even successful ones, will involve limited price swings. The same principles govern the taking of a position for a limited gain as for an unlimited gain; the trader must perceive that the price is out of line with where he thinks it ought to be, and the trader must be prepared to recognize that he cannot always be right.

The last thing I want to do is specify a set of pedantic trading rules. However, the reader may find the following guide helpful as a base for building a winning style. I call this the *Two-for-One Rule*. It is simple to execute, and is disciplined without being restrictive:

> If a trade is worth attempting, it should have a profit target of at least twice the amount risked. Once positioned, the trader should allow the market either to take out his stop or realize his profit. Winning trades, therefore, will win double what losing trades lose. On the other hand, there *will* be more losers than winners.

> A position should not be taken against the direction of the market on any given day. If you want to get long, do so only if the market is up on the day; likewise, get short only on a down day. This restriction might appear to fly in the face of the logic that markets, short-term, are almost totally random. The reason for not going against the daily momentum is that it will force the trader to resist the worst of his natural instincts—to buy into an avalanche and sell into a volcano.

Within these confines, the trader is free to choose and execute any trade, any way he likes. Apart from ease of handling, a discipline like this provides the trader with a trading record on which to assess his fundamental forecasting ability.

With the *Two-for-One Rule* the trader, to stay even, has to be right one time out of three. With this target in mind, I see nothing wrong with keeping one's batting average clearly posted. Rank beginners *lacking any knowledge whatsoever* will bat higher than 0.333, provided, of course, that they can maintain their discipline. That's a very big proviso, however.

Let me put it another way. Consistently trade two-for-one, never going against the daily direction in the market, and it will be difficult for you to lose money in the long run. I, for one, would not care to bet against you.

8

MONEY MANAGEMENT

Conundrums

I once attended a commodity seminar on money management at which a speaker stated that no more than 2 percent of one's equity should be risked on any one trade.

"Why not 4 percent?" I asked.

"Too risky," said the speaker. "You will experience unacceptable drawdowns to your equity."

I felt intuitively that the speaker was on shaky ground and tried to keep things going.

"Surely the trader risking 2 percent is going to be stopped out *twice as often* as the trader risking 4 percent. Aren't these traders equally vulnerable to equity drawdowns?"

"No," said the speaker, emphatically. "Survival is your number one priority. Extensive testing has shown that the maximum amount a trader may lose on a single trade without damaging his long term prospects is 2 percent of his equity. Any more questions?"

Whenever I hear that "extensive testing has shown" and see no numbers to back up the tests, I am naturally skeptical. I thought I'd try another tack.

"What about the size of the trader's position?"

"What about it?"

"You don't think *exposure* is relevant?"

"Limiting your loss to 2 percent is what's relevant."

"So a trader who habitually risks $1,000 on a five-belly position is at no greater risk dollar-wise than a trader who consistently risks $1,000 on a single contract?"

The audience was growing restless. Someone wanted to know if gold was entering the fourth leg of an Elliott Wave. I figured it was time to shut up.

> *Proposition:* You increase your chances of survival by risking smaller percentages of your equity on each trade. True or false?

No one else at the seminar questioned the 2 percent rule. Since it had been "extensively tested," what was there to question? Rather a lot, I thought. Later, informally, I resumed the conversation with the speaker.

"Let's say, for the sake of argument, I accept your 2 percent rule," I said. "How many *independent positions*, each risking 2 percent of equity, can I safely trade at the same time?"

"It doesn't matter," said the speaker. "If the positions are truly independent, it doesn't matter."

That stopped me cold; it did not jibe with my trading experience at all. I often trade several commodities at the same time, and when they all start going against me at the same time, it's surprising how much damage they can do—truly independent or not.

"You're saying an account trading one soybean *and* one sugar is no more vulnerable to a drawdown that an account trading one soybean contract alone?"

"If sugar and soybeans have the same volatility, yes, that's what I'm saying," he repeated.

At this point, a horse racing expert who also liked to trade futures joined in the conversation. He was very much in agreement with the speaker, and claimed he could settle the point with a very simple demonstration. He produced a nickel from his pocket and tossed it. Then he picked it up and tossed it again.

"The result of *this* toss," he said, "is independent of the result of the previous toss."

I knew that already, but listened politely.

The horseman then produced a second nickel and proceeded to toss both coins together.

"And the results of tossing these two coins together are also independent," he continued, pausing for my approval.

I nodded. The truth is a beautiful thing.

"But there's a difference between your two demonstrations," I said.

"What's that?"

I thought I was on solid ground.

"Let's say it's heads I win, tails you win."

The horseman accepted.

"In that case," I said, "you stand to lose *two* nickels when you toss both coins together, but only *one* nickel when you toss one coin."

"That's irrelevant in the long run," said the horseman, with a wicked smile. "Watch this."

He tossed both nickels again, but this time one nickel fractionally later than the other one. He covered both coins with his hands, then revealed them one at a time.

"This one here is sugar," he said. "And that one there is soybeans. Now, whether I trade them at the same time or one after the other, the net result will still be the same. I can win on both, lose on both, or there can be a split."

I stared at the nickels, perplexed. The horseman's logic seemed watertight.

"Well?" he demanded. "Does it matter if I trade two commodities at the same time, or one after the other?"

"It doesn't seem to," I said, distantly.

I thanked the horseman for his most convincing demonstration, and left. He called after me, laughing. "Probability and statistics, that's all it is."

> *Proposition:* Trading a soybean and a sugar at the same time entails no more risk than trading a soybean *after* a sugar? Any offers?

A Popular Delusion

A speculator shows up in a brokerage office with $20,000 and wants to open an account.

"How many contracts of the Swiss Franc can I put on?" he inquires of a salesman.

"You mean legally?"

"Yes."

The salesman consults the margin sheet.

"Eight," he says.

"How about cattle?" asks the trader. "How many cattle?"

"Thirty," says the salesman. "Or eighty spreads."

"You're talking pretty high leverage," says another salesman, listening in.

"So how many Swiss would *you* trade with $20,000?" asks the trader.

"Two."

"Two?"

"That's right, two," says the second salesman. "Otherwise, you risk getting your brains blown out."

"I'd go with four myself," says the first salesman. "But I'd use a tight stop."

"But I *can* trade eight if I want?"

"That's what it says on the sheet."

Commodity firms set minimum margins to protect themselves against clients suddenly incurring large losses. They do not recommend minimum margin financing, for no one can trade anywhere near exchange margin requirements and hope to survive for any length of time; one or two wrong calls and you're history.

Ask five commodity brokers what a prudent level of exposure in the market is, and you will get five different answers. This is a question to which there is no absolute answer; but it is a question worth probing, because proper money management will allow an account to prosper, while careless money management will surely break it.

Whether they realize it or not, all traders, regardless of ability, are going to run into very bad sequences of losing trades, *purely by chance*. The prudent trader must therefore anticipate the worst sequence he is ever likely to encounter in his career and make sure his account is adequately financed to withstand it. I am assuming here that a trader starts out with a fixed amount of capital, and that he has no intention of ever adding to it—a very smart decision to make before embarking on a trading career. (Many traders continually lose small amounts of money trading small positions and regularly write checks to their brokers. People who trade this way have no belief in what they are doing; they view commodity trading as a minor but rather expensive vice they have to pay through the nose to indulge in.)

The trader *I* am addressing should be deadly serious about his goals. He has a fixed amount of capital to risk. If this capital is lost, it will hurt, and it will be game over. A speculator should consider his commodity trading capital sacrosanct, to be preserved at all costs and never added to. If there is one true statement in this book, it is this:

> Writing a *second* check to a commodity broker is an admission of defeat; traders who arrive at this sorry state of affairs are psychologically damaged and have very little chance of ever breaking even—never mind winning.

I will be making the case that the severity of an equity drawdown to an account is almost exclusively a function of the *size of the positions* habitually put on in that account. Some commentators downplay the exposure issue, suggesting that the trader protect himself from "overtrading" by limiting the amount he risks on each trade to a fixed percentage of his equity. Some experts say 5 percent is the most that should be risked; others say 2 percent. I intend to show that the question of risk percentages is academic and that only *exposure* matters in the long run.

Let's say—from simulated trading results, charts, fundamentals, or whatever, a trader with $20,000 true risk capital anticipates capturing an 80 cent move in soybeans. (An 80 cent move in soybeans equates to $4,000 per contract.) The trader has been reading a book that cautions him to risk no more than 5 percent of his equity on any one trade. Accordingly, he risks $1,000 on one contract, hoping to make $4,000: a trade with a risk to reward ratio of 1 to 4.

Now, imagine this same trader reading elsewhere that he should risk no more than 2 percent of equity on any one trade. If he takes *this* advice, the trader may still trade one contract, but may risk only $400. He is still hoping to capture the same $4,000 per contract move and is therefore working on risk to reward ratio of one to ten—or so he may think.

Let us compare these two approaches to equity preservation and see where they are the same and where they differ. Both are equally exposed to a sudden sharp price change, since both are holding the same position size—one contract. Both are going for the same size of price move, determined, as it should be, from the potential the market seems to be offering. The two approaches differ only in the *amount initially risked*, and if both pursue the same consistent strategy of going for that 80-cent move in soybeans, the strategy risking $400 can expect to be stopped out *two and one-half times as often* as the strategy risking $1,000; it can therefore expect to experience the same magnitude of drawdown over the same period of time.

Estimating likely drawdown is vital in determining long-term financing needs. That the two strategies described above can expect to experience *the same equity drawdowns* leads inexorably to a little understood axiom of the market:

> Risk to trading equity *cannot* be reduced by reducing the amount risked on each trade.

You can drive from Toronto to Miami in one day, or you can spread the driving over three days; it still takes the same amount of gas to get there. The small amounts risked with very tight stops will be balanced by the higher frequency of occurrence of losing trades. And if amounts risked are reduced to absurdly low levels, the commission and slippage charges will begin to eat heavily into whatever trading edge existed in the first place.

Equity swings *can* be reduced by shooting for very small profits while taking very small risks. Ignoring commission and slippage, you could, in theory, risk $50 on each trade and try to grab $50 profit. Trading like this, you might last a very long time, but you would not be trading commodities with any expectation of winning.

Whether you risk 2 percent initially, or 5 percent initially, your costs of *completing* a trade will be about the same in the end. There really is no free lunch, and it is very much a question of paying now or paying later. The simple fact is that once you have made the decision to challenge a market

(and not chicken out prematurely), it is the *market*, not *you*, that decides how much you are risking. This paradoxical truth is perhaps clearer when you consider the operation of reversal systems—systems that reverse positions on trading signals, going from long to short to long again in a continuous chain. In a reversal system, market action dictates *absolutely* the amounts that are risked on each new position. Such systems cannot possibly risk fixed amounts, and it would be ludicrous to try to constrain them to do so.

Exposure

In the retail business, the three most important things are location, location, and location. In commodities, assuming you have acquired sufficient trading skills to have an edge in the market, the three main threats to the health of your account are:

> *Exposure*
>
> *Exposure*
>
> *Exposure*

By exposure, I mean simply the dollars of equity available to cover each open position. Exposure can be limited by good diversification, but big positions mean big risks. An account trading one contract of a commodity and risking $500 is a much less risky proposition than an account trading two contracts of that same commodity and risking $250 on each.

Risk to equity increases not just with exposure, but with time; the longer you trade commodities, the greater the opportunity for the unthinkable to occur. It is said, given a word processor, enough paper, and enough time, that a chimpanzee will eventually type out the complete works of William Shakespeare, and that a trader trading one contract of soybeans will eventually go broke, even if he starts out with all the money in the world. I believe it.

Fortunately, none of us is destined to trade forever (we hope). But, a commodity trader, if he is serious, ought to be thinking of trading for at least ten years, and he should certainly be thinking of financing his speculations in such a way that he never experiences an intolerable drawdown to his equity. Of course, what is tolerable to one trader may not be tolerable to another. It should be noted in passing that there is no way a trader can absolutely *guarantee* he won't be hit by a drawdown that knocks him out of the game. All traders face this possibility. There is a big difference, however, between *running into* trouble and *asking* for trouble, and a trader working with a properly financed account would be extraordinarily unlucky if he were blown out of the market by a bad run.

There used to be two inevitabilities in life. Now there are three: death, taxes, and equity drawdowns. How much of an equity drawdown should a trader allow for? I can only offer the reader recommendations based on what I, personally, would find intolerable. For example, on purely psychological grounds, I would never wish to see my equity shrink by 50 percent. Many traders watch their equities shrink by 50 percent in a week, or even a day, and trade with their checkbooks at the ready. The only check I ever wrote to a broker was the first one, and that's the way I intend to keep things.

Even if I postulate a 50 percent drawdown once in ten years as my outer limit, so to speak, I cannot arrange my trading pattern to guarantee that this will never occur. I can only reduce the probability to an acceptably small level. *My* optimum level of exposure in the market, which frankly I have gravitated to through experience and intuition rather than through statistical analysis, has a *one in four* chance of producing a 50 percent drawdown in equity in a *ten-year period*. It hasn't happened in twenty years, but it might be just around the corner.

Probability level, size of drawdown, and time period are all variables in the risk/reward equation, and other traders may put different premiums on the importance of each. In what follows, remember, these are *my* choices, and this is the speed of the track that appears to suit *me*. There is no reason in the world why others shouldn't run faster or slower—within reason.

Is there any way a trader can objectively estimate, at a given level of probability, the worst equity drop he can ever expect to encounter? Yes, there is. And all disciplined traders can expect about the same magnitude of drawdown at the same level of exposure, simply because drawdowns have little to do with trading ability. Drawdowns are a function of the intrinsic randomness of the market.

To get at an estimate of an expected drawdown, a few simplifying assumptions about wins and losses will have to be made. But once largest expected equity drop (LEED) is objectively estimated, the trader can then make a logical decision on how he wishes to finance this LEED. He can be aggressive, or he can be conservative—as long as he is aware of the risks he is running.

Why is LEED such a crucial number? For the very simple reason that an account may well start trading at the least favorable point in its cycle. If this should occur, LEED plus margin is the minimum amount the account could start with and *survive*, let alone prosper. The argument might be raised that it is unduly pessimistic to anticipate an account starting trading at the *worst possible moment*. It is true that the largest equity drop will, by definition, start from an equity peak (Figure 8-1), and that there would likely be a cushion of profits going into this peak which would partly cover the effects of the equity drop. Possibly true, but dangerous to assume.

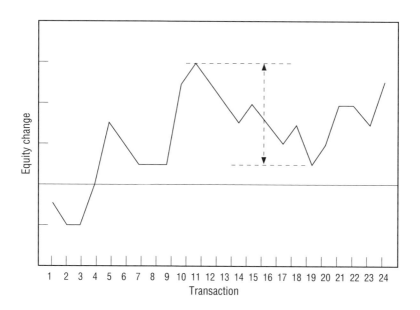

Figure 8-1 Strings of losses interrupted by intermittent profits are the bane of system traders. The *largest expected equity drop* (LEED) facing the trader is much larger than generally thought. Its magnitude increases indefinitely with time.

Successful commodity traders can expect to regularly increase the size of their positions in the market. As equity increases, so logically should position size, and if position size increases with equity, chances are the account will be trading at its optimum and consistent exposure level (to capitalize on profit opportunities) just at the moment the largest equity drop hits.

Largest Equity Drop

Let's proceed in stages, first considering the LEED in an account trading just one contract on a regular basis over a period of two years, say. It doesn't matter whether the trades are fundamentally or technically based. I am going to suggest a trading frequency of *one trade per month*—about the normal turnover rate for any mainstream system. In two years of system trading, then, we can expect twenty-four trades to take place.

Now we must make some assumptions about the distribution of wins and losses we might expect among these twenty-four trades. From experience trading PLODDER, I am going to suggest a win/loss profile (Table 8-1 and Figure 8-2) that should be typical of the results from trading *any* commodity, systematically and with discipline. The distribution of wins and losses is lopsided, with a long "tail" to the right, reflecting the fact that losses are cut short while profits are allowed to run. Although, numerically, there are more losers than winners, the *expectation* per trade is still a positive 0.1 (a 10 percent edge).

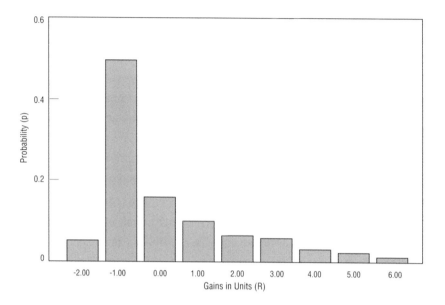

Figure 8-2 Distribution of wins and losses for sampling

Win/loss (ratio of R)		Probability of occurrence		Expectation
-2.0	x	.05	=	-0.10
-1.0	x	.50	=	-0.50
0.0	x	.16	=	-0.00
1.0	x	.10	=	+0.10
2.0	x	.07	=	+0.14
3.0	x	.06	=	+0.18
4.0	x	.03	=	+0.12
5.0	x	.02	=	+0.10
6.0	x	.01	=	+0.06
		Expectation per trade		+0.10

Table 8-1 A probability distribution of results of trades in a "disciplined" account with small positive expectation (0.1 or 10 percent). Although the result of any one trade is unpredictable, each trade can "expect" to result in a gain of 10 percent of the average daily trading range (R).

For convenience of analysis, I am also "binning" what is really a continuously variable probability distribution into discrete boxes, expressed in terms of (R), the average daily range from high price to low price. Expressing amounts won or lost in terms of the *average daily range* is an excellent way of standardizing results from commodities of vastly different contract sizes and dollar values, and of vastly different volatilities. Expressed in terms of (R) then, the profile of Table 8-1 should be as typical of the results from trading pork bellies as it is from trading gold or the Swiss franc. Results expressed in terms of (R) can easily be converted to the appropriate dollar amounts for particular commodities.

I deliberately chose a results profile with a very small profitable edge. Since the concern here is with the drawdowns, I would rather err on the side of conservatism by estimating drawdowns in a slightly profitable environment rather than in a hugely profitable environment. Even good traders go for long periods during which they make little progress, and these are the periods where drawdowns are most likely to occur.

To understand how equity drawdowns can be expected to increase as the number of transactions increase, consider a sequence of results (Table 8-2) drawn randomly from the distribution of Figure 8-2. The largest equity drop over twenty-four transactions is five units of R. Of course, this is but one sample for a simulated two-year period and subject very much to chance. What we need is a profile of the largest equity drops encountered in multiple simulations from this distribution over a much longer time period.

Trade	Gain/loss (in units)	Cumulative Equity	Largest Drawdown
1	-1	-1	1
2	-1	-2	2
3	0	-2	2
4	2	0	2
5	3	3	2
6	-1	2	2
7	-1	1	2
8	0	1	2
9	0	1	2
10	4	5	2
11	1	6	2
12	-1	5	2

Trade	Gain/loss (in units)	Cumulative Equity	Largest Drawdown
13	-1	4	2
14	-1	3	3
15	1	4	3
16	-1	3	3
17	-1	2	4
18	1	3	4
19	-2	1	5
20	1	2	5
21	2	4	5
22	0	4	5
23	-1	3	5
24	2	5	5

Table 8-2 Possible equity variation over the course of 24 trades drawn from the distribution of Figure 8-1. Note that the largest equity drawdown increases irregularly, in quantum steps, as the number of transactions increase. In theory if you trade indefinitely, you will experience an infinite drawdown at some point.

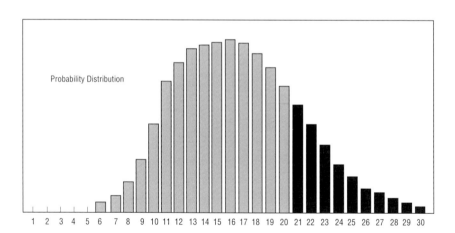

Probability Distribution

1 2 3 4 5 6 7 8 9 10 11 12 13 14 15 16 17 18 19 20 21 22 23 24 25 26 27 28 29 30

Figure 8-3 Distribution of largest equity drops arising from pure chance. Although the largest expected equity drop (LEED) over the ten-year period was 15 units, values ranged from 6 to 30, and a quarter of the values were above 20 (my arbitrary cut-off point). Even in the long run, the difference between good luck and bad luck is substantial. It pays to allow for bad luck.

Multiple simulations of sequences drawn from the probability distribution of Figure 8-2 produced the following information on the nature of drawdowns:

LEED in 5 years (60 transactions) = 11.2 units

LEED in 10 years (120 transactions) = 15.3 units

LEED in 20 years (240 transactions) = 21.2 units

Note how closely the relationship between LEED and time approximates a square root function. I expect a good mathematician could come up with a theoretical proof of this relationship. I have to work with empirical evidence only, which strongly suggests that:

A *quadrupling* of the trading horizon (number of transactions) *doubles* the expected largest equity drawdown.

It is appropriate to consider LEED as the real determinant of financing requirements, but it is worth remembering that one of the E's stands for expected—in other words, LEED is an *average*. A trader over his career might be luckier or unluckier than average. In an extreme case he might *never have a winning trade at all*. But we are not interested in extreme cases any more than we are interested in chimpanzees with word processors. If you tried to protect yourself from the worst thing that could *ever* happen, you would never trade at all.

It's worth noting that the difference between good luck and bad luck is substantial (Figure 8-3). Although the LEED for the ten-year period is 15 X (R), *one quarter* of the observed largest equity drops were over 20 X (R). I admit to being conservative, and if I am to stick to my stated objective of not flirting with a more than one-in-four chance of losing 50 percent of my equity at any point in a ten-year trading career, I would have to conclude that the financing requirements to trade one contract of *anything*, by itself, is 40 X (R). Perhaps this is worth emphasizing:

Dollars of equity needed to finance trading of one contract of *any* commodity = 40 X (R)

where (R) is the average daily trading range of the commodity, in dollars. Now we have the question of multiple positions to contend with. If forty units of (R) equates to $20,000 in terms of a soybean contract, say, does this *same* $20,000 allow us to trade *another independent* position such as a contract of sugar without increasing risk?

The horseman at the commodity seminar demonstrated very convincingly that in terms of expected drawdown, it made no difference whether a soybean and a sugar were traded sequentially or simultaneously. The horseman was right in one sense, but wrong where it matters. What he did not realize was that the simultaneous trading of two commodities essentially *speeds up time*, allowing more opportunity for a bad sequence to occur. However, his demonstration of the equivalence of the two situations made something clear to me that I'd had trouble articulating before:

> In terms of potential equity drawdown, trading N positions for one year is the same as trading one position for N years.

Trading a sugar and a soybean together for *one* year involves the same risk to equity as trading either, by itself, for *two* years. Since it has just been established that largest expected equity drop is a function of the *square root* of the trading time, it follows that:

> Largest expected equity drop is also a function of the square root of the number of independent positions being traded.

Two independent positions do not need *twice* the financing requirements of one. But neither can they be financed as though they were one position. The requirement lies somewhere in between. So, nice try horseman, but no cigar.

Dollars and Cents

I have spoken of wins, losses, and equity drops only in terms of (R), the average daily trading range. This has allowed me to generalize the discussion without having to refer to contract specifics. Since contracts come in very different sizes and trade with inherently different volatilities, one final step remains in determining dollar financing requirements by commodity.

Market	Current price	Daily range (R) (in pts)	Daily range (R) (in $)	Equity coverage/contract (alone)	Equity coverage/contract (with 1)	Equity coverage/contract (with 3)
Soybeans	$7.00	12 cts	600	24,000	17,000	12,000
Wheat	$3.00	6 cts	300	12,000	8,500	6,000
Corn	$2.40	5 cts	250	10,000	7,000	5,000
Bean Oil	21 cts	40 pts	250	10,000	7,000	5,000
Cattle	75 cts	60 pts	250	10,000	7,000	5,000
Hogs	50 cts	75 pts	300	12,000	8,500	6,000
Bellies	50 cts	100 pts	400	16,000	11,400	8,000
Cocoa	$1000	30 pts	300	12,000	8,500	6,000
Coffee	75 cts	200 pts	750	30,000	21,000	15,000
Sugar	10 cts	30 pts	350	14,000	10,000	7,000
O. Juice	$1.20	300 pts	450	18,000	13,000	9,000
Gold	$370	$5	500	20,000	14,000	10,000
Silver	$5.00	15 cts	750	30,000	21,000	15,000
Cotton	60 cts	100 pts	500	20,000	14,000	10,000
Crude	$20	30 pts	300	12,000	8,500	6,000
Swiss	68 cts	80 pts	1,000	40,000	28,000	20,000
D-Mark	60 cts	60 pts	750	30,000	21,000	15,000
Pound	$1.50	150 pts	1,000	40,000	28,000	20,000
Yen	90 cts	100 pts	1,250	50,000	35,000	25,000
T-Bonds	116.00	24 pts	750	30,000	21,000	15,000
T-Bills	97.00	8 pts	200	8,000	5,500	4,000
S & P	450.00	300 pts	1,500	60,000	42,000	30,000

Table 8-3 A guide to money management
Suggested financing requirements for different commodities, traded alone or in combination with comparable positions in other independent commodities

I argued earlier that it is the commodity that dictates how much a trader must risk to capitalize on a good move, and that overall risk cannot be minimized by risking artificially small amounts. The degree of risk in any trade is directly related to the current price volatility of the commodity in question, and this is reflected in the average daily trading range—a quantity I designated as (R). Because of different contract sizes and differing volatilities, the value of (R) is different for each commodity, and will vary over time in each commodity (Table 8-3). The (R) values here reflect market volatilities in the summer of 1993.

For example, according to Table 8-3, the dollars to adequately finance the trading of one contract of soybeans in the summer of 1993, with the average daily range around 12 cents ($600) would have been (40 x 600 = $24,000). The final two columns of Table 8-3 reflect the benefits of diversification; the reduced equity coverage per contract required when a commodity is traded with *one* other independent commodity, and with *three* other independent commodities.

As an illustration, the implied long-term financing requirement for trading T-Bonds alone is $30,000 per contract. However, if T-Bonds are traded simultaneously with gold, cattle, and cocoa, financing requirements for the T-Bond drop to $15,000 per contract. A balanced account (position-wise) trading one T-Bond, two bellies, and three each of cattle and cocoa would therefore require an initial equity of:

$$1 \times 15,000 \quad \text{(bonds)}$$
$$2 \times 8,000 \quad \text{(bellies)}$$
$$3 \times 5,000 \quad \text{(cattle)}$$
$$\underline{3 \times 6,000 \quad \text{(cocoa)}}$$
$$\text{Total} = \$64,000$$

These suggested financing requirements will look absurdly high to most traders. On the other hand, most traders will eventually blow themselves out of the market through *overtrading*. Granted, my figures are conservative, but they can hardly be conservative by more than a factor of *two*, and I humbly suggest that any active trader trading at more than twice the leverage implied in Table 8-3 can expect to run into problems somewhere down the road—and perhaps sooner than later. There is little doubt that traders consistently underestimate the power of the random forces in the market to inflict terminal damage to their accounts. The other day, someone with a surefire system to trade the S & P asked me how many contracts I thought he could trade with $50,000. I looked at Table 8-3, and gave him the answer. None.

A case can be made that many traders will trade much less frequently than the rate I am assuming—turning over positions on average once a month, and that consequently these traders can afford to trade less conservatively than I have suggested. I wouldn't argue with that. Also, my financing suggestions are based on equity drawdowns occurring in an account that does not reduce its trading level as it shrinks in value. In practice, it makes a lot of sense to reduce position sizes as equity diminishes, though not necessarily after every unsuccessful trade. Traders who are prepared to "retreat to victory" can also afford to be a little more aggressive with their financing.

Traders who consistently trade with a higher edge than 10 percent would also expect to experience smaller drawdowns and likewise be able to operate with reduced financing requirements. I'd be wary of this, all the same. The problem is with consistency. My guess is that even the best traders will go for lengthy periods where they do little better than break even. Of course, a major equity drawdown does not necessarily *have* to occur during every lean period; it's just more likely.

Technical traders who trade *many* different commodities at the same time get further benefit from their high degree of diversification in the form of *even lower* financing needs (on a per contract basis). They have to be careful that their positions are truly diversified, or make allowance for the instances where there is dependency. For example, while it is reasonable to assume that pork bellies, cocoa, and sugar vary independently, it is certainly not reasonable to assume that the Swiss franc and the D-mark vary independently; in fact, these contracts move in very close tandem, and trading one of each is very much like trading two of either. Certain interest rate markets may move in tandem at some times but not at others. Some judgment is needed in assessing the *increased financial risk* incurred by trading positions that are not truly independent.

Fundamental traders may be in the market less often than technical traders and have fewer independent positions on at any one time. Still, I would argue that the financing constraints of Table 8-3 are equally applicable. An active fundamental trader could easily be turning over positions once a month, risking small amounts in pursuit of big moves.

I know of a broker who has just begun operating a currency trading system. He trades a portfolio comprising one contract each of the Swiss franc, the D-mark, the yen, and the pound. These are all large contracts with high volatilities and a penchant for sudden overnight surprises. The accounts trading this system are financed, initially, with $20,000 equity. On the surface, this financing has the appearance of being sound—at least double exchange minimum margins, and a coverage of $5,000 per contract.

Yet, by my reckoning (Table 8-3) a prudent equity to handle this level of trading would be $80,000, almost *four* times what is being employed. And these contracts are nowhere close to being truly diversified!

Needless to say, the expected return that is helping to sell this system is very high indeed, based, as it is, on an artificially low equity base. The investors might strike it rich, but only if they get lucky fast—and pack it in early.

A Day at the Races

You are headed for the racetrack with $100 in your pocket, intent on betting each race on a six-race card. I accost you just before the first race and tell you that I am a clairvoyant and have information you can use. Since I have unusual powers of persuasion, you listen. I tell you that one horse in each race will start at odds of two to one against, and that *three* of these two to one shots will win. The problem is, I can't tell you which three. I also warn you that my clairvoyance will work only if you decide before the first race on the *fixed fraction* of the money in your pocket you are going to bet on each race.

"I'll divide the $100 into six, and bet equal amounts on each race," you say. "That way, I'm bound to win."

"No," I say. "You must bet the same *fraction of your equity* on each race, whatever that equity happens to be at the time."

You ponder. This is more complicated than you thought. But it is getting close to post time and you agree to try this staking scheme. You pay me $10 for the information, and I disappear.

> *Proposition.* What fixed fraction of your equity (your original $100 plus accumulated winnings or deducted losses) should you bet on each race, to end up with the most money in your pocket at the end of the sixth race?

The answer is $f = 0.25$; you must bet one quarter of your bankroll on each race. At the end of the sixth race you will end up with $142.37 (Table 8-4).

And it doesn't matter in which order the wins and losses occur; you will still end up with $142.37. Betting any other fixed fraction of your bankroll, higher or lower, will result in a lower profit. Betting f = 0.50, for example, will break even, and betting a higher value of f will produce a loss (Table 8-5).

f = 0.25		Starting dollars	Bet	Ending dollars
1st Race	Bet on loser	100.00	25.00	75.00
2nd Race	Bet winner 2/1	75.00	18.75	112.50
3rd Race	Bet on loser	112.50	28.13	84.37
4th Race	Bet winner 2/1	84.37	21.09	126.55
5th Race	Bet winner 2/1	126.55	31.64	189.83
6th Race	Bet on loser	189.83	47.46	142.37

Table 8-4 How equity would have grown, betting 25 percent (f = 0.25) of your bankroll on each race.

(As an interesting aside, a punter who consistently bet a quarter of his equity on 2/1 shots—and was able to win half of these bets—could turn $100 into $1 million after 162 bets (the equivalent of 27 race cards), *regardless of the order in which his winners appeared.*)

$(100 \times 1.4237^{27} = \$1,300,000)$

f = 0.50		Starting dollars	Bet	Ending dollars
1st Race	Bet on loser	100.00	50.00	50.00
2nd Race	Bet on winner 2/1	50.00	25.00	100.00
3rd Race	Bet on loser	100.00	50.00	50.00
4th Race	Bet winner 2/1	50.00	25.00	100.00
5th Race	Bet winner 2/1	100.00	50.00	200.00
6th Race	Bet on loser	200.00	100.00	100.00

Table 8-5 Betting 50 percent (f = 0.50) of your bankroll on each race only allows you to break even. With too high a stake (anything above f = 0.50) you will come out losing—even betting a series of results with a positive expectation.

Now, instead of a race card with three 2/1 winners and three losers, consider a card with one 8/1 winner and five losers (Table 8-6). Both these series of results have the same *mathematical expectation* (0.5 on each trial). Yet see what happens when you bet the 8/1 series at f = 0.25 (Table 8-6). This, remember, was the optimal fixed fraction for the other series.

Because the second series comprises one large gain and many small losses, it must be staked quite differently to produce its optimal profit (which turns out to be a rather modest $8.65 at f = 1/16). It seems two streams of betting results may be equivalent in terms of the bettor's edge (expectation), yet require very different optimal staking treatments, which in turn yield very different outcomes.

Later, I will show how this observation is relevant to commodity trading, where a typical success profile will comprise a few big winners and rather many small losers.

f = 0.25		Starting dollars	Bet	Ending dollars
1st Race	Bet on loser	100.00	25.00	75.00
2nd Race	Bet on loser	75.00	18.75	56.25
3rd Race	Bet on loser	56.25	14.06	42.19
4th Race	Bet winner 8/1	42.19	10.55	126.59
5th Race	Bet on loser	126.59	31.65	94.94
6th Race	Bet on loser	94.94	23.73	71.21

Table 8-6 Altering the distribution of winners and losers without altering the expectation. Starting with $100 and betting f = 0.25, you will have lost $28.79 by the end of the sixth race. The true optimal f for the series above is f = 1/16, yielding a profit of $8.65.

The concept of optimal f applied to futures trading is not mine; it belongs to Ralph Vince. In *Portfolio Management Formulas*, Vince provides a convenient equation, called the Kelly formula, for determining optimal f for a sequence of bets.

$$f = ((B +1)*P - 1)/B$$

where   B = the ratio of the amount won on a winning bet to the amount lost on a losing bet

P = the probability of a winning bet

and   f = the optimal betting fraction

For example, to find the optimal f for the sequence of Table 8-6, above:

$$f = ((8 + 1)*1/6 - 1)/8$$

$$= 1/16$$

Now hold on, you say. This whole concept is absurd. Since no one can know the results of a race card in advance, how could anyone devise a staking method in advance? Is this not optimization in another guise? And if so, surely this exercise is no more than a trivial pursuit better kept for passing a wet day at the cottage? Perhaps. But that's not the way a lot of people see it.

Optimal f

It's a big leap from racing imaginary horses to trading actual commodities, but some have made it with surprising ease. Ralph Vince, for example, in *Portfolio Management Formulas*, has attempted to stretch the "clairvoyant" horse-staking paradigm I described above into a full-blown theory applicable to commodity trading. Vince's books have enjoyed good press, and *optimal f* applied to commodities is something of the latest buzz among theoreticians, academics, and the usual suspects—people who have never traded commodities before. While I do not question Vince's mathematical integrity, I seriously question whether anything he proposes is remotely applicable in the real world.

Vince presents a persuasive theoretical argument in favor of fixed fractional trading, yet, in two books devoted to the subject—books positively drooling with statistics, he is unable to document even one example of optimal f operating on *real commodity data,* an omission that speaks volumes about optimal f's track record in actual trading. Optimal f does implicitly recognize that contract *exposure,* and not *amount risked per trade,* is the true threat to an account's survival. But that's about all that can be said in favor of it.

The tactic of continuously adjusting one's exposure in the market to an optimal level is an attractive and seductive one. But it is a seductive mirage. I already came up with what I considered to be logically based exposure levels (Table 8-3) for different combinations of positions being simultaneously traded. In essence, these are *my* suggestions for optimal f. You may find my numbers too high or too low, but that is a matter of taste. You don't have to be a genius to know that you should expand your trading level as your equity increases, and contract your trading level when your equity shrinks. Having determined beforehand the exposure level you are comfortable with, the dollar numbers of Table 8-3, applied with a little common sense, *will keep you close to your optimum level of trading* at all times.

In the trading of a commodity account, the distribution of amounts won and lost is almost certainly going to be highly variable. Trading a commodity is not like betting on a horse; you don't stake a fixed sum, knowing in advance that you will either *lose* that fixed sum or get back a *multiple* of that fixed sum. If you opened a commodity account with $20,000, it wouldn't make any sense to say, for example: "My optimal f is 0.15; therefore, I am going to risk $3,000 on my next trade." Why? Because that $3,000 could be risked on two contracts ($1,500 each) or on ten contracts ($300 each). Both these strategies could *hardly be optimal at the same time.* In horse betting, the quantity to be optimized is the fixed fraction of bankroll to bet each time, but the quantity to be optimized in commodity trading is the *number of contracts to be traded per dollar of equity*, because, practically, this is the only parameter than can be varied.

Suppose, after "extensive analysis" of your old trading slips, you discover that your optimal f for soybean trading, say, *would have been* one contract for every $8,541 of equity in your account. How can you use this information to make sure all your *subsequent* trading will be done at optimal f? For one thing, you will have to keep adjusting the number of contracts traded every time your equity changes—which is all the time.

But let's allow that you are still trading optimal f when you close out a position *before* adjusting a number of contracts. Unless you are trading gargantuan volumes, optimal f will dictate that you trade fractional contracts. Unfortunately, you cannot call the Chicago Mercantile Exchange with an order to buy 2.872465 contracts of pork bellies. On purely practical grounds, therefore, most traders would be unable to make the fine adjustments necessary to trade "optimally." If you round out to whole number contracts, you will not be trading optimally at all. And you may be way off the mark, because, as Ralph Vince points out, optimal f can be very sensitive around its optimal value.

Conclusion: Optimal f has severe operational limitations.

What if you are trading different commodities at the same time? Does optimal f mean anything in this real-life situation. Vince points out that optimal f is also very sensitive to the largest loss in a stream of results. While this *may* be true in a one-commodity trading situation, where every contract is being hit at the same time and no retreat is possible, it is certainly not true for an account trading more than one commodity (surely the norm). Practically, a drawdown resulting from a large loss in one commodity is *attenuated through diversification.* What's more, during the time a large loss may be building in one commodity, fresh positions in other commodities would surely be "sized" to reflect the decline in overall equity. Nowhere in his theory does Vince address this reality—a glaring omission, to say the least.

> *Conclusion:* Optimal f, as presently described, is only applicable, even theoretically, in a simplistic situation a trader will hardly be likely to encounter.

And I'm sorry, but there is more bad news. Ralph Vince has shown that optimal f is highly dependent on the size of the expected greatest loss that will be incurred on a single trade, thereby putting a very heavy premium on an *accurate* estimate of a most *nebulous* quantity. How can anyone possibly know what his greatest loss is likely to be? Prudent traders will try to limit their largest losses through the use of stop-loss orders set at predetermined risk levels. Traders operating reversal systems will have their largest loss *determined by the market,* and who knows what weird and wonderful price patterns may be in the offing?

Practically, no sensible trader ever trades to take a big loss. When he is finally hit with his biggest loss, it will most likely be the result of a market gapping through a stop point. A trader's prospective largest loss is therefore indeterminable in principle, and any estimate would be a wild guess. It follows, therefore, that a trader's optimal f is acutely sensitive to what is basically a random number.

Moreover, as I demonstrated with the two sequences of imaginary horse races, optimal f is very dependent on the *distribution* of winners and losers. (Even with streams of results where the net expectation is the same, optimal f's were vastly different.) No one can possibly know what his future distribution of wins and losses is going to be like, or even for that matter what his *expectation* is going to be in the future. A trader does not work with a fixed edge in the market any more than a hitter bats with the same batting average every season. My own batting average was quite different in the seventies than it was in the eighties. Who knows what it will be in the nineties?

Ralph Vince goes as far as to suggest that traders monitor their "batting averages" and adjust their optimal f's accordingly. What this means is that the hotter you get in the market, the higher your optimal f should be and the more aggressively you should trade. If you take this advice, you will find yourself trading at your highest exposure level just as you're turning cold— a recipe for disaster. There's one thing you can be sure of: Your performance level will regress. Hot streaks never last.

> *Conclusion:* On top of the practical objections already noted, the very *concept* of an optimal f is suspect in principle.

What can you expect from optimal f if, perchance, you were to accidentally apply it? Ralph Vince, himself, seems curiously ambivalent:

> Many traders have the mistaken impression that drawdown in terms of equity retracement is not as severe as it is. For instance, I can think of a system on bonds which, when traded on a 1-contract basis made $86,460 and drew down $2,890 over the test period, January 1982 to June 1989. One would think, then, that the drawdown wouldn't have been too bad on a fixed fractional basis. Well, let's take a look. The optimal f was .85, meaning that the drawdown, if one were trading at the optimal f over the historic test period, would have been at least 85% equity retracement. In fact it was 87.84%! Most people could never handle that. Yet that was the best mathematical route to take. In fact, trading at the optimal f value over this test period would have resulted in a gain in excess of $10 trillion. This is no more attainable than my hurling a brick across Lake Erie, yet it demonstrates the enormous power of using optimal f as well as the concomitant drawdowns to expect.

What is the author's conclusion about the applicability of his own theory? Do we use optimal f or not? If *not, why* not? Incidentally, anyone with real knowledge of trading would know that it is impossible to trade the bond market for seven years and encounter a drawdown of less than $3,000. And thereby, may well hang a tale ...

OPTIMAL F = 1.6 CONTRACTS/$10,000

Gain $/contract	Start equity	Number of contracts	Gain/ loss	Ending equity
-387	10,000	1.60	-619	9,381
1,425	9,381	1.50	2,139	11,520
-2,212	11,520	1.84	-4,077	7,443
800	7,443	1.19	952	8,395
1,675	8,395	1.34	2,250	10,645
-737	10,645	1.69	-1,255	9,390
325	9,390	1.50	488	9,878
11,212	9,876	1.58	17,720	27,598
-2,362	27,598	4.41	-10,429	17,169
1,762	17,169	2.73	4,840	22,009
-1,512	22,009	3.53	-5,324	16,685
2,037	16,685	2.67	5,437	22,122

Table 8-7 Optimal f as it would be calculated empirically for the results of trading the Japanese yen—described in Chapter 7. Ralph Vince makes rather heavy weather of explaining optimal f as applied to futures and, oddly enough, never uses real data. Traders interested in the after-the-fact calculation of optimal f for any stream of commodity results may find the calculation above easier to comprehend.

For convenience, it is easier to start with a round number for beginning equity and find the optimal number of contracts to trade, starting with that amount of equity. In the calculation above, we start at f = 1.6 and maintain that ratio of contracts to equity as we work through the table. How did I know f = 1.6 contracts per $10,000 was optimal? I didn't. It's a trial and error process (Table 8-8)— fascinating in a way for amateur mathematicians, but ultimately meaningless.

My advice to traders is to forget about optimal f and to keep things simple. Decide on your equity financing needs on a per contract basis and stick with it. You will *automatically* increase your position sizes as you get ahead, and decrease them when you have a setback. And you will avoid ever increasing your exposure in the market just because you are having a good run—as optimal f would have you do.

Contracts per $10,000	Starting equity	Closing equity
f = 0.50	10,000	15,760
f = 0.75	10,000	18,156
f = 1.00	10,000	19,628
f = 1.40	10,000	21,900
f = 1.50	10,000	22,076
f = 1.60	10,000	22,122
f = 1.70	10,000	22,050
f = 2.00	10,000	19,447
f = 3.00	10,000	12,374

Table 8-8 Returns from trading at different fixed fractional levels. The theoretical optimum f level to have traded the yen using PLODDER is 1.6 contracts per $10,000 equity, or about $6,400 per contract, a level of financing much too low for safe trading. Beware of unrealistic values of optimal f's derived from nonrepresentative sequences of wins and losses.

Remember my results from technically trading the Japanese yen? (These were listed in Chapter 7 and are repeated in Table 8-7). Had I "tracked" these results, measured optimal f, and used this value of f for further trading, I would be financing one contract of yen with $6,500, and could expect to have my brains blown out in very short order.

Conclusion Optimal f = phony optimization.

9

OPTIONS

An Offer You Can't Refuse?

How's this for a dream investment? You can't lose more than you put in, but you can multiply your stake many times over. And, should you change your mind at any time, someone else will be happy to take it off your hands.

These are the tantalizing prospects offered to purchasers of commodity futures options. They are also the prospects offered to purchasers of lottery tickets. Among savvy market players, the buying of options is widely regarded as a sucker play. But is it? If it is a bad deal for the option *buyer*, surely it must be a good deal for the option *seller*? Options must be purchased from sellers, or option *writers* as they are called.

Consider the prospects faced by the option writer; these are exactly the reverse of those faced by the option buyer. The option writer is making an investment where he may lose much more than he can possibly gain. If he wins at all, it will be at an agonizingly slow pace; if he loses, he may lose in a very big way, and it may happen very fast. What would induce anyone to assume an investment with such apparently unattractive features?

Apparent is the operative word here. In exchange for allowing the buyer the luxury of unlimited profit potential, along with limited loss liability, the writer wants to be paid, and paid rather well. If he charges a hefty premium and finds buyers willing to pay up, the option writer may turn the transaction odds substantially in his favor.

But what is the function of an option on a futures contract? People who have yet to trade commodity futures are unlikely to have come across a futures option. Most people, however, will already be familiar with the concept of an option in other fields. For example, the option is a common device in publishing and in the film industry, where the writer (literally) is paid a sum of money for selling the rights to publish his material or develop his screenplay.

These rights are granted to a publisher or a producer for a *limited period of time* only and at an *agreed upon price*. The option has an *expiry date*, and if the party optioning the material fails to act upon the rights he has purchased, the option agreement is null and void. The writer will then be entitled to keep the proceeds he received, and be free to option or sell his material elsewhere. The buyer of this kind of option is essentially buying time in which to test-market a product. If the test marketing turns out to be positive, the option buyer wants to be sure that the product will be available for him to develop.

There are, however, significant differences between an option on a piece of property and an option on a futures contract. In the case of property, the big unknown is the true value of the property. In the case of a futures contract, the price is known at all times during the life of the option; the big unknown is the value of the contract will have on the date the option expires. If, at the expiry date of the option, the price of the futures contract that has been optioned has *moved favorably*, the buyer will *exercise his option*. If the futures contract has not moved favorably, the buyer will let the option expire and forfeit the money he paid.

When a buyer purchases an option on a futures contract, he pays a *premium* to the writer in exchange for the right to buy or sell that futures contract at a fixed price, called the *strike price,* at any time during the life of the option. Options to buy are known as *calls*; options to sell are known as *puts*. The buyer of a call option hopes that the underlying futures contract moves above the strike price of the option before the option expires, thereby giving the option *real value*. The buyer of a put option hopes that the price of the underlying futures contract falls *below* the strike price, allowing the sale of goods at a higher price than they are presently worth. Needless to say, the hopes of all option buyers are diametrically opposed to those of their writers.

While the straightforward futures contract is symmetrical—in the sense that both the long and the short have the same exposure in the market and are subject to the same margin requirements, there is a distinct asymmetry in the terms of the options contract. Buyers have limited exposure, and need only deposit the option premium. No matter *what* happens, the buyer's risk is limited to the option premium he pays. At worst, his option will expire worthless.

Option writers, on the other hand, are faced with the same level of risk as those trading futures contracts; they have full contract liability and must put up margin. The reader might pause to marvel at the depths of human ingenuity which lies behind the creation of a commodity futures option. Consider, for example, the levels of abstraction implicit in a put option on a Treasury Bond futures contract. The buyer of a *T-Bond put option*, for example, is betting with an unknown adversary that the value of his government's obligation to an unknown lender, thirty years hence, will, within the short life of the option, decline by an amount sufficient to cover the price of his bet and still yield a profit. We've come a long way from the cave.

Because of the skewed terms of the option contract—limited risk, unlimited potential, options are attractive to traders who don't like using stop-loss orders. An option is a seductive instrument. For the buyer, it effectively removes the need to make any dynamic decisions. Since profits accrue slowly to option writers, and since writers can suffer severe financial damage when they are wrong, options are mostly written by professionals with the resources to cover many markets simultaneously—thereby minimizing the damage they may suffer from being very wrong on any one option. A writer has other defensive strategies, too. An option, once written, may be *laid off* by passing it to someone else. Option writing, in fact, is remarkably akin to bookmaking, casino management, or insurance broking—where the house doesn't mind making occasional big payouts as long as it is taking in sufficient funds to cover these payouts and still provide for a tidy profit.

Being concerned almost exclusively with probabilities, option writing is the one area of the futures business amenable to pure technical analysis.

Market professionals will tell you that the option game is stacked against the buyers because the premiums demanded by writers are sufficiently high to compensate them for the unlimited liabilities they assume. Buyers believe this, too, though it doesn't stop them from buying. Everybody wants to go to heaven; nobody expects to die.

Options Basics

The price of an option that is freely traded on a commodity exchange fluctuates in response to price changes in the underlying commodity future. The same anonymity exists between buyer and writer as exists between buyers and sellers of futures contracts, and any option position may be closed out at any time through simple transference to a third party, via the exchange. There are *fixed strike prices* at which options on futures contracts are to be contracted, and each option has a *fixed expiry date* preceding the expiry date of the underlying future by up to five weeks. Some actively traded commodities, such as gold, currencies, and the S & P index have options expiring every month.

The life of an option is usually less than the life of a futures contract, with six months about the maximum term. Since options are traded right up to their moment of expiry, it is possible to purchase an option with as short an expiry period as one minute. An option is defined by its strike price and its expiry date. For example, the buyer of an *August 360* gold call is buying the right to purchase a contract of gold at $360 per ounce, at any time during the life of the option (expiry is the second Friday in July).

The parties to an option (buyer *or* writer) can always transfer their positions to other traders in the pit, at the prevailing bid or asking price. And each option is traded independently; for example, an *August 360* gold call, an *August 370* gold call, and a *September 370* gold call are all separate and independent option contracts.

The price at which an option trades in the free market depends on the *strike price* of the option, the *prevailing futures price* to which the option is attached, the *anticipated price volatility* in that futures contract, and the *time remaining* until expiry of the option. Day to day, any increase in the price of a futures contract will result in *higher* call option values and *lower* put option values for that future. Any decrease in the price of a futures contract will result in *higher* put option values and *lower* call option values.

An option is a *derivative* trading vehicle, which means that its value is determined by the action in another market—the futures market. For this reason, and because there are so many options for each futures contract, price charts are not normally kept for options. There would be little point; where the future goes, the option must follow.

Option statistics are published daily in the pages of the financial press. Table 9-1 (for options on gold futures) reflects prices prevailing on June 30, 1993.

Strike	Calls			Puts		
Price	Aug	Sep	Oct	Aug	Sep	Oct
350	29.40	31.70	33.20	0.20	0.90	2.10
360	19.50	23.00	24.30	0.30	2.20	3.30
370	10.00	15.50	17.50	1.00	4.60	6.40
380	3.90	10.20	12.80	4.70	8.80	11.60
390	1.50	6.50	8.30	12.30	15.00	16.60
400	0.60	4.20	6.10	21.10	22.70	24.10
410	0.30	2.80	4.20	30.90	31.00	33.50

Table 9-1 Gold options quoted in dollars per ounce. Option prices as of close on Wednesday, June 30, 1993. (August gold futures closed at 379.1.)

In the case of a call option, when the future is trading higher than the strike price, the option is said to be *in-the-money*, in the sense that it has real value if exercised immediately. Otherwise, the option is said to be *out-of-the-money*, its current value deriving entirely from its potential—the potential for the future to rise above the strike price during the remaining life of the option. Reverse arguments hold for *put* options. A put option is *in-the-money* when the futures price is under the strike price. An option with a strike price exactly equal to the futures price is said to be *at-the-money* and is the option in which trading is likely to be most active. Options are available at strike prices so far out-of-the-money, and with such short lives to expiry, that only a massive economic dislocation could give them any terminal value. These options can be purchased for as little as $25, and occasionally, like lottery tickets, they pay off.

Working *down* the columns of Table 9-1 above, note how the values of call options *decrease* as one moves from in-the-money strikes to out-of-the-money strikes, and how the values of put options vary in the reverse direction. Working *across* Table 9-1, from left to right, note how the values of options increase as the amount of time expiration increases. On

June 30, for example, the August options have less than two weeks to run, the Septembers have six weeks, and the Octobers, eleven weeks.

Pay particular attention to the row entry starting with the strike price of 380. Since the future is trading at 379.1, the 380 options are trading very close to the money. Put and call options trading close to the money will have similar values. Options are derivative products and reflect only probabilities. Since a temporary equilibrium always exists in the market, the odds neither favor the up side nor the down side. Hence the equivalence of put and call options when these are trading at-the-money.

Option values also increase with market volatility. As of June 30, 1993, the gold market was rather volatile, having risen $60.00 in less than three months. The five-week at-the-money option was valued at $10.00. In early 1993, with gold in the doldrums, a similar five-week option was valued at less than half this amount.

Option values are determined by the free interplay of supply and demand in the marketplace. You will hear analysts talk about *overvalued* or *undervalued* option prices. If an option were obviously undervalued, it would clearly be worth buying, and if it were obviously overvalued, it would clearly be worth writing—purely on technical grounds. In practice, things are never that clear.

The question of whether an option represents fair value is ultimately subjective. Option premiums may drop sharply when the related future begins to trade in a narrower daily range, leading some observers to deduce that such options are "bargains." This need not be so. Option values reflect volatility, and a commodity future exhibiting reduced volatility is less likely to experience a big move, the very thing the option buyer is paying for. Falling premiums reflect falling expectations. Option premiums on currencies, for example, tend to hold steady the week before a meeting of the G-7 (the major industrial countries), and then to contract after the meeting, if, as is normally the case, no world-shattering statement or policy shift is announced.

A lot of sophisticated software is devoted to analyzing options to determine overvalued and undervalued situations. Indeed, the theory behind option pricing has filled a number of academic textbooks and, doubtless, a few doctoral dissertations as well. The available literature is liberally sprinkled with complex mathematical functions such as *gammas, thetas, deltas,* and *vegas.* It makes for very interesting theoretical reading, but my inclination when considering an option is to take the prevailing market price to be the fair value and to look for other reasons to be in an option position. For my money, the free market is likely to have a better intuitive fix on the true probabilities than any academic or any computer.

The Writer's Edge

Rather than introduce endless complex strategies involving combinations of futures and options—as many books on options do—I prefer to investigate what I call *the writer's edge.* It is commonly accepted that option buyers are at a disadvantage because they consistently pay more for their options than the probabilities warrant. An edge to the writer is believed to exist, but I am not familiar with any studies supporting that particular hypothesis. The reasons, no doubt, have a lot to do with the difficulty of digging out historical data for testing (no charts or compendiums of statistics are kept on options). But analysis is still possible.

As a first step, consider Table 9-2 and Figure 9-1, which present the data of Table 9-1 in a slightly different way; here, the values of the puts and calls at each strike are *combined into one price,* representing the amount a writer would receive for writing both sides of an option simultaneously. A combined put and call written on the same future at the same strike price is known as a *straddle.* Note (Figure 9-1) that the straddle has its *minimum* value when the strike price is *at-the-money.* And further note that, except in the case of options with very short times to expiry, the straddle value remains close to its minimum at-the-money value at strike prices on *either* side of the at-the-money strike price. This "flatness" of the curve expresses the simple truth that you can't get something for nothing; the underlying future is *bound to fluctuate.* Therefore, what the call gains the put must lose—within limits. The flatness of the straddle curve makes it possible to test hypothetical trades made at-the-money, even though a future never closes exactly at a strike price.

Strike	Straddles (Puts and Calls Combined)		
Price	Aug	Sep	Oct
350	29.60	32.60	35.30
360	19.80	25.20	27.60
370	11.00	20.10	23.90
* 380	8.60	19.00	24.00 *
390	13.80	21.50	24.90
400	21.70	26.90	30.20
410	31.20	33.80	37.70

* = the at-the-money strike

Table 9-2 Gold options (straddles) quoted in dollars per ounce. Option prices as of close on Wednesday, June 30, 1993. (August future closed at 379.1.)

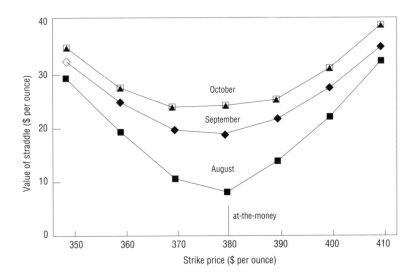

Figure 9-1 Pricing of gold straddles

The straddle curve is very flat at-the-money. Over a wide range of futures price, the call will gain what the put loses—and vice versa. The market offers no prizes for information everyone knows—futures are *bound* to fluctuate.

With futures it is possible to test theoretical trading strategies in hindsight; records are kept of daily highs, lows, and closes. Not so, in the case of options. Without daily ranges to work with, the testing of dynamic option strategies is severely limited. There is no way of knowing whether a stop-loss order would have been triggered, and even if there were, it would be impossible to estimate what a fill would be. Liquidity in options is rather low.

These limitations, however, do not preclude research into the size and nature of the writer's edge. I have not come across any studies confirming or denying the existence of the writer's edge. To come up with appropriate data, I had to spend many hours in the microfilm department of the public library, searching back issues of the financial press. Anyone researching this topic is likely facing the same problem.

Why should anyone be interested in the writer's edge at all? Well, let's say a trader is contemplating becoming an option writer. If he is to approach option writing seriously, the aspiring writer must be prepared to write both puts and calls, and be prepared to do this more or less continuously.

Before taking on such a task, the writer ought to have some idea of his expectation. After all, he will be assuming unlimited liability in exchange for limited profit potential; he will be embracing dullness, and excitement will be his enemy; he will be entering a world where no news will be good news, and where time can never pass quickly enough. That's a tall order and an order begging for a few answers up front. Conventional insurers have a fair estimate of their expected annual profitability. Why not option writers?

A serious option writer is more concerned with assessing probabilities than he is with price forecasting. He is as likely to be writing put options as call options, and he knows the greatest demand will be for at-the-money options. One way of getting an idea of the long-term net profitability of option writing is to investigate the historical profitability of continuously writing straddles at strike prices as close to *at-the-money* as possible and holding these options until they expire.

In this quest for the writer's edge, let's imagine these straddles are written ten weeks before they are due to expire. This gives the writer at least four writing opportunities per year per commodity. While the option writer can be lucky or unlucky on any one option he writes—depending on market behavior after the option is written, he should be able to get an idea of his long-run expectation by testing enough historical data to produce a statistically significant result. (I am talking here about returns from pure uncovered writing, with no defensive strategy to deal with an option that turns heavily against the writer. Whether the writer can improve his edge with dynamic strategy is another interesting question, but not a question amenable to testing on historical data.)

Study the entries in Table 9-3. This information is compiled from five years of wheat price data (options and futures) from 1988 to 1992. The table summarizes the results of writing *twenty* at-the-money straddles, each with *ten* weeks to expiry, and holding these straddles until they expire.

Take row five of Table 9-3, for example. On December 1, 1989, the closest at-the-money March 1990 wheat option had a strike price of $4.20 per bushel. This option was scheduled to expire on February 17, 1990; it had ten weeks to run. The proceeds from writing the *March 420* call and the *March 420* put, on December 1, 1989, amounted to 29.2 cents. On February 17, 1990, March 1990 wheat futures closed at $4.245. Since the put and the call were written at the same strike price, only one of them could expire with value, and that value was the difference between $4.245 and the strike price $4.20, in other words, 4.5 cents. Ignoring commissions for the moment, this particular transaction can be seen to *favor the option writer* over the option buyer. The writer takes in 29.2 cents premium and pays out 4.5 cents, for a net profit of 24.7 cents per bushel.

Over the five-year test period, the straddle strike prices more or less track the price of wheat, since options are always written as near to at-the-money as possible. The writer's profits are always limited to the premiums he receives from writing the straddle, while his losses are potentially unlimited. After *twenty* transactions in wheat, the writer comes out slightly ahead. Tables 9-4 through 9-8 contain comparable results for writing options in five other actively traded markets. The results are rather surprising.

OPTIONS ON WHEAT
(CENTS/BUSHEL)

Option Month & Year	Strike Price	Write Option on	Option Expires on	With Futures at	Option Writer Pays	Option Writer Receives	Writer's Profit (loss)
MAR 88	320.0	Dec 1	Feb19	322.0	2.0	28.2	26.2
JUL 88	310.0	Apr 4	Jun24	381.5	71.5	23.2	(48.2)
SEP 88	360.0	Jun 1	Aug19	391.7	31.7	41.0	9.3
DEC 88	410.0	Sep 1	Nov18	411.0	1.0	38.5	37.5
MAR 89	420.0	Dec 1	Feb17	424.5	4.5	29.2	24.7
JUL 89	400.0	Apr 3	Jun23	397.5	2.5	33.0	30.5
SEP 89	400.0	Jun 1	Aug18	392.2	7.8	28.2	20.4
DEC 89	400.0	Sep 1	Nov17	410.0	10.0	21.7	11.7
MAR 90	410.0	Dec 1	Feb16	384.0	26.0	19.5	(6.5)
JUL 90	340.0	Apr 2	Jun22	334.0	6.0	18.5	12.5
SEP 90	340.0	Jun 1	Aug24	285.0	55.0	21.0	(34.0)
DEC 90	270.0	Sep 3	Nov16	250.0	20.0	20.5	0.5
MAR 91	260.0	Dec 3	Feb15	256.5	3.5	18.0	14.5
JUL 91	300.0	Apr 1	Jun21	271.5	28.5	24.0	(4.5)
SEP 91	300.0	Jun 3	Aug23	296.5	3.5	18.7	15.2
DEC 91	320.0	Sep 3	Nov15	350.5	30.5	24.0	(6.5)
MAR 92	370.0	Dec 2	Feb21	415.5	45.5	25.5	(20.0)
JUL 92	350.0	Apr 1	Jun19	357.7	7.7	28.5	20.8
SEP 92	360.0	Jun 1	Aug21	315.5	44.5	30.0	(14.5)
DEC 92	340.0	Sep 1	Nov20	370.5	30.5	23.3	(7.2)
				Average	21.6	25.7	4.1

Table 9-3 Results of writing straddles (puts and calls) on wheat over a five-year period.

OPTIONS ON SILVER
(CENTS/OUNCE)

Option Month & Year	Strike Price	Write Option on	Option Expires on	With Futures at	Option Writer Pays	Option Writer Receives	Writer's Profit (loss)
MAR 88	700.0	Dec 1	Feb12	639.0	61.0	92.5	31.5
JUL 88	700.0	Apr 4	Jun10	701.5	1.5	64.5	63.0
SEP 88	700.0	Jun 1	Aug12	674.0	26.0	62.0	36.0
DEC 88	675.0	Sep 1	Nov11	641.0	34.0	58.0	24.0
MAR 89	625.0	Dec 1	Feb10	583.5	41.5	53.5	12.0
JUL 89	600.0	Apr 3	Jun 9	519.0	81.0	42.0	(39.0)
SEP 89	525.0	Jun 1	Aug11	521.8	3.2	40.0	36.8
DEC 89	525.0	Sep 1	Nov10	526.0	1.0	36.0	35.0
MAR 90	575.0	Dec 1	Feb 9	527.3	47.7	53.0	5.3
JUL 90	500.0	Apr 2	Jun 8	503.3	3.3	32.0	28.7
SEP 90	525.0	Jun 1	Aug10	499.4	25.6	37.0	11.4
DEC 90	475.0	Sep 3	Nov 9	423.7	51.3	36.5	(14.3)
MAR 91	425.0	Dec 3	Feb 8	383.3	41.7	44.0	2.3
JUL 91	400.0	Apr 1	Jun14	442.7	42.7	42.7	0.0
SEP 91	425.0	Jun 3	Aug 9	397.5	27.5	38.0	10.5
DEC 91	400.0	Sep 3	Nov 8	400.3	0.3	29.6	29.3
MAR 92	400.0	Dec 2	Feb14	415.0	15.0	28.5	13.5
JUL 92	400.0	Apr 1	Jun12	412.5	12.5	27.7	15.2
SEP 92	400.0	Jun 1	Aug14	379.2	20.8	24.4	3.6
DEC 92	375.0	Sep 1	Nov13	375.0	0.0	22.8	22.8
				Average	26.9	43.2	16.3

Table 9-4 Results of writing straddles (puts and calls) on silver over a five-year period.

OPTIONS ON THE S & P INDEX

Option Month & Year	Strike Price	Write Option on	Option Expires on	With Futures at	Option Writer Pays	Option Writer Receives	Writer's Profit (loss)
MAR 88	260.0	Jan 4	Mar17	270.6	10.6	26.1	15.5
JUN 88	260.0	Apr 4	Jun16	270.2	10.2	24.3	14.1
SEP 88	275.0	Jul 1	Sep15	267.8	7.2	21.0	13.8
DEC 88	275.0	Oct 3	Dec15	277.3	2.3	16.8	14.5
MAR 89	280.0	Jan 3	Mar16	299.7	19.7	15.9	(3.8)
JUN 89	300.0	Apr 3	Jun15	319.8	19.8	15.7	(4.1)
SEP 89	325.0	Jul 3	Sep14	343.5	18.5	17.7	(0.8)
DEC 89	355.0	Oct 2	Dec14	350.3	4.7	16.7	12.0
MAR 90	360.0	Jan 2	Mar15	338.3	21.7	19.0	(2.7)
JUN 90	345.0	Apr 2	Sep14	363.3	18.3	22.2	3.9
SEP 90	365.0	Jul 2	Sep20	311.5	53.5	20.4	(33.1)
DEC 90	320.0	Oct 1	Dec20	330.3	10.3	27.4	17.1
MAR 91	325.0	Jan 2	Mar14	373.6	48.6	26.4	(22.2)
JUN 91	355.0	Apr 1	Jun20	375.8	20.8	22.5	1.7
SEP 91	380.0	Jul 1	Sep19	387.1	7.1	23.7	16.6
DEC 91	390.0	Oct 1	Dec19	382.9	7.1	22.2	15.1
MAR 92	420.0	Jan 2	Mar19	409.9	10.1	22.1	12.0
JUN 92	405.0	Apr 1	Jun18	400.6	4.4	21.7	17.3
SEP 92	410.0	Jul 1	Sep17	420.2	10.2	19.3	9.1
DEC 92	415.0	Oct 1	Dec17	436.1	21.1	22.2	1.1
				Average	16.3	21.2	4.9

Table 9-5 Results of writing straddles (puts and calls) on the S & P index over a five-year period.

OPTIONS ON CRUDE OIL
(DOLLARS/BARREL)

Option Month & Year	Strike Price	Write Option on	Option Expires on	With Futures at	Option Writer Pays	Option Writer Receives	Writer's Profit (loss)
MAR 88	18.0	Dec 1	Feb12	17.28	0.72	1.73	1.01
JUN 88	16.0	Mar 1	May13	17.74	1.74	1.83	0.09
SEP 88	18.0	Jun 1	Aug12	15.26	2.74	1.62	(1.12)
DEC 88	15.0	Sep 1	Nov11	14.04	0.96	1.49	0.53
MAR 89	15.0	Dec 1	Feb10	17.11	2.11	1.73	(0.38)
JUN 89	17.0	Mar 3	May12	20.09	3.09	1.71	(1.38)
SEP 89	18.0	Jun 1	Aug11	18.48	0.48	2.10	1.62
DEC 89	19.0	Sep 1	Nov10	19.84	0.84	1.48	0.64
MAR 90	20.0	Dec 1	Feb 9	21.74	1.74	1.29	(0.45)
JUN 90	21.0	Mar 1	May11	18.95	2.05	1.55	(0.50)
SEP 90	19.0	Jun 1	Aug10	26.23	7.23	1.60	(5.63)
DEC 90	28.0	Sep 3	Nov 9	33.89	5.89	5.72	(0.17)
MAR 91	28.0	Dec 3	Feb 8	21.92	6.08	7.30	1.22
JUN 91	20.0	Mar 1	May10	21.27	1.27	2.72	1.45
SEP 91	21.0	Jun 3	Aug 9	21.62	0.62	1.69	1.07
DEC 91	22.0	Sep 3	Nov 8	22.91	0.91	1.51	0.60
MAR 92	21.0	Dec 2	Feb 7	19.87	1.13	1.62	0.49
JUN 92	19.0	Mar 2	May 8	20.86	1.86	1.52	(0.34)
SEP 92	22.0	Jun 1	Aug 7	21.22	0.78	1.42	0.64
DEC 92	21.0	Sep 1	Nov13	20.08	0.92	1.57	0.65
				Average	2.16	2.16	0.00

Table 9-6 Results of writing straddles (puts and calls) on crudle oil over a five-year period.

OPTIONS ON THE SWISS FRANC

Option Month & Year	Strike Price	Write Option on	Option Expires on	With Futures at	Option Writer Pays	Option Writer Receives	Writer's Profit (loss)
MAR 88	78.00	Jan 4	Mar 4	71.52	6.48	3.89	(2.59)
JUN 88	74.00	Apr 4	Jun 3	69.57	4.43	2.90	(1.53)
SEP 88	67.00	Jul 1	Sep 9	64.07	2.93	2.70	(0.23)
DEC 88	64.00	Oct 3	Dec 9	68.12	4.12	2.24	(1.88)
MAR 89	67.00	Jan 3	Mar 3	63.56	3.44	2.56	(0.88)
JUN 89	61.00	Apr 3	Jun 9	57.38	3.62	2.03	(1.59)
SEP 89	61.00	Jul 3	Sep 8	58.10	2.90	2.76	(0.14)
DEC 89	62.00	Oct 2	Dec 8	62.69	0.69	2.62	(1.93)
MAR 90	63.00	Jan 2	Mar 9	66.30	3.30	2.62	(0.68)
JUN 90	66.00	Apr 2	Jun 8	68.92	2.92	2.52	(0.40)
SEP 90	71.00	Jul 2	Sep 7	76.58	5.58	2.45	(3.13)
DEC 90	77.00	Oct 1	Dec 7	79.54	2.54	3.58	1.04
MAR 91	79.00	Jan 2	Mar 8	73.05	5.95	3.55	(2.40)
JUN 91	70.00	Apr 1	Jun 7	65.78	4.22	3.24	(0.98)
SEP 91	63.50	Jul 1	Sep 6	66.35	2.85	2.69	(0.16)
DEC 91	68.50	Oct 1	Dec 6	72.16	3.66	2.89	(0.77)
MAR 92	72.50	Jan 2	Mar 6	65.98	6.52	3.20	(3.32)
JUN 92	65.50	Apr 1	Jun 5	68.78	3.28	2.71	(0.57)
SEP 92	72.00	Jul 1	Sep 4	79.94	7.94	2.82	(5.12)
DEC 92	79.50	Oct 1	Dec 4	69.88	9.62	4.94	(4.68)
				Average	4.35	2.95	(1.40)

Table 9-7 Results of writing straddles (puts and calls) on the Swiss franc over a five-year period.

OPTIONS ON THE JAPANESE YEN

Option Month & Year	Strike Price	Write Option on	Option Expires on	With Futures at	Option Writer Pays	Option Writer Receives	Writer's Profit (loss)
MAR 88	82.00	Jan 4	Mar 4	77.69	4.31	3.79	(0.52)
JUN 88	81.00	Apr 4	Jun 3	79.47	1.53	3.20	1.67
SEP 88	75.00	Jul 1	Sep 9	74.86	0.14	2.63	2.49
DEC 88	75.00	Oct 3	Dec 9	81.73	6.73	2.48	(4.25)
MAR 89	82.00	Jan 3	Mar 3	78.37	3.63	2.51	(1.12)
JUN 89	77.00	Apr 3	Jun 9	68.36	8.64	2.24	(6.40)
SEP 89	71.00	Jul 3	Sep 8	68.09	2.91	3.20	0.29
DEC 89	72.00	Oct 2	Dec 8	69.32	2.68	2.77	0.09
MAR 90	68.00	Jan 2	Mar 9	66.14	1.84	2.17	0.35
JUN 90	63.00	Apr 2	Jun 8	65.19	2.19	2.56	0.37
SEP 90	66.00	Jul 2	Sep 7	71.47	5.47	1.98	(3.49)
DEC 90	73.00	Oct 1	Dec 7	76.50	3.50	2.69	(0.81)
MAR 91	75.00	Jan 2	Mar 8	73.09	1.91	3.20	1.29
JUN 91	71.50	Apr 1	Jun 7	71.20	0.30	3.08	2.78
SEP 91	72.00	Jul 1	Sep 6	73.66	1.66	2.24	0.68
DEC 91	75.00	Oct 1	Dec 6	78.04	3.04	2.25	(0.79)
MAR 92	80.00	Jan 2	Mar 6	75.84	4.16	2.73	(1.43)
JUN 92	74.00	Apr 1	Jun 5	78.85	4.85	2.43	(2.42)
SEP 92	79.50	Jul 1	Sep 4	81.20	1.70	2.47	0.77
DEC 92	83.00	Oct 1	Dec 4	80.03	2.97	3.27	0.30
				Average	3.21	2.70	(0.51)

Table 9-8 Results of writing straddles (puts and calls) on the Japanese yen over a five-year period.

Silver was by far the most profitable market for the writer. The S & P index was also good, while wheat was moderately profitable. Crude oil balanced out exactly, but the two currencies were *big losers*, especially the Swiss franc. The options market, it seems, has consistently exacted high premiums in silver and stock index options yet seriously undercharged for currency options. Is the market stupid? Perhaps, but I don't think so.

In 1988, memories of the incredible drop in the stock market (October 1987) were fresh in traders' minds. Writers of put options on stock indexes had been severely burned in the crash (Table 9-9), and their immediate response was to charge very high option premiums. These high premiums have persisted for several years now, and consequently the S & P options market has been a good one for writers, *despite a doubling of the stock market*. Are premiums too high? Who can say for sure? Another stock market debacle can never be entirely ruled out, in which case, despite the high premiums, option writers stand to be massacred again.

Strike Price	Value of put option October 9	Value of put option October 19
260	0.25	61.00
265	0.45	66.00
270	0.65	71.00
275	1.00	76.00
280	1.65	81.00
285	2.25	86.00
290	3.35	91.00
295	4.50	96.00
300	6.10	101.00
305	8.00	105.00
310	10.20	110.00
315	12.75	115.00

Table 9-9 The December 1987 S & P put option

For once, the Doomsday scenarists were right. Buyers of wildly out-of-the-money put options on October 9, 1987, must have felt like lottery winners just ten days later. During this period, the S & P stock index future fell from 320.0 to less than 200.0, a decline of unprecedented proportions. A *December 260 put option*, bought for $125 on October 9, was worth $30,000 on October 19. This windfall for the option buyers was a disaster for the option writers. Just as maritime insurance rates rose sharply after the Titanic went down, so too did S & P option premiums; they have remained high ever since.

As noted, silver options have been fertile territory for writers in recent years. Normally, large absolute moves in futures prices are bad for option writers. Yet, despite a decline in silver from $7.00 to $3.75 per ounce, opportunities for option buyers have been scarce. Like stock index options, the silver options market may be suffering a kind of writer's hangover lingering from the early eighties, when writers took tremendous beatings—both on the upside and on the downside—as silver prices spiked at an almost unbelievably high price of $50.00 per ounce.

Crude oil neither favored the buyer nor the writer, but it had a tumultuous ride. Note the enormous rise in premiums demanded by writers around the time of the Gulf War, and the subsequent rapid decline to historical norms.

Currency options are hard to fathom. Indiscriminate buying of Swiss franc options would have been profitable almost any time within the last five years; on only one occasion (out of twenty checked) would writers have received premiums exceeding their payout. Could it be that currency futures trading is too recent a vehicle for traders to get a true reading of its volatility, or are traders perpetually anticipating a quiescent market in currencies that just never materializes? Or, is the whole thing a statistical fluke? Usually these anomalies *are* statistical flukes, though it is certainly puzzling that premiums have failed to rise given the consistent losses currency option writers have endured. If currency option premiums do not rise soon, I know of one writer who will be happy to let someone else do the writing.

What can be said about the *overall* result? Six markets were covered for a period of five years, and during this period 120 theoretical straddles were assumed to have been written. Admittedly, there is a substantial random element present in the result of any one trial. For example, the amount a writer will eventually pay out to a buyer is very much dependent on the strike price he writes at, and that in turn is sensitive to the precise timing of the writing of the option. And 120 trials still constitutes a rather small sample size. For all that, I find the results surprising: The writer's edge is very much smaller than I would have anticipated.

The *expected return* to an option writer is 1.7 percent of the combined premiums he will receive for writing a straddle (Table 9-10). For example, on a typical $2,000 premium, the writer can expect to net $34, an insignificant amount considering that he can expect to pay $100 in commissions to complete the transaction ($60 for writing the straddle plus $40 for the side that is exercised). In other words, if this data is representative, there is effectively *no writer's edge*. Nor, for that matter, is there a buyer's edge, for the buyer is faced with the same commission problems—on top of a negative $34 expectation.

	Options Written (1988–1992)	Average Premiums Received	Average Writer's Profit	Profit as % of Premiums
Wheat	20	25.7	4.1	15.9
Silver	20	43.2	16.3	37.7
Crude Oil	20	2.16	0.0	0.0
Yen	20	2.70	-0.51	-18.8
S. Franc	20	2.95	-1.40	-47.7
S & P	20	21.2	4.9	23.1
			Average	= 1.7%

Table 9-10 Option writing—overall expectations

The option writer appears to have a positive edge, but a small one—insufficient to cover even commission charges.

When I set out to test the writer's edge hypothesis, I fully expected to confirm the prevailing wisdom that option writing, in general, is a *clear* winning proposition. I think we can dispel that notion, or at least cast serious doubt upon it. Even allowing for my sample to be accidentally nonrepresentative, I feel it is large enough to conclude that option writing is not the dairy cow it is cracked up to be. It's always nicer to confirm a hypothesis than refute it, but there you have it. I would be curious to know if others have come to similar conclusions.

If my numbers *are* representative, the options market turns out to be *remarkably efficient overall*, but seemingly *inefficient in individual commodities*. Were option values to remain where they are and futures profiles to remain the way they are, it would clearly be good business to *write* silver and S & P options but to *buy* currency options. However, it's my guess we are entering a period where silver and S & P option premiums will gradually decline, while currency premiums gradually rise.

Practical Writing

I have been looking at generalized option trading—the indiscriminate buying and selling of every option. This approach I consider a valid one for determining the *pure writer's edge*. In the real market, writers who have written options need not watch powerlessly as a big move develops against them. There is always the possibility of *covering* an option by repurchasing it on the exchange, or by *offsetting* it with a futures position.

In general, I don't see much reason to buy options—the Swiss franc performance, notwithstanding. The limited liability aspect of the option *is* attractive to traders who hate placing stops, but there is a cost. To profit from an option purchase, one must forecast not only the direction of a price move but also its *timing*. There are few more discouraging experiences than watching a price evolve in one's favor and then finding that it has not moved fast enough to compensate for the time erosion of the option premium. The reality of option buying is that most of the time buyers are simply delaying the taking of a loss they would have incurred in trading the future itself. I'd rather take the loss quickly and get on with something else. Being stopped out of a futures position is unpleasant, but watching an option erode to nothing is positively masochistic—unless you are the writer, of course. I don't believe there is *any* option buying strategy that cannot be improved upon by the simple use of futures, *provided the trader is able to take small losses and re-enter the market if necessary.*

I once watched a broker who was enjoying considerable success as an option buyer. He was winning regularly and attracting a lot of money. His strategy was simple: buy both sides of an option—called buying the straddle—and shoot for a small predetermined profit (20 percent). For example, if he paid $2,000 for the straddle (combined put and call premiums) and the straddle increased in value to $2,400, he would immediately cash it in.

Three times out of four, this worked. If the profit never materialized, he would let the options expire, and because he was buying straddles, one option would always expire worth *something*—anywhere from zero to $2,400. There were never any margin calls (options are paid for in cash), and the broker could truthfully claim that eight out of ten trades were winners. Not only did it sound attractive, the system worked for a while— I think it started off trading currencies. But as soon as the program was expanded to other options, its performance dropped off and has been grinding down equity ever since. Unaware of the true probabilities working against them, the "investors" in this program will eventually be commissioned to death, for it is doubtful the wasting disease will ever be diagnosed.

Although the *pure* writer's edge appears minimal, I believe any options strategy worth pursuing has to be from the writer's side. An option writer may improve his *own edge* relative to the pure writer's edge in several ways.

First, *through timing*. Options need not be written every day, nor any particular day. If the writer can detect a *trading range* in a future and write puts and calls within that trading range, he will be in a much stronger position than if he writes at a market peak or at a market trough. Accurately predicting when a market will do nothing is just as much a skill as predicting when it will trend. The trader who bets on nothing happening does have one advantage; most of the time markets do *not* trend. Maybe it's my Scottish blood, but I consider a well-written straddle a trade to be savored. Where else in this world can you be paid handsomely for forecasting that absolutely nothing will happen?

The second way a writer can increase his edge is by *writing only one side* of the straddle. Returns improve if you write only puts in a bull market and calls in a bear market. Problem is, of course, to *identify* bull markets and bear markets. This strategy also pays off when absolutely nothing happens.

Finally, a writer can *hedge problem options*. An option that is increasing rapidly in value can be neutralized, either by offsetting the option or hedging via futures. We are strictly into damage control here, and trying to minimize or contain a loss. How does a writer decide when an option has increased enough in value to warrant protection? This is subjective, but I would say that a straddle that has doubled in value is in danger of becoming a headache for the writer.

It's worth noting that the odds against *any* put, or *any* call, doubling from its current value are *always less than 50 percent*. If this were not true, the indiscriminate buying of options would be a positive strategy. For the value of a *straddle* (put plus call) to double, the odds are considerably longer. A future would have to make a very substantial move for an at-the-money straddle to double in value. The straddle curve (Figure 9-1) is very flat, *at-the-money*, since any increase or decrease in the value of the call side is balanced by a similar but opposite change in the value of the put side.

Options are best written at the strike price closest to where the future is trading; this is the strike price where there is greatest demand, and where the market is most liquid—not that the options market is ever particularly liquid. Lack of liquidity is not a big problem when initiating a position, and the trader can take his time to make sure he gets fair market prices. However, when the trader is faced with offsetting a bad option position, the option will have moved well *into-the-money*, and have lost so much of its liquidity that it may be hard to offset at a fair price. When you want to get rid of a problem option, you want to act quickly, and an illiquid market is the last thing you need.

An alternative to offsetting an option is to hedge a losing option via a future. Once an option is hedged via a future, the trader prays for the trend that caused the problem to continue. If the trend reverses again, the future begins to lose. At first this loss is balanced by a corresponding retreat in the value of the option, but eventually the future will start to lose more than the option is giving back and will have to be jettisoned. Balancing losing options with futures can be tricky for the writer, but it is all part of the business. Option writing is not for amateurs.

There are many, many possible strategies for writing options and a lot of avenues worth exploring. For example, is it better to write *out-of-the-money* options, and accept the smaller premiums in exchange for the reduced likelihood of having them exercised? Is it better to write short-term options than long-term options and to accept the lower premiums in exchange for a reduced waiting period?

The answers lie in the microfilm departments of public libraries everywhere. And they're free.

10

RETROSPECT

Summary

It was always my intention to describe the world of commodity trading rather than alert the reader to specific trading situations. For one thing, I hold to a fundamental philosophy that calls for a dynamic approach to trading. Whatever fundamental insights into particular markets I may have at this time of writing will hardly be relevant to the markets the reader will face at the time he reads this book. What I hope the reader will find of enduring value is a way of looking at the markets with an open mind, because, as I have tried to show, there aren't any routine mechanical approaches that work consistently. And there simply aren't any obviously right or wrong trades.

On the other hand, there are obviously right and wrong ways of making inferences from available evidence; these I have tried to point out. Whether my suggestions are useful or not, they do represent a lot of thinking about the problems and an insistence on a logical interpretation of the facts.

I felt it important to talk first about the many wrong-headed notions that prevail in this business, to clear the decks so to speak, and to put the reader in a better position to look at the markets as they truly are. Many foolish articles disguised as scholarship have been written about trading. An intelligent person would see through most of these by himself, in due course. If I have speeded up this awareness in the reader, so much the better. Time is valuable and best used for positive thinking and planning.

When I mock commodity brokers and their clients, it is not that as individuals I see them as particularly deserving of scorn. The commodity market is a three-ring circus, and a circus needs performers. In many ways, brokers and players are simply prisoners of the situation they find themselves in, albeit prisoners of their own device. The market is a monster we have created to satisfy our speculative desires. And a monster demands respect. If we taunt it, it will be quick to lash out at us, showing no mercy and exposing our every weakness.

If you choose to become a commodity trader, you will encounter many entertaining but irrational characters. It seems reasonable that I, who have been around this business for so long, should forewarn you. Though I recognize its marginal relevance to trading, I still feel it appropriate to describe and comment upon "the scene" as accurately as I can.

Regarding soothsayers and self-proclaimed experts peddling advice, I have no compunction about deflating some overly inflated egos and exposing some very third-rate minds. Though greedy people are easily hoodwinked and often deserve what they get, that does not entitle charlatans of the market to prey upon human frailty.

After describing the circus, I talked about coping with uncertainty. Chartists I accused of suffering from tunnel vision, of trying to solve a dynamic space-*time* problem with the methods of geometry. Seasonality predictions, and predictions made from trendlines, I showed to be facile in concept, and worthless in practice. I also showed that there was no evidence to support interpretation of mass psychology as being in any way useful in price forecasting.

Next, I examined the causes of the characteristic bad habits most traders seem naturally to fall into, habits that almost guarantee they will fail. Evidence from actual trading results suggested that winning was not a chance matter at all, and that losing was systematic, behavioral, and predictable, among those who lost.

These observations led to the hypothesis that it was possible to beat the market *by pure technique*—without regard to economics at all—on the grounds that losers were so singularly successful at *losing* by pure technique. The hypothesis was tested using a trading system typical of the genre. A positive result was indicated and shown to be valid at a statistically high level of confidence. Though positive, the rate of return on investment with this system turned out to be much lower than first appearances suggested. Furthermore, the system was shown to be vulnerable to strings of losses, with sobering implications of the kind most technical traders either downplay or choose to ignore.

I cautioned the reader against following the fashionable trend among traders, operators, money managers, and commodity pools—away from economic analysis and towards system trading; away from using imagination and towards using surrogates. I produced evidence that commodity funds achieved results at the level of pure chance.

I then argued that it was only fair for real returns to accrue to the creative fundamentalist. I talked about imagination, flexibility, and open-mindedness; dispositions anathema to the technical trader, but dispositions that enable the fundamentalist to take advantage of evolving opportunities in the market.

I presented fundamental data on specific commodities to show how a fundamental trader might come up with a judgment on whether to take a position or not. And then I constructed logical disciplines for getting in and out of the market. I argued for facing the tough questions before a position is actually put on, when stress is not a complicating factor.

I argued that three needs had to be satisfied to ensure successful execution of a big trade: the need to limit initial risk, the need to persist after an initial setback, and the need to get out and stay out of a market after a trade is over. I used the yen bull market of 1992–93 as a data base for testing a fundamentally based strategy. I pointed out that trading results achieved by this strategy were hypothetical, that the wisdom of hindsight can be blinding in its brilliance, and that paper–trading is for exploring strategy and not for predicting what that future is going to be like.

Finally, I devoted a chapter to exploring money management in depth, and a chapter to options—a trading vehicle that hardly existed ten years ago, when I wrote the first edition of this book.

Truth and Consequences

I neither trade for other people, write a newsletter, nor offer advice on a day-to-day basis. Nor do I have any affiliations with brokers or promoters. I keep in touch with the business though, and I consider myself a keen observer of the scene. Having finished this book, I feel well-satisfied that what I have offered is an accurate description of the commodity market and what *really* goes on there.

In nonfiction, the best motive a writer can have for writing is to spot a void in a body of knowledge—a void he thinks he can fill. What I saw missing in the commodity library was a good critique for the general reader, combined with enough real "stuff" to get the attention of active traders. In terms of the commodity scene, I am very much an outsider, but an outsider with inside knowledge—a one-man Greek chorus, if you will. It is not my business to promote commodity trading or to rail against it, only to describe it so that the reader gets good value and closes the back cover of this book better informed.

In what way better informed? For one thing, the reader should now appreciate that commodity trading is neither exclusively science nor art, but a bit of both. Certainly, if you wish to understand it, you must begin with the methods of science. The job of the scientist is to gather evidence of the world without trying to alter that world, and then to proceed, by measurement and deduction, to identify whatever relationships might exist among the variables of the world he is studying.

Grab a physicist who has been ensconced in a laboratory all his life and thrust him into the world of economics. Ask him to study the economics of sugar, say, and he will soon tell you that historically an inverse relationship has existed between the world supply of sugar and the world price of sugar. Broaden the physicist's field of study and he will tell you that this supply-price relationship appears to be a general rule of commodities, but that the strength of the relationship is more pronounced in sugar than in other commodities. A simple notion, admittedly, but this is the method by which science proceeds from first principles: observation, deduction, and prediction.

Now, invite the physicist with his new-found scientific knowledge of economics to trade sugar futures. Almost for sure he will fail at first, and he will be frustrated with the seemingly irrational responses of the market, particularly to news. Then, one of two things will happen. If he is unimaginative, the scientist will give up, deducing, correctly, that the trading of futures is a game that cannot be played with the methods of science alone. But, if the scientist is a man of imagination, he will try to learn from the unfavorable outcomes of his trades, and discover the nuances of timing that can turn his losers into winners. By this process, he will realize a winning style through the use of his imagination as well as his rationality. He will then, perhaps subconsciously, be visualizing favorable outcomes and exploiting his prophecies.

A peculiar word, prophecy, with all its attendant biblical baggage. I like Northrop Frye's definition. Talking about William Blake, the visionary and mystic, Frye says: "A prophet has unusual powers of perception rather than clairvoyance. There is no inevitable future, and it is not the prophet's job to foresee it. What a prophet sees that others don't is a likely outcome of a present line of policy" (fundamental inputs?).

Hunch and common sense. Imagination and knowledge. Could these all be bound up in the great commodity trade? And might there be something else? Disposition, perhaps? Some highly able individuals seem to possess all the prerequisites to be good traders, but for some reason just can't cut it.

> A successful speculator is not someone who doesn't lose or has never lost. Quite the contrary. You know you are going to be a successful speculator if you have been totally wiped out two times and you still have enough confidence in yourself and determination to win, to go out, work, and earn enough to come back a third time. The difference between successful and unsuccessful speculators is that unsuccessful speculators quit after they are wiped out. We are not quite sure about the need to be actually wiped out in practice, but what does seem to be correct is that the character structure of a successful speculator involves the capacity to compete even if the initial outcomes are destined to be unsuccessful. Is it that the psychological structure of successful speculators differs from ordinary people, e.g., do they manage aggression, shame, rage, and the like, differently?
>
> —excerpted from *The Rosenthal Report*, circa 1977

Of course, the writer exaggerates; successful speculators do not by definition get wiped out. However, he touches on an important ingredient in the makeup of the successful trader: determination. And I would agree with him that successful traders are extraordinarily determined people.

They also must learn to handle success. Big money can come very fast; values can get distorted and respect for money fall. The market may suddenly look easy, even to the trader who understands full-well how fearsomely difficult it really is. The market has an uncanny ability to punish those who treat it disrespectfully. You would think that a successful speculator would increase his distance from the market the more successful he becomes—learn to enjoy his liberation and good fortune. It doesn't always work out that way. It is a huge error to become addicted to commodity trading, or to make trading one's reason for living. I've seen it happen, and it is not a pretty sight.

Parting Shots, Winning Thoughts

The commodity market is a unique institution, offering unique attractions. Where else can you get immediately recompensed for eschewing conventional truisms and acting solely on the strength of your own convictions?

I strongly urge the reader to trade for himself; to approach trading with high expectations, and to trust himself (or herself) *to the exclusion of all others*. I also urge the reader to remember that winning in the market buys time as well as money, and that a winning style may, in a curious way, be connected with that understanding.

I urge the reader to think big, to find the right perspective on space and time. While the screen-watcher is thinking in terms of minutes, the smart trader is thinking in terms of weeks, even months. A smart trader gives free rein to his imagination. By seeing in his mind's eye a great trade developing as he believes it might, a trader may subliminally evolve a plan to capitalize upon it. I don't consider it any accident that my best trades were formulated far from the madding crowd, where I had time to reflect. Nor is it any accident that my worst trades were made after staring at a quotation machine all day.

If you stray too close to the action, you risk becoming a slave to the very latest price tick, and you will be prone to make foolish impulsive decisions. Take it from one who has been there. Commodity trading can easily take over your life and ruin you; the world is full of commodity junkies who have to call their brokers twenty times a day for a fix. *Irrelevant information is your number one enemy.* Do not be seduced by it, and keep your distance. Accept that from time to time the market is going to make an enormous fool of you; that is its nature. Smile at its contrariness, and in the end you will have the last laugh. Winners don't worry about the market; they don't have to, for they are secure in their own knowledge.

I'll give the last word to Bob Dylan: "I just write a song and know it is going to be all right. I don't even know what it's going to say."

GLOSSARY

Artificial Intelligence - As applied to commodity trading, the attempt to link the learning processes in the brain with the cracking of the information thought to be encoded in the historical price series. The search for the talented soybean.

Asking Price - The lowest price at which any seller is prepared to sell. Or, the price a buyer would have to pay to guarantee purchase of a contract.

Bearish - Descriptive of a market that is trending lower, or of the disposition of a trader who believes that a market will decline.

Bid Price - The highest price any buyer is prepared to pay. Or, the price a seller would have to take to guarantee sale of a contract.

Book Squaring - A term invoked by commentators to explain a daily price change when no other explanation can be thought up. It has a plausible ring, but no one knows what it means.

Broker - The intermediary who relays client instructions to the trading floor; and who solicits such business from the general public.

Bullish - Descriptive of a market that is trending higher. Or, of the disposition of a trader who believes a market will rise.

Call - An option to buy a future at a fixed price for a specified period of time.

Chartist - A trader who attempts to forecast prices by looking at past price formations drawn on charts with price as one axis and time as the other.

Choppy Market - A market characterized by large swings around a mean value, where traders, both long and short, get "chopped-up" trying to establish positions. See also *Trading Range*.

Commercials - Large traders who are involved in the trade of physical commodities.

Commission - The cost of trading one contract of a commodity. With a futures position, commission is charged only when the position is closed out. With options, commission is charged both on entry and on exit.

Commission House - Also known as a *Commodity Brokerage Firm*. If you want to trade commodities you must open an account with a commission house.

Commitments of Trader Report - A report released every other week showing, in macro terms, who-is-holding-what in the various futures markets. Why the government should choose to waste taxpayers' dollars in this way is a mystery.

Commodity Fund - Basically a mutual fund trading commodity futures. Fees can be high, and average performance is mediocre at best. If you invest in the right one, you might get lucky, but don't be surprised to lose 50 percent of your investment in rather a short period of time.

Commodity Futures Trading Commission (CFTC) - A government regulatory body.

Confirmation Bias - The tendency to hear and see what we want to see rather than what is there.

Curve Fitting - See *Optimization*.

Cyclical Price Change - All markets experience booms and busts to some degree. Excessively low prices induce conditions that result in excessively high prices. The timing of cyclical price changes is irregular, however, making the simple observation that a price is cyclical of little value in price forecasting. See *Periodic Price Change*.

Day Trader - A trader who tries to capitalize on short-term price swings within one trading session (about five hours). Day traders often become *Position Traders* unintentionally—when they cannot accept taking a loss.

Deficit - Arises when a client owes his brokerage firm for losses not covered by his margin deposit. If exchange margin requirements were rigorously applied by commodity brokers, deficits would be rare. In practice, however, they're rather common.

Delivery - The fulfilling of a contract by making physical presentation of the goods rather than *Offsetting* a trade in the futures market.

Diversification - The simultaneous trading of several unrelated markets. Reduces risk level for any given level of *Exposure*.

Equity - The total value of an account; consists of cash on deposit plus profits or minus losses on *Open Trades* held in the account.

Evening up of Positions - A meaningless term like *Book Squaring*—much used but never defined.

Execution Costs - In system trading, the sum of *Slippage* and *Commission*.

Execution Price - The actual price at which a transaction takes place. In an unstable market, the execution price on a *Stop Order* may be quite different from the stop order price. **Execution Costs** - In system trading, the sum of *Slippage* and *Commission*.

Exposure - The overall size of one's contractual obligations. Risk increases with exposure, but can be reduced through effective *Diversification*.

Fading - Simply stated, doing the opposite. Often used, sarcastically, to suggest that doing the opposite of what another trader does *must* be a good strategy.

Floor Broker - The last link in the order chain. Floor brokers exchange, buy, and sell tickets in a trading ring on the floor of the exchange, in response to instructions from commodity brokers who in turn are relaying instructions from clients.

Fundamental Trader - A trader who takes positions in the market based on his perception of current economic realities. Philosophically opposed to the *Chartist* and the *Technical Trader*.

Futures Contract - The mechanism whereby a buyer and a seller of a commodity strike a deal on goods for future delivery. One will gain what the other will lose.

Futures Exchange - The arena where commodity futures contracts are "exchanged"—by public outcry.

Head and Shoulders - Not a shampoo, but a chart formation alleged to have predictive value. Many examples of corroboration are displayed in the literature. Example of non-corroboration rarely get press. Other formations favored by *Chartists* include flags, pennants, and ascending and descending triangles. There is no hard evidence to suggest that these formations have any substance outside of the imaginations of the people who perceive them.

Hedging - Taking a futures position in a market for price insurance rather than for speculative gain. Hog farmers who sell hog futures and chocolate manufacturers who buy cocoa futures are hedging. In reality, hedgers are prone to become speculators by default—such are the temptations of the market.

Hindsight - What we all wish we had before the fact. Traders must be careful not to draw too may conclusions based on hindsight. It's tempting, but unhelpful.

Initial Margin - See *Margin*

Insider - A market participant believed to be privy to information not available to the general public, and thus to enjoy an unfair advantage. Certainly true of the stock market. Not so true in the commodity market.

Largest Expected Equity Drawdown (LEED) - The worst conceivable losing streak a trader can expect to ever encounter—and therefore the amount he must budget for.

Leverage - What makes commodity trading so exciting. $100,000 worth of commodity may be controlled with a $5,000 security deposit, so that small price changes can result in huge profits or losses.

Limit Move - The maximum permissible change in a price in one day. This number is specified by the exchange and is particular to each commodity. When a market reaches the limit, trading stops—either there are no buyers or no sellers. Limits are supposed to minimize excessive price volatility, but there is little evidence to support this.

Liquidity - A liquid market is one that can absorb large orders with little effect upon price. Illiquid markets can be expensive to exit in a hurry, since buyers or sellers may be scarce. *Option* markets are notoriously illiquid; interest rate futures are among the most liquid.

Long - A trader who has purchased futures expecting the price to rise. Also used adjectivally as in to be "long" the market.

Maintenance Margin - The equity you must have in your account to allow you to hold your positions. If your account falls below this amount, your brokerage firm will ask you to put up more money or get out of your positions.

Margin - A dollar amount, required by a brokerage firm as security, which must be on deposit in an account before a futures position may be taken. Also known as *Initial Margin*. Margins are different for each commodity, and may be altered from time to time by the exchanges, as *Volatility* increases or decreases.

Market Order - An instruction to a *Floor Broker* to execute a buy or sell order at the prevailing price level when he receives that order. To buy or sell "at the market" is the usual term.

National Futures Association (NFA) - an industry watchdog organization whose bark appears to be much stronger than its bite.

Neural Network - See *Artificial Intelligence.*

Null Hypothesis - A statistical test to determine whether chance is a likely explanation for a set of results.

Offering Price - See *Asking Price.*

Offsetting Trade - To liquidate (cancel) an open position by selling a contract when long, or buying a contract when short.

Open Interest - The number of contracts outstanding at any time in a given future of a given commodity. It starts out at zero, may rise to any value, and declines towards zero as delivery approaches.

Open Trade - A long or short position which has yet to be cleared by an *Offsetting Trade.* When all open positions have been cleared from an account it is said to be flat.

Opening Price - The price at which the first trade of the day is executed. Often expressed as a range with the opening *Bid Price* as the low value and the opening *Asking Price* as the high value.

Optimization - A fallacious projection of nonrepresentative theoretical trading results into future expectations. Also known as *Curve Fitting.*

Option - A right to buy or sell at a fixed price for a fixed period of time.

Option Writer - The trader who assumes the contractual obligations to fulfill an option contract should the buyer wish to exercise his option.

Overbought - A nonsense word used by frustrated players to describe a bull market they have missed or want to go short in.

Oversold - See *Overbought*

Overtrading - Controlling too much commodity with too little money. A dangerous practice which will get you in the end. Most traders chronically overtrade without realizing it.

Paper Losses - See *Paper Profits*

Paper Profits - Profits which have accrued from open positions but have not yet been cashed in. Paper profits are just as real as cash—as are *Paper Losses.*

Periodic Price Change - A periodic price change is one that occurs at regular time intervals. Few commodities exhibit this pattern, and where it does occur (in the hog market for example), futures prices will discount the effect by selling at premiums or discounts to the cash price.

Positive Feedback - An instability in a system resulting from an internal short circuit. The excessive amount of meaningless information now being flashed at market players is conducive to the creation of highly unstable markets.

Premium - The amount an option buyer must pay an *Option Writer* in exchange for the rights to an option.

Profit Taking - A classic nonsense word originating in the stock market—where there are few short sellers. It is used to make edgy stockholders feel better after a sharp reaction in a bull market. The obvious converse, *Loss Taking*, is an expression you will never hear.

Promoter - An individual whose trading experiences have taught him that it is smarter for him to advise others than to speculate for himself.

Put - An option to sell a future at a fixed price for a specified period of time.

Pyramiding - Using *Paper Profits* (which are real enough) to finance additional positions in commodity futures contracts.

Random Walk - A hypothesis that price changes evolve in a totally random fashion similar to the numbers generated off a roulette wheel or from a set of dice.

Regression - The tendency for excellence to gravitate to mediocrity. The offspring of two geniuses are rarely geniuses too, and it's hard to stay hot in the market for any length of time.

Resistance Level - A price level that a rising market has repeatedly failed to break through.

Seasonality - A belief that seasonal price patterns recur, patterns which the "clued-in" trader can exploit. An illusion.

Short - A trader who has sold futures expecting a price decline. See *Long*.

Short Squeeze - An unusual situation occurring when a future comes up for delivery and there are more outstanding contracts than can be fulfilled by delivery of physical product. The problem is normally solved by a sharp price advance, but defaults are not unknown.

Slippage - The difference between actual trading results and theoretically projected results.

Spread - The difference in price between contract months of one commodity; or between the same month of different but related commodities.

Stochastic - According to the dictionary, stochastic means "random" or "proceeding by guesswork." The word has been seized upon by a number of market theoreticians to add pizzazz to some rather mundane indexes derived from price action. Often used in the plural, as in "What do the stochastics say?" Meaningless.

Stop-Limit Order - Same as a *Stop Order*, with one difference. The transaction may only be made at the specified price or at a more favorable price. Occasionally, a stop-limit order will *not* be executed (whereas a stop order guarantees execution). You can't have your cake and eat it too.

Stop Order - A contingency order held by a *Floor Broker* to buy or sell at the best available price whenever the market trades at the price specified on the stop order. Used by smart traders to initiate positions in the direction of the market, to limit losses to a predetermined amount, to protect profits after a favorable move, and generally to protect themselves from making stupid decisions under stress.

Straddle - A combined put and call option on the same future, having the same expiry date and exercisable at the same strike price.

Strike Price - The price at which an option may be exercised.

Support Level - A price level that a declining market has repeatedly failed to penetrate.

System - See *Trading System*.

Technical Analysis - The manipulation of historical price data to predict the future. Economic realities do not influence the forecasts of technical traders.

Technical Trader - Almost synonymous with a *Chartist*, although he may work strictly with numbers rather than pictures. Uses *Technical Analysis* to forecast prices. Philosophically opposed to the *Fundamental Trader*.

Trading Range - A bandwith of prices within which a commodity has been constrained for some considerable period of time.

Trading System - A non-subjective, mechanical rule for making trades based on signals generated from evolving price patterns.

Treasury Bills - Monies held on deposit in a commodity account may be invested in government interest-bearing securities, called Treasury Bills. If your broker is not doing this for you, change brokers.

Trending Market - A market that has shown a tendency to persist in one direction for an exceptionally long period of time. A subjective judgment, really. Opposite of a *Choppy Market* or of a market in a *Trading Range*.

Trendline - A line drawn on a commodity chart connecting a series of peaks or a series of valleys. The breaking of a trendline is thought to signal a key reversal in a market. A million chartists will disagree, but there is no evidence to support the trendline theory is in any way useful in price forecasting.

Undermargined - Having insufficient funds on deposit to cover the exchange *Maintenance Margin* requirements. The solution is to put more money or liquidate some positions. The latter action makes more sense.

Volume - The number of contracts exchanged on a given day in a given month of a given commodity.

Whipsaw - A sharp reversal in a market followed very quickly by another sharp reversal in the opposite direction.

Zero–Sum Game - a contest in which the winners take only from the losers. A private card game is the best example. Commodities would be a zero–sum game were it not for the commission charge which turns it into a decidedly non–zero–sum game.

INDEX

ABOUT THE AUTHOR

William Gallacher is a commodity trader living in Toronto. A professional engineer by background, Mr. Gallacher has traded the market successfully for nearly 20 years.